The Peculiar Democracy

WALLACE HETTLE

The Peculiar Democracy

*Southern Democrats
in Peace and Civil War*

The University of Georgia Press
Athens & London

Paperback edition, 2012
© 2001 by the University of Georgia Press
Athens, Georgia 30602
www.ugapress.org
All rights reserved
Designed by Walton Harris
Set in 10/14 New Caledonia by Walton Harris
Printed digitally in the United States of America

The Library of Congress has cataloged the hardcover
edition of this book as follows:

Hettle, Wallace, 1962–
The peculiar democracy : Southern democrats in peace
and Civil War / Wallace Hettle.
xi, 240 p. ; 24 cm.
ISBN 0-8203-2282-2 (alk. paper)
Includes bibliographical references (p. 211–233) and index.
1. Jackson, Andrew, 1767–1845—Influence.
2. Democratic Party (U.S.)—History—19th century.
3. Politicians—Southern States—History—19th century.
4. Political culture—Southern States—History—19th century.
5. Sectionalism (United States)—History—19th century.
6. Secession—Southern States.
7. Southern States—Politics and government—1775–1865. I. Title.
F214 .H48   2001
324.2736'0975'09034—dc21   00-045134

Paperback ISBN-13: 978-0-8203-4098-2
          ISBN-10: 0-8203-4098-7

British Library Cataloging-in-Publication Data available

For Leslie

Contents

Acknowledgments *ix*

Introduction *1*

1. Jefferson, Jackson, and the Southern Foundations of Democratic Politics *11*

2. The Approaching Storm: Southern Democrats and the Sectional Crisis *39*

3. The "Self-Analysis" of John C. Rutherfoord: Democracy and the Manhood of a Virginia Secessionist *57*

4. An Ambiguous Democrat: Joseph Brown, Secession, and the Confederacy *84*

5. The Price of Moderation: Francis W. Pickens and the Factionalism of South Carolina *102*

6. Curing the "Sir Walter Disease": The Politics and Fiction of Jeremiah Clemens *122*

7. Jefferson Davis and the Confederacy's Dysfunctional Democracy *142*

Conclusion *165*

Notes *173*

Works Cited *211*

Index *235*

Acknowledgments

I am indebted to my mother, Dona Hettle, for too many things to mention. Most important, she found children's biographies of Frederick Douglass and Abraham Lincoln when I was seven years old and obstinately refused to read fiction. When I went to college, David Roediger's courses heightened my interest in race and U.S. history. Dedicated to changing the world at the height of the Reagan-Bush era, the political activists of the International Socialist tendency greatly influenced the way I think about history. Years before I worked on this project, my good friend David Kopman gave me a tape with Bob Dylan's homage to slain civil rights leader Medgar Evers. The song declares:

> The South's politician preaches to the poor white man
> You've got more than the blacks don't complain . . .
> But the poor white is used
> In the hands of them all like a tool
> He's taught in his school
> That the laws are with him
> To protect his white skin
> To keep up his hate
> So he never thinks straight
> About the shape that he's in
> But he ain't to blame
> He's only a pawn in their game.

Dylan undoubtedly learned about the dynamics of racial oppression and class divisions in white society from the civil rights activists of the early 1960s. While his words are a bit overstated by scholarly standards, I should acknowledge that they have profoundly affected this study.

In graduate school at Northwestern University, T. H. Breen offered rigorous course work and an insightful critique of my dissertation. Nancy Maclean was in turns friend and trusted adviser. Her admonitions that I think harder about gender scarcely made a dent on my dissertation but would have a profound impact on this book. My dissertation adviser, Jim Oakes, has a tremendously infectious intellectual enthusiasm that made graduate work exciting. We spent hours in his office debating a variety of topics ranging from the "republican synthesis" to the latest Spike Lee movie. Jim always encouraged me to follow my beliefs about the elitist nature of the Democratic Party in the slave south. He should not, however, be held responsible for my conclusions.

As a beginning graduate student, I had an extraordinary talk about scholarship and the profession with Stephen Hahn, who bolstered my confidence. My friend Mary Pyke Gover generously copyedited my dissertation. David Zimand shared his wide-ranging knowledge of antebellum political history with me. Eric Foner provided an insightful reading of a key dissertation chapter. The late Arthur Cohn provided a model of scholarly productivity that I may never match. At different times, Barb Hettle and Lois Cohn both taught me the meaning of southern hospitality.

As the book took shape, Mills Thornton suggested sources to consult regarding Jeremiah Clemens and Mark Twain, and Anthony Carey helped me to think more carefully about Clemens and southern honor. Lou Faulkner Williams kindly assured me that the chapter on Francis Pickens and South Carolina was on the right track. At the University of Northern Iowa, Nancy Isenberg and Greg Bruess provided intellectual stimulation and guidance in adapting to the strange and all-too-stressful role of assistant professor. UNI colleagues Andy Burstein and Paul Horton read parts of the manuscript, providing encouragement and helpful suggestions.

Financial support was provided by a dissertation fellowship from the Graduate College at Northwestern University. As the manuscript evolved into a book, the Graduate College of the University of Northern Iowa furnished a summer grant that funded additional time in the archives. The Virginia Historical Society extended a Mellon Fellowship that helped me to use its extraordinary collection.

John Inscoe helped sharpen my thinking about Joseph Brown and guided the publication of an essay on Brown and Georgia's road to secession in the Fall 1997 issue of the *Georgia Historical Quarterly*. I am grateful for his help on the piece, which gradually evolved into chapter 4 of this book. Jeff Jakeman helpfully edited an article on Jeremiah Clemens, which appeared in the *Alabama Review* in February 1999. It appears here in revised form as chapter 6.

Everything else pales in comparison to the many contributions made by Leslie Cohn. At various times she aided this project by serving as breadwinner, sounding board, and first reader. More important, and in ways that only she knows, she lent indispensable moral support every step of the way.

The Peculiar Democracy

Introduction

In an 1863 speech in New York's Cooper Union, Frederick Douglass described the end of slavery as a potentially liberating event for nonslaveholding southerners. The former slave asserted that slavery had been built with the cooperation of white nonslaveholders who had been "deluded into the belief that to degrade the black laborer is to elevate the white." In fact, said Douglass, the nonslaveholders "have been looked down upon and oppressed by the slaveholders." Portraying the Confederacy as a tenuous and uncompromising combination of slave states, he declared that the "first grand error this war is likely to cure is: That a nation can outlaw one part of its people without endangering the rights and liberties of all the people." In his view, American history taught that nonslaveholders could not "put a chain on the ankle of the bondsman without finding the other end of it about their own necks."[1] The abolitionist leader hoped that members of the yeoman class would struggle to remove the chain and in doing so hasten the collapse of the Confederacy. Behind his words lay the belief that in the plantation South, slavery and meaningful democracy—even for white men—were incompatible.

Southern newspapers and politicians portrayed the South in very different terms, of course. In 1856, when the *Richmond Enquirer* stated that "freedom is not possible without slavery," it was repeating a sentiment invoked so often that it was practically a cliché, a means for antebellum politicians, especially Democrats, to trumpet their devotion to the popular will. The *Montgomery Advertiser*, the official Democratic Party organ in Alabama, proclaimed that "the masses of the party and the people at large . . . are the sovereigns who make governors."[2] Such pronouncements had a mass appeal that continued into the Civil War, when loyal Confederates insisted they fought for "slavery for negroes" because they valued "freedom for whites." The view that black slavery buttressed the freedom of whites by raising them above a permanent lower class of slaves, summarized best in J. D. B. De Bow's 1860 pamphlet *The Interest of the Southern Nonslaveholder in Slavery*, was ubiquitous.[3]

Douglass and De Bow represent opposite poles, which historians have generally allowed to stand as testament to the hardened biases that made war inevitable. Certainly, Douglass was invested in the abolitionist crusade in a way that could affect his analysis of the South, just as the newspapermen and politicians of the Old South adhered to a self-protective ideology of their own. The ideal means of comparing the views of Douglass with those of slavery's defenders would be to seek the views of the people whose democratic rights were in question: nonslaveholders. Yet few of these people kept written records on matters related to political activities, so their estimation of southern liberty and democracy is elusive. Yeoman testimony is too scarce to settle the controversy between Douglass and the statesmen of the Old South.

Therefore, this study attempts to illuminate the question of southern democracy in another way, by asking a simple question: How democratic was the Democratic Party? As we examine the party and some of its individual leaders, we must distinguish between two key terms: *democracy* and *Democrats*. As a system and theory of self-government, democracy dates from ancient Greece. The Democratic Party, however, is a modern, distinctively American political organization that emerged during the presidency of Andrew Jackson. Since this book discusses both democracy and the Democratic Party, it is worth emphasizing that these similar words do not always mean the same thing. Indeed, the actions taken and the ideas expressed by southern Democrats from the antebellum period through the Civil War reveal much about the limitations of white man's democracy in the South.

The Democratic Party was for all practical purposes the only political party in the South by 1855 and arguably the most important voluntary organization in the region. Indeed, it was the Democratic leadership that most strongly voiced the idea that the antebellum and Civil War South was a popular white man's democracy. Democrats fashioned themselves as the champion of the yeomanry and played a crucial role in managing the sometimes touchy relationship between slaveholders and nonslaveholders throughout the antebellum period. While a few Confederate leaders were former Whigs, Democrats dominated the key positions in the new government. If one were to find evidence of popular self-rule in the slave South, it would be in the workings of the Democratic Party.

Historians have produced a considerable body of literature relating to antebellum politics. Following the lead of J. Mills Thornton's work on Alabama, the prevailing view among historians for the last twenty years has been that the antebellum political system was extraordinarily responsive to voters. Indeed, the argument that antebellum politics were based on an egalitarian model of activist democracy is now "nearly a scholarly paradigm." Numerous writers have taken the words of southern statesmen seriously in trying to reconstruct the system of beliefs, values, fears, and commitments that constituted political ideology.[4] Their interpretation of antebellum southern politics emphasizes the unity of white men and the great responsiveness of popular politics, which they argue buttressed equality within the master race by allowing white men to share in a republican political order based on tyranny over slaves.[5] These studies have contributed much to our knowledge of politics in the Old South: it is no longer tenable, if it ever was, to dismiss southern democracy as a fraud masking the unchallenged power of slave owners. But these studies have gone too far, veering dangerously close to taking at face value southern politicians' pronouncements that slavery promoted freedom for white men.

In recent years, a growing number of historians have followed Eugene Genovese in emphasizing planter dominance of the Old South and the limits of southern white men's democracy. These scholars have shown the manner in which plantation society and the political world could reflect the habits of patriarchal domination of men on the plantation, illuminating the complexity of antebellum political culture and emphasizing the limits of southern egalitarianism by focusing on issues such as gender, class, and honor. But much of the best work on the limits of southern equality has been done by social historians, and none of the historians emphasizing elite power has systematically studied the Democratic Party.[6] *The Peculiar Democracy* uses this body of historiography to offer a distinct critique of the southern Democrats' egalitarian rhetoric.

Despite the resonance of Jacksonian political rhetoric during the secession crisis and war, few studies have linked the contentious politics of the antebellum period with the notorious infighting of the Confederacy. Indeed, many of the best works on proslavery politics end in 1861, four years before the final destruction of slavery. Much of this useful scholarship aims to answer a big question for southern historians: What caused secession and the Civil War? Although such explorations have been valuable, exclusive attention to the road to disunion has elicited many complaints of a "Civil War synthesis" that distorts the past by focusing on a single event, secession.[7] Too often, southern political history has become a teleological process in which all roads lead to Fort Sumter. Single-minded emphasis on explaining disunion may have had the unintended consequence of exaggerating southern political unity by ending the analysis at a high point for white racial solidarity.

This study focuses instead on the relationship between the South's heritage of Jacksonian democracy, as embodied in the Democratic Party, and the events of the secession crisis and Civil War. Exploring how the political process worked under the pressure of disunion should advance our understanding of its dynamics. During the Civil War, Democrat L. Q. C. Lamar of Mississippi noted that the war had brought previously existing problems to the forefront: "The tendency of all such struggles as this, is to throw to the surface those moral disorders which, in quiet times, lie concealed in the bosom of society."[8] Lamar understood that latent conflicts in the political order became manifest in the midst of social upheaval. The Democratic leadership of the South, personified by Jefferson Davis, floundered as it suffered from public attacks that accused it of favoring measures that served a monied elite and centralized power. Although the political squabbling that racked the Confederacy was hardly the sole factor contributing to its collapse, bitter factionalism certainly did not help the cause of the fledgling nation.[9] To help find answers to this problem, five chapters of this book focus on individual Democratic leaders, both prominent and obscure men, as they negotiated the uncharted terrain of secession and Civil War. The point of these biographical chapters is to illustrate the limitations of the South's white man's democracy by linking the antebellum period with disunion, thus bringing into sharper relief the tendency of the Democratic Party to favor the slaveholders. Of course, no selection of five men could amount to a scientifically representative sample. There is no such thing as a typical Jacksonian Democrat; examined closely they all have their quirks. My interest was drawn to peculiar Democrats, leaders whose stories illuminate the paradoxical nature of democracy in a society dominated by the peculiar institution.

Thornton's seminal work on Alabama was based on the premise that politicians follow the will of voters and therefore "democracy as a form of government is merely a mirror of men." In contrast, this study is inspired by political theorists who, through examining the Western world's dysfunctional politics in the late twentieth century, argue that equal participation in a system characterized by inequalities is not possible.[10] Social stratification plays a crucial role in Jürgen Habermas's now classic account of the declining vitality of public debate in Western democracies. Inequality can distort the democratic process, as formally democratic systems witness participation that "becomes largely passive for the majority," who are subject to the manipulation of elites.[11] The slave South differed in many ways from the modern West, but both societies' political systems have been corroded by social inequality. If the Democratic Party was a mirror of men, it was more like a fun-house mirror, distorted by the manner in which the slave-based economy generated economic stratification between slaveholders and nonslaveholders, especially in the 1850s.[12]

Chapter 1 begins by recognizing the profound influence of Thomas Jefferson and Andrew Jackson on southern Democrats, exploring their role in shaping Democratic Party thought. Jefferson idealized a romantic version of the yeoman farmer, and Jackson personified the ideal of rural manhood. During his presidency, Jackson in particular led the Democrats as they developed a series of interlocking political propositions that made them the leading party in the South for a generation. Suspicion of nationally sponsored internal improvements such as canals and roads provoked Jackson to use his veto power more than any previous president. Jackson's famous war with the Second Bank of the United States, in which he vilified Philadelphia banker Nicholas Biddle as a symbol of privilege, would remain a touchstone of the party for decades. As historians such as John Ashworth have shown, the Democratic Party's clashes with financial elites such as bankers resonated with deep-seated fears among voters, especially farmers, of the formation of an aristocracy of privileged men. Precisely for this reason, Jacksonian warnings against the growth of aristocracy appealed to no group more than to southern yeomen. Democrats pledged to protect the independence of subsistence farmers against the encroachments of a market economy that would concentrate wealth in the hands of a few. Jacksonian Democrats so refashioned political debate that the term "Age of Jackson" seems appropriate even to historians skeptical of the notion that great men shape history.[13]

For white southern men, especially nonslaveholders, Andrew Jackson remained the most important symbol of the Democratic Party. New candidates came to the fore after Jackson left office in 1837, but Old Hickory remained central to the party's image. One Alabama wit remarked in 1853, eight years after Jackson died, that "it would be somewhat dangerous to tell [the voters] that the Jin'al is not a candidate this election." Many Democratic voters were "voting for Jackson" long after his death.[14] While part of Jackson's lasting appeal lay in his identification with popular issues such as opposition to centralized banking and internal improvements, his enduring reputation owed as much to popular affection for his personal character. In 1855, Whig writer

Joseph Glover Baldwin accounted for Jackson's political success by remarking that "the strong will . . . is the strong man."[15] Thus chapter 1 explores the paradox that this man who most symbolized democracy was in fact admired as a militia leader possessing outstanding qualities of masculine strength and determination, who effectively dominated other white men both in battle and in the political arena.

Chapter 2 deals with party conflict during the 1850s and culminates in the secession crisis. After Jackson, Democrats defined themselves in opposition to their Whig opponents, a party that they derided as "aristocratic" because it sought government-sponsored privilege such as subsidies to business. Unlike Whigs, whom Democrats accused of sponsoring economic programs that would undermine the yeoman farmer, Democrats claimed that they could preserve the independence of white men. Yet without Jackson, the party offered no compelling national leader from the South, and many Democrats worried that voters would begin to view self-interested elites as the mainstay of their party. Such fears intensified after the Whigs' self-destruction in the early 1850s left the party without meaningful competition and resulted in the entry of many conservative Whigs into the Democratic Party. Once their image as confident boosters of rural democracy became increasingly difficult to sustain, southern Democrats engaged in politics based on fear: dread of abolitionists, anxieties regarding economic development, and, by 1860, the concern of many leading politicians that nonslaveholders were a potentially unreliable lower class. Fears of yeoman discontent in 1860 may have been exaggerated, but such worries had an enormous impact in limiting popular democracy in the secession crisis.

After surveying antebellum politics, this study examines and interprets the stories of five Democrats whose lives span the gap between antebellum and Civil War politics. Their careers raise questions about the limits of popular democracy as the antebellum period gave way to secession and war. Jeremiah Clemens of Alabama, John C. Rutherfoord of Virginia, Francis Pickens of South Carolina, Joseph Brown of Georgia, and Jefferson Davis of Mississippi all have unique histories. Yet their tribulations help to isolate common themes, as each struggled with the boundaries of democratic practice in political lives that bridge the gulf between peace and war. Together, these narratives encompass a cross-section of crucial states at the heart of the Confederacy and illustrate ways in which Democratic theory and practice limited the scope of egalitarianism for white men.

Jeremiah Clemens, an abrasive personality and Alabama Democratic partisan, was elected to the Senate in 1849. After capturing attention with his vehement opposition to the sectional Compromise of 1850, Clemens dramatically (and mysteriously) changed course, championing the compromise after its passage. As his politics evolved from states' rights to Unionism, he found his political career hampered, and then destroyed, by his failure to live up to the system of southern honor. Accusations of dishonorable political behavior drove him from the Democratic Party. Clemens's political course was one of twists and turns that seemed to invite insults upon his character. In 1856, he began to publish works of fiction that reveal the link between his Jacksonian political values and southern honor. States' rights politicians used the language of honor to discredit him as he tried to advance his pro-Union politics. Clemens struck back during the Civil War, delivering a novel about Alabama's guerrilla fighters that questioned the system of honor observed by southern statesmen. Ultimately, Clemens's life suggests that the community-based conventions of chivalry worked to undermine the individual autonomy central to Democratic Party rhetoric and the practice of genuinely democratic politics.

The code of honor limited the autonomy of Alabama Democrats in subtle ways, but in the South Carolina of Civil War governor Francis W. Pickens, democracy was openly crushed. Pickens, an upcountry politician with close ties to the national Democratic Party, came under the suspicious eye of secessionists who viewed him as insufficiently enthusiastic about the southern-rights cause. Opposition to Pickens grew in early 1861 as he refused to be rushed into confrontation with the Union over Fort Sumter. South Carolina's secession convention ultimately stripped Pickens and the state legislature of power, and a dictatorial Executive Council composed of five men replaced them. Politics in South Carolina during the Civil War illuminated stark fissures scarcely apparent to observers before the war, as states' rights extremists forcefully suppressed the governor's power. The roots of Pickens's clash with South Carolina's secession convention lay in antebellum squabbling among Democrats. The emergence of the Executive Council dictatorship in South Carolina, which has often been described as the most united state in the Confederacy, not only suggests the limits of white men's democracy in that state but reminds us that no place was immune from the factional infighting that characterized the Civil War South.

Virtually all his contemporaries viewed Georgia's Joseph Brown as idiosyncratic. There is something to be said for this characterization, for at first glance it seems odd that a professed upcountry radical would play a crucial role in bringing his state to secession. Moreover, Brown angered opponents with apparent political flip-flops. Brown's politics reveal an ambiguous Democrat, desperate to please both the upcountry yeoman constituency that elected him and planter-class political leaders who selected him as a gubernatorial nominee. The story of Brown, who worked to maintain his upcountry base of support while currying favor with the state's Whiggish elite, shows the manner in which the most talented sons of the upcountry could serve the ends of the planter class through the Democratic Party. Although he engaged in blistering criticism of the Confederate government during the Civil War, he nevertheless displayed genuine enthusiasm for the larger cause of southern independence. Despite his vacillating political positions as he worked to serve both the slaveholding leadership of the Democratic Party and the north Georgia yeomanry, Brown's goal of uniting white Georgians behind slavery provides the underlying logic that makes this quirky character comprehensible.

Like Joseph Brown, Virginia's John C. Rutherfoord fashioned himself a Jacksonian Democrat opposed to banks and internal improvements. Rutherfoord had embraced radically democratic politics in his college days. As he grew older, this leader in the Virginia House continued to espouse the reason and democracy of Thomas Jefferson and denounced railroad and bank subsidies in Jacksonian language. But in his extensive diaries and commonplace books, he began to record his doubts about the democratic process, even as he headed the Virginia Democratic Party. Preoccupied with attaining a position of personal power as a politician and gaining posthumous distinction, he hoped to achieve prominence as a leader and believed he could do so if he succeeded in disciplining himself to rule over other white men. In his commonplace books, Rutherfoord painstakingly recorded efforts to improve himself by cultivating qualities of masculine self-discipline. Increasingly he viewed the domination of other white men as crucial to political success. In Rutherfoord's Virginia, Democratic politics were integrally bound to the imperatives of a society based on mastery.

Confederate president Jefferson Davis has been the subject of numerous books and articles, but he remains an enigmatic figure.[16] One aspect of his presidency that has been overlooked is the problems generated by the clash between Davis's rigid constitutional doctrine, which he derived from John Calhoun, and the Confederacy's Democratic Party heritage. Jacksonian rights rhetoric had shaped debate in the Mississippi Democratic Party, in which

Davis had emerged as a leader. Nevertheless, the Confederate president found himself unable to please Jacksonians as he led the war effort. Davis's uncompromising, elitist, and sometimes muddled constitutional doctrine alienated him from the common people of the Confederacy who feared the growth of centralized power in Richmond. Calhoun's constitutional creed, central to Davis's conception of the Confederacy, did not provide answers to problems such as the existence of social divisions within the master race. Davis's fear of unchecked popular power and relative disregard for individual rights created an unresponsive national government. His insistence on proving himself right in constitutional matters and his relative indifference to antebellum ideals of limited government diminished popular support for his administration.

Although this book emphasizes the limitations of the antebellum Democratic Party and its even greater failure to measure up to democratic principles in the Civil War, it is necessary to underscore the distinction between the Democratic Party, which became increasingly elitist, and the ideals of Jeffersonian democracy, which are not. Historian Joseph Ellis's recent biography of Jefferson concludes that Newt Gingrich and the politically disastrous 1994 Republican Contract with America were Jefferson's ideological offspring, a conclusion that seems misguided.[17] The problem with the ideals of Jefferson and Jackson was not that they were inherently elitist; rather, they were marred by the constant presence of slavery. Jefferson wrote that a man must be a "prodigy" who could remain with his democratic manners intact in a state based on "tyranny" over the slave.[18] He was right. The tragedy of the Jeffersonian creed in the antebellum South was that democracy, even of the limited white man's variety, became hopelessly entangled in the politics of slaveholding.

Abraham Lincoln understood the way that slavery could undermine democracy. Lincoln may seem an unlikely expert on Jacksonian democracy, but he grew to maturity in southern Indiana and Illinois surrounded by emigrants from the slave states, especially Kentucky, and lived in a political culture dominated by Jacksonian Democrats. Indeed, his cousin Dennis Hanks told pioneering Lincoln biographer William Herndon that Lincoln was "originally a Democrat after the order of Jackson—so was his father—so we all were."[19] In the Civil War, Lincoln incisively identified the problem of taking the pronouncements of slaveholding Democrats at face value: "We all declare for liberty; but using the same *word*, we do not all mean the same *thing*." For Lincoln, the problem with the South was not solely or even primarily that it enslaved African Americans. After all, as Douglass noted, Lincoln was a "white man's President." Lincoln acted against slavery because it endangered the freedom of all Americans, declaring, "We cannot escape history. . . . In *giving* freedom to the *slave*, we *assure* freedom to the *free*."[20]

Ironically, Lincoln's most celebrated statement of his democratic principles was a call for the United States to return to the ideals of Thomas Jefferson. Historian Garry Wills has written that Lincoln's Gettysburg Address, delivered a year after the Emancipation Proclamation, revolutionized Americans' ideas of constitutionalism by tying the document to ideals of liberty and equality. Lincoln "not only put the Declaration [of Independence] in a new light as a matter of founding law, but put its central proposition, equality, in a newly favored position as a principle of the Constitution."[21] However, the revolutionary impact of this single oration has been exaggerated. Lincoln, like the abolitionists, had long interpreted the Constitution in light of the Declaration, and no less an authority than John Quincy Adams argued as early as 1842 that a president could end slavery under martial law. Lincoln himself anticipated themes of the Gettysburg Address in the months approaching the speech. In the summer of 1863, he drew on Jefferson's words to inform a Fourth of July crowd, "We have a gigantic Rebellion, at the bottom of which is an effort to overthrow the principle that all men were created equal."[22]

Lincoln's ideas were not original, but they did help build the war effort by expanding the justification for the conflict. By contrast, the South increasingly lacked a popular foundation for the struggle. The president defended the idea that all men are created equal and resolved that the Union would experience a "new birth of freedom—and that government of the people, by the people, for the people shall not perish from this earth."[23] He practiced his democratic values by facing the electorate in a dangerously uncertain 1864 campaign. W. E. B. Du Bois has pointed out that emancipation "came not simply to black folk in 1863; to white Americans came slowly a new vision and a new uplift, a sudden freeing of hateful mental shadows. . . . At last there could really be a commonwealth of freemen."[24] Lincoln made democracy the central issue of the Civil War. In doing so, he brought forth a new potential for freedom for all Americans, including southern white men.

1. Jefferson, Jackson, and the Southern Foundations of Democratic Politics

While today's southern historians have only recently explored the connection between male identity and politics, antebellum writers emphasized the manliness of Andrew Jackson in emphatic terms. Nineteenth-century biographer James Parton argued that the key reason for Jackson's political popularity lay in the fact that "what man supremely admires in man is manhood."[1] From the time of the Battle of New Orleans in 1815 to his death thirty years later, Jackson's image as a paternal figure would prove crucial to his appeal. Although antebellum Democrats professed to embody the popular will, they actually practiced a distinctive kind of deferential politics, following the lead of a single man, Andrew Jackson. That Jackson's image as a strong man proved crucial to developing his remarkable political power should not be surprising. In a variety of societies, political discourses of masculinity have been tied not to egalitarianism but to "the politics of domination."[2] Jackson inherited a broad range of rural ideals from Thomas Jefferson, but Old Hickory's extraordinary masculine reputation marked his own distinctive contribution to Democratic politics. His self-fashioning as a rural patriarch, intertwined with his role as a leader of the citizens' militia, proved central to the formation of Democratic politics, especially in the South, where Jackson's crucial base of support lay.[3]

Jefferson has become a national icon, and his ideas have been invoked for a variety of causes, including the abolition of slavery, secession, low taxes, and a balanced budget.[4] But antebellum Democrats claimed his legacy first and made his writings their political touchstone. The image of an ordered society of farmers buttressed by the militia, which would be central to Jacksonian democracy, drew on a web of associations about rural life popularized by Jefferson. For Jefferson, agriculture was more than a material grounding for a democratic way of life; it was sublime. In his ideal of agrarian society, which emerges most eloquently in the *Notes on the State of Virginia*, farmers are the repositories of virtuous practices. In agriculture, Jefferson discovered a basis for a harmonious society that grew out of habit, custom, and community opinion. In a sense he had overcome the problem of individualism that dominated so much early liberal thought. His agricultural ideals differed from the model of liberal individualism that Thomas Paine called "self-business." The community of farmers celebrated in pastoral literature such as Virgil's *Ecologues*, which Jefferson copied from in his notebooks, embodied his hopes for the good life. His evocation of Virgil's sacred fire in the dome at Monticello signaled that he fashioned his plantation as a pastoral ideal.[5] When Jefferson praised "the power of the people," he meant rural people, not the centralizing schemes of manufacturing that created inequality he believed would subvert democracy.[6]

In his *Notes on the State of Virginia*, Jefferson directly juxtaposed his portrait of the ideal farmer with his bleak vision of slavery. He denounced African American slavery because of its effects on white society: "There must doubtless be an unhappy influence on the manners of our people produced by the existence of slavery among us. The whole commerce between master and slave is a perpetual exercise of the most boisterous passions, the most unremitting despotism on the one part, and degrading submissions on the other.... The man must be a prodigy who can retain his manners and morals undepraved by such circumstances." Slavery damaged the character of Virginia's young men: "The parent storms, the child looks on, catches the lineaments of wrath, puts on the same airs in the circle of smaller slaves, gives loose to the worst of his passions."[7] This condemnation of the culture of slavery in Virginia, the strongest denunciation of the peculiar institution by Jefferson, reflected his fears that slavery could doom his democratic vision. As a relatively young man in the 1780s, he insisted on the incompatibility of republican principles and slavery.[8] Normally hopeful about the future, here he confronted the painful truth that human bondage could distort white society by distorting the social education of young men. He worried that tyranny on the plantation would produce a society of petty dictators inured to habits of domination.

Jefferson examined slavery and quickly, after predicting its gradual demise, changed the subject. He substituted for Virginia's slave society his idealized vision of the yeoman farmer: "Those who labour in the earth are the chosen people of God, if ever he had a chosen people, whose breasts he has made this peculiar deposit for substantial and genuine virtue. It is the focus which keeps alive that sacred fire, which otherwise might escape from the face of the earth. Corruption of morals in the mass of cultivators is a phaenomenon of which no age nor nation has furnished an example."[9] The language here is not the dispassionate logic of political economy but the imaginative leap of a man with an extraordinary creative intellect. The words of the normally secular Jefferson in his praise for the yeomanry—"the chosen people of God"—places the self-sufficient farmer above politics and economics as the basis for a nearly perfect society.

This idealization of the yeoman helped Jefferson resolve his nagging concern with slavery. If a man must be, as Jefferson supposed, a "prodigy" to mature with his morals unaffected by slavery, the independent farmer maintained his democratic manners as a matter of course. Jefferson, with his faith in agrarian virtue, possessed sufficient optimism to walk past the slaves on his plantation thinking grand thoughts of human progress without much sense of any contradiction. Sometimes his rural nostalgia led him to odd flights of fancy, such as when he asked, "Is it not better that we return at once into that happy system of our ancestors, the wisest and most perfect ever yet devised by the wit of man, as it stood before the eighth century?"[10] Jefferson's impulse to turn back the clock could not be realized. Nevertheless, he found consolation in the notion that American manufacturing workers, if employers tried "to reduce them to the minimum of subsistence . . . will quit their trades and go to labouring the earth."[11]

The pastoral tradition provides a useful framework to discuss Democratic views of yeoman life, since the literary imagination served as a crucial source of Jeffersonian ideals. Jefferson's literary commonplace book provides evidence that he immersed himself in pastoral writers he felt could teach moral lessons about social relations. Writers such as Virgil, Ossian, and Goldsmith confirmed his emotional conviction of the superiority of rural life. Fiction, Jefferson believed, had a greater "moral utility" than political economy. He admonished a young friend that "considering history as a moral exercise, her lessons would be too unfrequent if confined to real life. We are therefore wisely framed to be as warmly interested for a fictitious as a real personage."[12]

Jefferson also read, and assimilated into his thinking, English Whig oppositionists, John Locke, and Scottish moral sense philosophers, but his ideas have been described as unsystematic and "eclectic."[13] The single consistent thread running through his career, and the distinctive element of his thought, is his commitment to rural life as the basis for democracy. Jefferson's ideal of rural virtue appealed to both planters and plain folk and reflected an idealized vision of existing social practices. Jefferson portrayed the good life as already existing on Virginia farms. His rhetoric, which he drew from everyday life, provided a material basis for democracy. America witnessed profound social and political transformations during Jefferson's long life, but he remained committed to the beauty, stability, and harmony of rural life.

Jefferson's imaginary ideal sprang from discomfort with his twin problems of slavery and personal indebtedness. In an Anglo-American world witnessing the erosion of rural tradition, many eighteenth-century writers, popular in both England and America, created an ill-defined country way of life. Part of the attraction of the pastoral vision of history lay in the possibility of romanticizing a mythic rural life as eighteenth-century farmers faced threats to their way of life. Virginia planters, for example, faced the problems of debt and exhausted soil. While maintaining a lavish lifestyle, Jefferson himself faced the specter of failure and in 1816 admitted to his grandson Thomas Jefferson Randolph, "I am indeed an unskillful manager of my farms." As Raymond Williams has pointed out, the pastoral ideal has gained adherents when essentials of agrarian life seem threatened by impositions of the market such as debt: "The contrast . . . is between the pleasures of rural settlement and the threat of loss and eviction."[14] The ideal of agrarian life remained, but America's market economy grew. Ongoing hostilities with Jefferson's traditional enemy, England, produced the Embargo Act and the War of 1812, both of which halted trade and effectively weaned the United States from British manufactures. Determined to avoid "dependence on that foreign nation [England]," Jefferson reconciled himself to the growth of American commerce and industry, placing "the manufacturer by the side of the agriculturalist."[15] While he hoped agriculture would predominate, within the confines of his devotion to limited government, he could not imagine government taking active measures to ensure that it would prevail.

Jefferson's ideal of manhood, not surprisingly, was intertwined with rural life. His attachment to country life, and the type of manhood it fostered, is reflected in his extraordinary regard for the poems of the purported Celtic bard Ossian. The Scottish writer James MacPherson claimed to have collected and translated traditional ballads composed by Ossian, and these poems captured a wide audience in the eighteenth century. Jefferson became fascinated with this primitive Gaelic verse, especially with its celebration of romantic untamed heroes of a distant past. He wished to learn to read it in the original language and transcribed much of this now forgotten poetry in his literary commonplace book. MacPherson declared that among the primitives of the Celtic fringe, one found crucial lessons about manners, a topic that had bedeviled Jefferson in the *Notes on the State of Virginia*. MacPherson wrote, "If our fathers had not so much wealth, they had certainly fewer vices than the present age.... The general poverty of a nation has not the same influence, that the indigence of individuals, in an opulent country has, upon the manners of the community."[16] In the prefeudal era depicted by Ossian, Jefferson found a society based on communal ideals. Masculinity was linked to an ideal of family, as warriors fought while preserving the memory of their "fathers."[17]

In his original draft of the Declaration of Independence, Jefferson appealed to the "manly spirit" of the colonists.[18] But his model of independent manhood differed from bourgeois individualism. He focused on man's role as head of the household and member of the community. The connection between yeoman independence and community attachments appears when Jefferson describes the yeoman as one whose "estate provides a good table, clothes himself and his family with their ordinary apparel, furnishes a small surplus to buy salt, coffee, and a little finery for his wife and daughter, enables him to receive and to visit his friends and furnishes him pleasing and healthy occupation."[19] He envisioned the farmer as the cornerstone of a virtuous society.

Jefferson's picture of agrarian life reflected his belief that man was created for a "social state." Moreover, his ideal yeoman was part of a society that was based not just on "rights" but on "duties." Every young man should be taught, Jefferson argued, "to observe with intelligence and faithfulness all the social relations under which he shall be placed." Young men should learn military skills while still "at that age of aptness, docility, and emulation of the practices of manhood."[20] The independent farmer was to reaffirm his ties to society by participating in a popular organization that blended authority and democracy: the people's militia. Anglo-American political thinkers had long cherished the supposed invincibility of propertied men organized in a militia, as the armed citizenry played a key role preserving a society based on popular sovereignty.[21]

Blending family and work, Jefferson's agrarian vision offered something that was at a premium for the "doomed aristocrat" of early national Virginia: hope for the future.[22] George Tucker, an early Virginia novelist and acquaintance of Jefferson's, underlined the wishful, imaginative roots of Jeffersonian democracy in his novel *The Valley of the Shenandoah*. In the book, a character complains of the impossibility of arguing with "your thorough going democrat" because "it does no good to reason with him." Democracy, in this view, was as much a bundle of emotional associations as a rational political credo.[23] Tucker's work illustrated not just the passionate nature of the agrarian disposition but an emotional attachment to a community of households. He portrayed the sense of loss felt by a generation of Virginia aristocrats in the state's troubled post-Revolutionary economy, as sons saw their patrimony disappear. This love for landed independence was intensified by the specter of debt.[24] Fear for an agricultural society threatened by the market was the wellspring of democracy.

Weary of debt and anxious about slavery, Virginia's eighteenth-century gentlemen ceased to think of themselves as aristocrats. Influenced by republican political thought, which highlighted the virtue of the yeomanry, planters shifted the language that they used to describe their agricultural life. In revolutionary Virginia, gentlemen came to identify with the independent yeomen, and, in theory at least, "*planters* became *farmers*."[25] Men like Jefferson were never exactly farmers; hence Jefferson's farm book duly records, without comment, the hiring and even sale of his slaves as he worked to pay his debts and satisfy his luxurious tastes.[26] At the time of the "revolution of 1800," which brought Jefferson into the presidency, a small elite still dominated American politics. Virginia's yeomen did not proclaim their virtue. Planters such as Jefferson did it for them. In doing so, they evaded the distinction between slaveholder and nonslaveholder, declaring the virtue of a unified agricultural interest. As Jefferson declared, "All can be done and peaceably, by the people confiding their choice of representatives & Senators to persons attached to republican government and the principles of 1776, not office-hunters, but farmers, whose interests are primarily agricultural. Such men are the true representatives of the great American interest."[27] When he talked of farmers in office, he referred to planters such as Washington, Madison, Monroe, and himself.

Jefferson worked to make Monticello economically independent as he tried to reduce his personal debt. Yet his debt to merchants diminished his ability to see himself as truly independent. Jefferson's ideal of community required that when he thought about abstract political and social questions, he had to ignore the presence of slaves at Monticello. The reader of Jefferson's correspondence can almost forget the fact that he spent most of his life surrounded by African Americans: the slaves, like the peasants in the European pastoral, are unobtrusive gardeners just out of sight. Jefferson, who had an enormous capacity for "self-deception," could sometimes imagine Monticello as nearly self-sufficient even as he plunged deeper in debt. Ironically, even as he praised the independent farmer, he started a nail-making factory on his plantation, which he attempted to run with an efficiency that twentieth-century readers associate with the scientific management theorist Frederick W. Taylor.[28] The man most influential in articulating an ideal of yeoman independence found himself immersed in a market society that gave rise to manufacturing and commerce.[29]

While Jefferson concentrated his energies on the political defense of the agriculturalist, Virginia political theorist John Taylor of Caroline provided the intellectual bridge between the hierarchical world of Jefferson and that of Jacksonian democracy. After the end of slave importations into the United States and the invention of the cotton gin, slave prices increased. Not surprisingly, the increasingly lucrative nature of slavery dampened emancipationist sentiment, and many planters wished to reconcile slavery with the ideal of pastoral democracy. More than any other theorist, Taylor would try to reconcile the competing strands in Jefferson's beliefs, combining a proslavery argument with pastoral nostalgia and a celebration of the independent farmer. When Taylor celebrated agriculture as the "architect of the complete man," he conflated the manhood and independence of planters with that of yeomen. In his most widely read work, *Arator*, he blended the material necessity of farming with a sublime creation, the well-rounded man. As with Jefferson, slavery figured little in Taylor's defense of pastoral republicanism. Nevertheless, he felt no qualms about human bondage and defended the lot of the slave by comparing his situation to the plight of the wage laborer in manufacturing.[30] But while Taylor, unlike Jefferson, had no misgivings about slavery, the slaves still remain absent in his rural ideal, and no clear distinction is made between planter and yeoman. His modest dress and demeanor made him seem the embodiment of rural simplicity: "I can hardly figure to myself the ideal of a republican statesman more perfect and complete," declared Thomas Hart Benton.[31]

James Madison described Jefferson as "in raptures" over Taylor's writings, which assembled in systematic form a philosophy that resembled the statesman's own scattered musings on manufacturing and agricultural society. Taylor's work appealed to Jeffersonians because it portrayed agrarian life as the best way to develop young men. He drove home the connection between agrarian independence, democracy, and manhood.[32] Yet Taylor never resolved the problem that bedeviled Jefferson: how to protect agricultural independence within the framework of an economy based on private property, which naturally generated dependence and inequality. Whereas Jefferson remained ambivalent about commerce, Taylor embraced it wholeheartedly. Steeped in classical economics, he echoed Adam Smith in his belief that "the commerce of the towns contributed to the improvement of the country."[33] Taylor's differences with Jefferson's views on commerce reflected changes in the nineteenth century, which witnessed increased market activity, even as the agrarian dream persisted.

Taylor's writings pushed agrarian democracy even further than Jefferson's work. In Taylor's view, all men, including officeholders, pursued their own self-interest. Politicians representing the manufacturing class must be restrained by the political virtue of farmers and the framework of a strictly construed Constitution. He outdid Jefferson in opposing the rule of elites: no aristocracy of talent could be trusted when "neither parties nor individuals will voluntarily diminish power in their own hands, however pernicious they have declared it in the hands of others." He demanded rigid adherence to the Constitution and strongly contested deferential politics because "abuses can never be corrected, where confidence and authority have subverted national political principles."[34] As Jefferson's influence waned during his retirement, Taylor emerged as the leading philosopher of the nineteenth-century movement for agrarian democracy. Taylor believed the most talented planters would no longer be seen as a "natural aristocracy" fit to rule, as his ideas reflected the increasing demand of white men, especially on the frontier, for self-rule. As the economy witnessed the development of market relations, demands for debt relief and a return to agrarian equality increased popular pressure for democratization, prompting the adoption of new state constitutions providing universal suffrage.[35]

Despite his commitment to democracy, the writer failed to answer the question that faces all systems of government based on popular sovereignty: how the ruling few chosen for office would represent the many. Citizens of colonial Virginia had selected representatives from a hereditary elite of leading families, but the agrarian ideal espoused by Taylor undermined this old style of deferential politics. Andrew Jackson helped solve this problem of representation in a republic by exemplifying the ideal of a dynamic ruler who spoke for the people. Jackson would gain extraordinary power in the political arena through validation on the new basis of popular responsiveness as well as his superior manhood. In his classic book *The Mind of the South*, Wilbur Cash argued that the "emergence to power" of a southern ruling class based on property rather than hereditary privilege "can be exactly gauged by the emergence of Andrew Jackson." Despite his hyperbole, Cash's point remains valid: a ruling class of frontier slaveholders coalesced in the 1820s, exemplified not only by Jackson but by younger men such as John Calhoun and William Lowndes Yancey.[36]

While Jefferson and Jackson presented strikingly different personalities, party leaders in the 1830s considered Jefferson's writings and ideals indispensable.[37] Yet Jefferson fashioned a relatively meek public persona when compared with the combative Jackson. Historian Henry Adams perhaps exaggerated when he described Jefferson as "almost effeminate," but the contrast with Jackson was evident.[38] The general was renowned for fighting the Creek and Seminole Indians and for winning the Battle of New Orleans. Jackson fought his way to the top, confirming his social stature on the dueling field, whereas Jefferson, a member of the eighteenth-century gentry, saw himself as part of a "natural aristocracy" of talent and breeding. Both came from master class backgrounds. Although Jackson's parents, who appear to have been small-scale slaveholders, were relatively humble, he benefited from classical schooling and a modest patrimony. His career exemplified the ambition of the slaveholding "parvenu aristocrat" rather than the virtues of the plain folk.[39]

The differences between Jefferson and Jackson as leaders reflected changes in American society and politics. As colonial deference gave way to a more open political system, new ways of selecting and evaluating leaders emerged. The period between the revolutionary era and the age of Jackson signaled a shift in attitudes toward authority. The South became a world in which political equality mixed with economic inequality.[40] With Jackson's rise to prominence, manhood offered a new way to talk about authority in a democracy. His extraordinary will and manhood made him a leader who differed from the colonial gentry. In other words, Jackson's exceptional manhood, intertwined with his performance in the South's culture of honor, legitimized his rule over other white men.[41] As historian Thomas Abernathy has pointed out, Jackson "from the beginning of his career set himself up to be a 'gentleman.' . . . On the frontier a gentleman was a man who could play the part, and Jackson played the part convincingly." Part of becoming a gentleman was attaining a reputation for honor, since the principles of honor meant to bind men such as Jackson to a "privileged group and to classify the ranks of its members for the purposes of establishing order."[42] Jackson inherited a set of political values, based on an ideal of the manly agriculturalist, that political scientist Mark E. Kann has noted "legitimized democratic deference" based on a coded language of paternal and fraternal authority.[43]

Jackson played a variety of roles in his life: he was a lawyer, a speculator, a planter, a general, and a politician. He resembled the slaveholding professionals that James Oakes has dubbed "middle-class" slaveholders. His ties with the powerful and wealthy Donelson family in Tennessee separated him socially from the humble yeoman. Moreover, his frontier legal practice, which was based on collecting rural foreclosures from bankrupt farmers, starkly contrasts with the agrarian ideals he promoted during his presidency. He had sufficient polish to mix with the best of Charleston society as a young man and to read law with a distinguished attorney. Frontier lawyers were the "shocktroops of capitalism": their role, Tocqueville remarked, was to restrain the "faults of democracy." Jackson's use of foreclosures meant that his legal practice played a role in bringing Tennessee into a world system of commodity circulation.[44] Andrew Jackson was a gentleman, but he was also the quintessential man on the make.

Yet despite his nouveau riche background, Jackson soon developed a public identity as the embodiment of the Jeffersonian ideal of the sturdy yeoman—a role closely bound to a prescribed masculine identity. In the War of 1812, he led an organization that embodied the strength of the yeomanry: the people's militia. After his spectacular victory at the Battle of New Orleans in 1815, many proclaimed him as the symbol of agricultural virtue. As the eighteenth-century notion of a natural aristocracy faded, Jackson's success as a leader drew on his ability to master the Old South's language for talking about inequality between men—the language of pastoral independence and masculine hierarchy. Some men were manly, but the way Jackson's supporters discussed him reveals that they saw him as especially powerful and virtuous.

Tocqueville believed that Jackson owed his political prominence to "military glory." The brilliant analyst of the antebellum United States declared Jackson a "man of violent temper and middling capacities" whose ascension to the presidency was "all due to the memory of a victory he won twenty years ago under the walls of New Orleans."[45] But the writer did not fully appreciate the cultural impact of the victory. The initial accounts of the Battle of New Orleans, in which a dramatic triumph over the British brought Jackson's name to national prominence, emphasized his role as a leader of the yeomanry. Jackson had inspired "a mass of farmers, hastily collected, with invincible ardor." Congressman George Troup of Georgia underscored the connection between the yeoman militia's actions in defending its country and its masculine prerogatives. These men were "leaving their wives and children and fire-sides at a moment's warning." Thus the American yeoman, and the long-standing tradition of the popular militia, seemed to be vindicated after several years of humiliation against well-trained British regulars. Jackson himself later underscored the connection between the combativeness of the yeomen and their role as men. They saved New Orleans from the specter of rape: "pollution and ravage by an infuriated British soldiery" had been stopped.[46]

Tillers of the soil could represent themselves on the battlefield and were thus superior to professional armies. As Jackson declared, "The farmers of the country were triumphantly victorious over the conquerors of Europe. *I came, I saw, I conquered*, says the *American husbandman*, fresh from his plough." He was especially satisfied with the enthusiasm that brought "the proud yeomanry of our country, to support its eagles." Troup noted that the effective "triumph of militia over regular troops" vindicated the ideal of the steadfast yeoman militia. Jackson, in a letter to the secretary of war, emphasized the importance of the militia performing with "firmness.... More could not have been expected from veterans inured to war." But while Americans lauded the militia, many also praised the remarkable "brilliancy of General Jackson."[47]

For the rest of Jackson's life, writers, political associates, and the general himself would embroider the picture of the man of the people, yet somehow above the people. One petition from the battalion of uniform companies at New Orleans thanked him for the "paternal care with which you watched over our comforts." The same document referred to him as one of the yeomen's "brothers in arms," a "fellow citizen."[48] Simultaneously a brother and a father, he was the yeoman's equal but also his superior. The presentation of Jackson as a yeoman predominated after New Orleans, but that image was contradicted by a letter from Jackson's friend General John Coffee to the *Richmond Enquirer*. Coffee emphasized that Jackson "received a liberal education and at an early age commenced the practice of law." No mere frontiersman, Jackson "was esteemed eminent in his profession.... He was pointed out to [Coffee] as an eloquent scholar." General Coffee emphasized that although Jackson came from humble origins, "his industry soon made him rich."[49]

Jackson's position as the first among equals is evident in his address to his troops, written by his close friend John Eaton and delivered as the army prepared to leave New Orleans. Jackson hailed his men as "full of honor" and expressed pleasure that they would now return to their roles as heads of households: "Go then to your homes, to those tender connexions and those blissful scenes which render life so dear." Yet even though he used the language of shared familial responsibility with his men, he also invoked his prerogatives as a superior, as he asked the men to "continue . . . to preserve on your passage to your homes, that patience, that subordination, that dignified and manly deportment which has so ennobled your characters." In appealing to his soldiers to be both "subordinate" and "manly," Jackson suggested that his ideal of agrarian manhood was based on an orderly community. Jefferson would later criticize Jackson, declaring that "his passions are terrible" and describing Jackson's tendency to "choke with rage" on the Senate floor.[50] Despite their differences in temperament, Jackson shared Jefferson's goal of preserving a harmonious rural society, and Democrats would invoke the Virginian's legacy.

In portraying Andrew Jackson as a farmer, his supporters and biographers stretched the truth, or at least blended the line between the upwardly mobile planter and the working farmer, effacing the presence of the slaves on whom Jackson depended to do the agricultural labor at his plantation, the Hermitage. One biographer wrote that before the war Jackson had "the determination to spend the rest of his life in tranquility and seclusion, on a beautiful farm belonging to him." In reality, Jackson at times seemed detached from matters of business on his plantation. John Henry Eaton, who stayed in Washington with the general in 1824, remarked that "if the Genl had remained at home, I am satisfied he would not have enjoyed such [good] health. His farm would have annoyed him." Before the presidential election in 1824, Eaton claimed that Jackson would prefer "that he should remain upon his farm and at his plough." The planter at the Hermitage became a farmer in political rhetoric. And like Taylor, Jackson linked agrarian independence with masculinity: "Independance of mind and action, is the noblest attribute of man," he remarked.[51]

Political literature promoting Jackson dramatically emphasized his masculinity. Jackson's authorized biography emphasized the connection between his manhood and the coming of age of the Revolutionary generation. When he was fourteen, Jackson had spontaneously joined in the fighting in the Carolinas alongside the militia. After he had been taken captive by the British, an officer demanded that the youngster clean his boots. Seizing on this chance to show both his Revolutionary fervor and his manhood, Jackson refused, demanding to be treated as a prisoner of war. He claimed his manhood at the risk of death: "The officer aimed a blow at his head with drawn sword, which would, very probably, have terminated his existence, had he not parried its effects by throwing up his left hand, on which he received a severe wound."⁵² The literal accuracy of the authorized account of this incident, drawn from Jackson's version of the story and closely followed by subsequent biographers, is less important than its symbolic resonance. By fighting and risking death, Jackson had proven his manhood in a spectacular matter. He took part in what one scholar has called an American "revolution against patriarchal authority." By claiming the rights of a prisoner of war in his dispute with the officer, the young Jackson simultaneously proclaimed his personal manhood and America's independence from Britain. In cultures based on slavery, honor and manhood have been closely associated with the willingness to risk death.⁵³ One need not be a Freudian to note the frequency with which portrayals of the fight emphasize the risk that he would lose his arm, a critical bodily appendage, in the act of asserting his manhood. They refer to the wounds left by the officer's attack, "the mark ... he bore to his death." As a biographer pointed out, "when we reflect that he was only fourteen years of age . . . his manly firmness and exalted sense of honor" deserved admiration. One man later praised "the manly spirit of the noble boy." A Whig writer of the 1830s noted with some pique that for Jackson the confrontation "has proved a most fortunate event, yielding a large portion of that glory which constitutes him the hero of two wars."⁵⁴ Thus the young man wore permanently the mark of his honor.

In Jackson's military service during the War of 1812, he learned to rule over farmers as subordinates. Militia service, like the army, depends on a respect for officers that is based not just on the voluntary decision to join but on the power of officers to coerce their men. Although Jackson made much of the strength of the yeoman militia at New Orleans, discipline under his command came primarily through his authority. His official biographers explained Jackson's execution of semimutinous subordinates in 1814 by referring to the special nature of yeoman militia, since "composed, as this army was, of troops entirely raw, it was not to be expected that any thing short of the greatest firmness in its officers could restrain that course of conduct and disorder." Without his willingness to extract the ultimate penalty from unruly soldiers, discipline would suffer because "militia, when at their fire-sides, at home, might boast an exemption from control, yet, in the field, those high notions were to be abandoned, and subordination observed."⁵⁵ In the people's militia, men gave up their domestic prerogatives and submitted to Jackson's power.

According to campaign literature, Jackson's ability to maintain subordination in his men came not only from his military rank but also from his strong will. In the Creek War, Jackson faced mutiny from restive, frustrated, and underfed militiamen. He successfully stood down rebellion, while displaying considerable physical courage. According to a Whig writer, Jackson revealed "the development of the organ of combativeness," which proved him "sadly deficient in the arts of conciliation." The execution of a militiaman during the Creek campaign highlighted his habitual reliance on force. By killing a fellow soldier, Jackson seemingly cast in doubt his claims that he was a paternal leader. Jackson's political allies justified the execution through its salutary effects in maintaining discipline: "Order was produced, and that opinion, so long indulged, that a militia man was for no offence to suffer death, was, from that moment, abandoned, and a strict obedience afterwards characterized the army."[56] Under Jackson, yeoman farmers were assembled in a popular institution, but they still met limitations on their independence.

General Jackson's power, exercised on both the plantation and the battlefield, had a familial character. His blending of personal concern with arbitrary power is the essence of slaveholding paternalism.[57] Young men of the frontier were accustomed to relative autonomy but found discipline and the authority to bind them together as a community through Jackson's leadership. As one of his admirers later explained, the general had to contend with the fact that his troops were composed of volunteers who were "young men educated in unrestrained freedom, accustomed to no . . . words of authority." This made his task difficult. Yet Jackson managed his army as a father figure, since, "like Moses called from the land of Jethro to deliver his people from bondage, Jackson had now come from his retirement that he might avenge his family and his fatherland, and save his country."[58] The militia led by Jackson revealed a community of men who were somewhat independent and not completely equal men.

During the Seminole War in Florida, Jackson showed his remarkable nerve by exceeding his orders and attacking the Spanish, touching off a congressional investigation of his conduct.[59] Henry Clay typified the wrath vented against Jackson when he accused him, as a military leader, of endangering the Republic, arguing that the most common cause of the downfall of republics was military dictatorship. He asked citizens to "recall to your recollection, the free nations that have gone before us. . . . How have they lost their liberties? . . . Ask a Grecian if he did not fear some daring military chieftain would one day overthrow his liberties. No! No! The confident and indignant Grecian would exclaim. . . . Remember that Greece had her Alexander, Rome her Caesar, England her Cromwell, France her Bonaparte." Clay tapped into genuine anxiety, as fears of military dictatorship abounded: British traveler Harriet Martineau was told soon after she arrived in the United States that the country was on the verge of military despotism. Despite Jackson's image as a democrat, his opponents feared the "absolute rule of a single man."[60] Jackson clearly had exceeded his military authority. Yet even these charges failed to dampen Jackson's popularity with southern farmers, men who valued their personal autonomy.

Jacksonians' deft use of his image as a father figure helps explain why complaints about his willingness to use arbitrary authority so often fell on deaf ears. For example, opponents noted that early in the War of 1812 Jackson defied government orders to discharge his troops. Yet the incident redounded to the general's advantage. Jackson had refused a direct order when, as eulogist Hugh Garland later pointed out, "an ordinary man would have complied." He disregarded his superiors because he felt their orders endangered men who had become like a family. Garland imagined Jackson's train of thought: "What!" said he, "shall the word of Andrew Jackson be forfeited? Did I not promise to be a father and friend to these young men, when, in obedience to my call, they flocked to the standard of their country? What did I promise to the daughters of Tennessee. . . . Did they not gather around me with tears in their eyes and say, General! General! I trust my father to you—my husband—my son—general! I know you will take care of them."[61] Jackson's role as a patriarchal ruler of his troops helps explain his notorious inability to coexist with civil authority, most notably evinced in New Orleans when he declared martial law, arrested civil officials, dismissed the legislature, and defied a writ of habeas corpus. Jackson and his proponents argued that his role as a strong and caring father tempered his demands for subordination.

Jackson also benefited from his association with the people's militia. He noted in his first inaugural address that he would rely on the militia rather than a standing army because so long as the government "is worth defending a patriotic militia will cover it with an impenetrable aegis." Jackson demanded, and received, obedience from his men. The distance between the general and his image as popular democrat is best displayed just at the moment he came to popular fame—in the campaign that led to the Battle of New Orleans. In the days after the battle, Jackson maintained a "police state" in the city, despite unofficial knowledge by inhabitants that the war was over. He ruled through dictatorial powers. Later his official biographers claimed that "he did it . . . to obtain, through fear, that security which could not be had through love of country."[62] Jackson's friends realized that his reputation for unrestrained passions could pose a political problem, and they artfully massaged his image. Eventually, supporters formed "a standing committee to defend his character and reputation against slander."[63]

The Jackson camp's deft blending of the pastoral and paternal image helps explain why accusations of despotism did not stick. Jackson played the role of the reluctant farmer turned politician even more convincingly than Jefferson. In replying to inquiries about his availability for the presidency in 1824, Jackson declared that those who thought he had ambition "do not know me." He "had never dreamed of . . . any higher future part, than that of the private citizen. . . . On my own farm, to have been a spectator rather than an actor, in events to come, I should have been contented and happy. . . . A man of fifty-seven, should be without any feelings of ambition, except what duty to the interest of his country and a regard for his own honor and character may dictate." His image as a working farmer undercut depictions of him as another Napoleon and provided continuity with Jeffersonian traditions. Like Jackson's followers, Clay supporters promoted their man as disinterested in the presidency. Yet the Whig leader was portrayed by backers as devoted to an occupation bound to be less popular with the yeomanry: "the regular practice of law."[64]

Like Jefferson, Jackson enjoyed pastoral literature. Jackson biographer Robert Remini notes that Jackson "prized the Vicar [of Wakefield] above all other books after the Bible."[65] James Parton alleged that this was the only secular book that the president ever read from cover to cover. Jackson's affection for this book suggests that he outgrew the impulsive personality of his youth. His preference for the *Vicar of Wakefield* speaks to the similarity between the virtuous community Goldsmith depicts in eighteenth-century rural life and Jackson's social mores. The novel, which was also a favorite of Jefferson's, is one that blends the values of rural society and patriarchal authority. Its lessons dovetailed neatly with the Democratic ideal of a community of independent men.

As the novel opens, Goldsmith portrays a happy family. The father works as a vicar but maintains a gentry lifestyle because of a patrimony of ten thousand pounds. He is thus able to provide his six children with "education without softness." The vicar could, because of his inheritance, be "careless of temporalities." Early in the novel an embezzler takes the money, forcing the vicar to become a working farmer. Financial ruin forces the family to "give up all pretensions to gentility." They move to a rural community that sounds much like Jefferson's agricultural ideal, "consisting of farmers, who tilled their own grounds, and were equal strangers to opulence and poverty." These people lived between poverty and luxury and "retained the primeval simplicity of manners."[66] The vicar drops aristocratic ostentation and inhabits a middle-class world, similar to the Jeffersonian vision of a society of working farmers.

The vicar enjoys his rural surroundings and benevolently dispenses his paternal authority. The yeoman life praised by Goldsmith was a model for a virtuous political system. Yet it was not exactly democratic: the vicar calls his family "the little republic to which I gave laws," a phrase that suggests that in his familial politics the vicar had paramount authority. The vicar's family cannot afford many luxuries but because of the virtue of rural life does not decline into absolute poverty. Instead, the family continues to "keep up some mechanical forms of good breeding." While maintaining the manners that represented the best of the upper class, the vicar abandons customs that encourage feminine luxury. Determined to conform to the mores of a community of humble farmers, he demands that his wife and daughters avoid wearing ostentatious "frippery," arguing that "these ruffles, and pinks, and patchings will only make us hated by all the wives of our neighbours."[67] The novel shows the need for paternal guidance, as domestic harmony is repeatedly subverted by the follies of the vicar's wife and daughters.

The vicar echoes the rural ideals that Jackson had imbibed as his political creed. In this pastoral setting, the work of agriculture is absent, like the slaves at Jefferson's Monticello. The author describes no labor by the wife, daughters, hired men, or, for that matter, the vicar himself. The vicar resembles both Jefferson and Jackson by being in, but not of, the farming class. Jackson had fashioned himself both as a gentleman and as an ordinary farmer. The vicar fits the same mold: he begins the novel with wealth and breeding, then maintains the polish of gentry habits while dispensing with useless luxury as his family lives in reduced circumstances. Miraculously at the end of the novel, he returns to affluence as his embezzled funds are returned. The vicar has visited the world of the working agriculturalist and absorbed his virtues. Nevertheless, he is not a simple yeoman. By returning his hero to comfortable independence from agricultural toil, Goldsmith suggests that lessons can be learned from the yeomanry, but he also signals that a man of the vicar's breeding should retain his class prerogatives.

As literary critic Dana D. Nelson has argued, early national elites such as Jackson maintained a nostalgic longing for a stable masculine order. Clearly the *Vicar* helped satisfy that sentiment for Jackson.[68] Jackson, who was intensely conscious of social hierarchy, charted a course between the world of the wealthy and that of the common farmer. His understanding of class distinctions is evident in advice he gave to his young ward, Andrew Jackson Donelson. Like the vicar, Jackson upheld a rigorous code of conduct for young gentlemen: "You should alone intermix, with the better class of society, whose characters are well established for their virtue. . . . Shun the intercourse of the others as you would the society of the viper or the base character." In this context, "character" became a way to order a society without hereditary status. This process of judging character was crucial in defining not only class relations but also those between the sexes: he fervently believed that "we should shun base women as a pestilence."[69]

The *Vicar of Wakefield* appealed to Jackson because it mirrored the agrarian identity he had fashioned for himself. As one campaign biography put it, he spent time on his farm "happy in the indulgence of his fondness for rural occupations, and in the society of an affectionate wife and a number of honest friends."[70] Like the vicar, Jackson enjoyed the tranquility of rural life while still having education and wealth. Thus he had the ability to lead not just his family but the rural community as a whole. Jackson and the vicar had the best of two worlds: they were both yeoman farmers and gentlemen patriarchs. This blurring of social distinctions would become crucial to southern democratic thought.[71]

Jackson's paternal authority helps explain the Peggy Eaton affair. His old friend John Eaton served as a cabinet member in his administration, but members of the cabinet and their wives shunned his young wife, Peggy Eaton. Rumors abounded that the couple had had an affair before they married, which caused Mrs. Eaton's first husband, John Timberlake, to slit his throat. Some historians have argued that the fight was a distraction from the real business of the administration, arguing that the Eaton dispute drew Jackson's attention because he wrongly believed that the attacks on Mrs. Eaton were part of a "conspiracy" against his administration. Others have maintained that his anger at rumors that had surrounded his wife, the late Rachel Jackson, inspired him to defend Mrs. Eaton. Therefore, tangled infighting detracted from the substantive issues of his presidency such as bank wars, Indian removal, internal improvements, and tariffs, providing mere "comic relief" to the historian. Yet Jackson's response to the Eaton affair reveals that "symbolic conflicts over cultural issues" can influence disputes over political power. Indeed, the fight was as much about the authority of Andrew Jackson as the reputation of Mrs. Eaton.[72]

The Peggy Eaton affair provides a window to the relationship between

Jackson's paternal authority and political power.⁷³ The conflict became public after a falling out between Jackson and his vice president, John Calhoun. Jackson attacked Calhoun in 1831 regarding his conduct of more than a decade earlier, when the South Carolinian served as secretary of war. While Jackson conducted a campaign against Creek Indians, he had antagonized the Spanish by illegally encroaching on their territory at Pensacola. He assumed he had Calhoun's support. But he learned early in his presidency that, contrary to appearances, Calhoun had not supported him while in the Monroe cabinet. Instead, Calhoun had undermined him politically. Jackson was infuriated less by the old political squabble than by the fact that Calhoun misled him while "endeavoring to destroy [his] reputation." He accused Calhoun of "deception" and declared "in the language of Caesar, et tu Brute." The *Washington Globe*'s assertion that the falling-out of Jackson and Calhoun "was a mere private difference" concerning "only the bearing of two gentlemen towards each other" seems strange considering that these men were president and vice president.⁷⁴ But it reflects the culture of honor in which Jackson and Calhoun grew to manhood.

The Eaton affair was central to a power struggle between Jackson and Calhoun, as the machinations of politicians exposed the fragility of barriers between public and private life. Calhoun's delicate letters to Jackson, attempting to explain his course during the Creek War, and Jackson's belligerent responses make sense within the culture of southern honor. Jackson's letters questioned Calhoun's honor and impugned his manhood. Calhoun's attempts to prove to Jackson that he had not made any "disguise" of his conduct in the Creek War proved unconvincing.⁷⁵ Worse, Calhoun's efforts to reconcile with the president never cut to the real issue at hand: the reputations of the two gentlemen. Calhoun followed a course that Jackson denounced as "uncandid and unmanly."⁷⁶ In the culture of southern honor, these were fighting words, and they would likely have produced a duel if not for Jackson's status as president. Instead, the Eaton affair reached the newspapers as Jackson's fight with Calhoun had escalated. Mrs. Eaton convincingly argued in her autobiography that "John C. Calhoun and his friends were at the bottom of this whole business." She explained that several members of the administration wished to force her husband out of the cabinet. Therefore Calhoun's close associate Duff Green ran an article in the *Telegraph* making the first public allegations against Mrs. Eaton. She was seen as a "good card to play" in Calhoun's rivalry with Jackson.⁷⁷

Jackson refused to condone a system that allowed his cabinet members to interfere with the harmony of his administration. His fervent attempts to root out the source of the Eaton rumors and resolve the issue, including firing cabinet officers, speaks to his belief that, as the head of government, he should control Washington's social scene. Elizabeth Fox-Genovese has argued that in the South the continuing centrality of the household as "the dominant unit of production and reproduction" fashioned distinctive gender relations. As South Carolina's C. G. Memminger wrote, "The Slave Institution of the South increases the tendency to dignify the family. Each planter in fact is a Patriarch—his position compels him to be a ruler in household."[78] Like Memminger's patriarch, Jackson refused to accept the limits on his authority implied by a division between public and private life. He reserved the right to regulate the lives of his subordinates because as a father figure his authority was absolute.

Opponents of Peggy Eaton within the Jackson cabinet disclaimed any responsibility for her ostracism in Washington society. Calhoun attempted to explain the reason that his wife, Floride, a leader among Washington matrons, snubbed Mrs. Eaton: "She knew nothing of Mrs. Eaton, or the truth, or falsehood of the imputation on her character; and that she conceived to be the duty of Mrs. Eaton, if innocent, to open her intercourse with the ladies . . . who had the best means of forming a correct opinion of her conduct." He argued that he knew his wife's course would cause him political difficulties but that the question involved was "paramount to all political considerations." Ultimately, the question was not of Mr. Eaton's right to serve in the cabinet but the admission into private "society" of someone who had been excluded.[79] Calhoun and his allies stated that women should judge women and that the ladies of Washington should decide Mrs. Eaton's place. The political importance of the move was unmistakable because before the rise of mass parties, social ability among officials weighed heavily in their ability to make political friends and contacts integral to their political success.[80]

Jackson believed, just like his favorite author, that "men are most capable of distinguishing merit in women." He refused to accept the notion that the shunning of a cabinet officer's wife could be a mere private affair. He considered the sensational rumors about Mrs. Eaton "the basest lie ever told." Jackson used his defense of Mrs. Eaton's virtue to assert his own authority. He emphatically declared that he "did not come here to make a cabinet for the Ladies of this place, but for the nation." In maintaining his right to defend Mrs. Eaton, the president noted that he had been chosen by the "voice of the people."[81] His power, interwoven with the power of the people, gave him the right to make the final determination regarding Mrs. Eaton's virtue.

Jackson has been described as "engaged in a lunatic campaign in which he had no business." Yet because of his long-standing image as a benevolent father, Jackson's ferocious loyalty to Mrs. Eaton dovetailed with his political identity and most cherished beliefs about the nature of his responsibilities as a leader. The president ultimately carried out an exhaustive investigation into the charges, found their source to be unreliable, and gave a young minister charged with starting the rumor a dressing down before the entire cabinet. Of course, in declaring the twice-married Mrs. Eaton to be "as chaste as a virgin," Jackson may have stretched the truth, but he effectively asserted his power.[82]

Jackson's patriarchal authority, as the Eaton case demonstrates, trumped the power of other men. When the family of his ward, Andrew Jackson Donelson, snubbed Mrs. Eaton, she appealed not to Donelson but to the president himself. Donelson was gravely offended by this encroachment on his familial prerogatives: "Instead of coming to me as the head of my family for explanations . . . they have invariably approached the President." Yet Jackson never apologized for interfering in the domestic relations of the masters of other households, even to his ward. Instead, he derided two of his cabinet members because they "could not controle their families." Jackson's role in the Eaton battle cemented his image as a protector of women to the last as he declared, "The exalted sphere of the ladies which his heart appreciated, his hand was ever ready to acknowledge." Yet it is important to note that for Jackson Peggy Eaton's well-being was a secondary consideration. By defending her, he "used her as a device to enforce standards of personal loyalty on the men around him."[83]

Jackson biographer James Parton, writing in 1855, recognized the importance of this struggle in the formation of the Jacksonian Democratic political style. Referring to Martin Van Buren, he slyly observed that "the political history of the United States, for the last thirty years, dates from the moment when the soft hand of Mr. Van Buren touched Mrs. Eaton's knocker." The writer underlined that while Van Buren, in siding with the Eatons, effectively curried favor with Jackson, more was at stake than his presidential aspirations. This Eaton imbroglio marked a watershed in antebellum political history because of the fight's symbolic importance in building Jackson's powerful image.[84] Jackson not only defended Peggy Eaton's virtue; he demonstrated his own political tenacity. He used the press to warn wavering supporters of their obligations, and if such attempts at persuasion failed, men could be effectively driven out of the party.[85]

Mrs. Eaton, by all accounts an intelligent woman, offered insights into how Jackson's public persona as a politician and his private life were intertwined. She described him as a gentle man: "The world knows the hard side of Genl. Jackson's character—and I think that side came out specially in his defense of me—but they do not know how gentle and tender and kind he was toward all his friends—men and women." Yet even as he revealed his "tender" side, Jackson could not stand any suggestion that his manhood had been impugned. In a famous incident during his presidency, a disgruntled officer attacked General Jackson, attempting to pull his nose. Such an action, Kenneth Greenberg has demonstrated, would be a terrible indignity. The frail, elderly Jackson fought back, and his subordinates offered to kill the attacker if they would be pardoned. Jackson rejected such a rash suggestion but could not shrug off the incident. In her old age, Peggy Eaton fondly remembered teasing Old Hickory about having his nose pulled, noting "the violence with which he would always repel" the story. Mrs. Eaton recalled that "he invariably sprang to his feet, shook his fist, and said, 'No; by the eternal God, madam, no man ever pulled my nose.'"[86]

South Carolina's nullification crisis, in which the state defied national authority by asserting its right to refuse to pay tariffs, provided the denouement to the rivalry between Jackson and Calhoun. Certainly the crisis threatened something beyond constitutional principles, although Jackson and Calhoun both took those principles very seriously. Thus Jackson, determined to put down this dissent, threatened, despite his poor health, to "march two hundred thousand men in forty days to quell any and every insurrection." He again appealed to the tradition of the people's militia, the institution that had made his reputation. Armed citizens would, he believed, put down treason in South Carolina because "the united voice of the yeomanry of the country" was on his side.[87] Jackson made a remarkable departure from ordinary Democratic rhetoric, which asserted that slaveholders and nonslaveholders constituted a united agricultural interest. His reference to the "united voice of the yeomanry" suggests that he understood that many viewed South Carolina as a bastion of aristocracy and expected to win nonslaveholder support against its ruling elite.[88]

That Jackson planned to lead the militia personally shows he interpreted the nullification doctrine from the perspective of an injured gentleman. In the initial draft of his second inaugural address he declared, "I feel in the depths of my soul, that it is the highest, most sacred and most irreversible part of my obligation to preserve the union of these states, although it may cost me my life." Southerners proved their manhood and honor with their willingness to risk death, and Jackson, the hero of two wars, signaled his readiness to fight another. Carefully, he invoked the legacy of Thomas Jefferson to justify his course.[89] Jackson acted as a man of southern honor: he accused Calhoun of dishonesty, threatened him with mortal combat, and forced him to back down. In doing so, he showed that his indomitable will could protect the interests of the plain folk. He concluded that "the free people of these United States [had] spoken, and consigned these wicked demagogues to their proper doom."[90]

Jackson's blending of equality and authority would serve him well in the most famous battle of his administration, his war with the Bank of the United States. Jackson identified the leader of the bank, Nicholas Biddle, as a threat to the liberty of the people and personally directed an audacious campaign to destroy his opponent's power. This conflict has long been seen as one of the central political events of Jackson's presidency. The Bank War's resonance with Jackson's image of paternal authority and popular fears of the market ensured that the incident would frame political discourse for the next generation. Jackson framed the Bank War as one that pitted him, representing the people, against the encroaching forces of privileged aristocracy. His choice of opponent exemplified his celebration of the pastoral middle state and commitment to defending the yeomanry. The president risked his public reputation with his bold action and justified his course as embodying the will of the people. For Jackson, a strong man leading the resistance was essential to preserving the sovereign will of the people. Moreover, the Bank War provided Jacksonians a chance to claim continuity with Jeffersonian tradition. Jackson ally Francis P. Blair clearly alluded to Jeffersonian principles when he declared that "the only legitimate object" of government was "to protect man in the pursuit of happiness." In a letter defending Jackson's stance against Biddle, James K. Polk praised "the political principles of Thomas Jefferson! They can never be overturned or destroyed by the corrupt power of an irresponsible corporation, which seeks by its money to controul public affairs."[91]

Jackson's conflict with the Second Bank of the United States was "in terms of party history the single most important event during the entire middle period of American history" as it became the instrument by which Old Hickory strengthened presidential powers.[92] Jackson suspected the bank of undermining him politically and using its deposits to influence a decision on renewing its charter. His aide Roger Taney accused Biddle of increasing the bank's loans in 1831 in order to "exercise a controlling influence over the action of the government in relation to its charter . . . to compel the people to continue its monopoly and privileges." Amos Kendall, an auditor at the Treasury, accused the bank of "subterfuges and falsehoods" and hence dishonorable behavior. Jackson's aides linked the fight with the bank to preserving republican manhood: "The pure men of the country are watching the course of the administration with intense anxiety. . . . If the first blow shall be to cripple the bank . . . the true men of the country will rally around the administration."[93]

To Jacksonians, the bank seemed dangerous because it undermined men's independence, which was closely bound up with yeoman conceptions of masculinity. Paper currency and a moneyed aristocracy, many Democrats feared, could endanger the autonomy of farmers.[94] Alabama writer Joseph Glover Baldwin explained the problem of credit to the yeoman class in a novel about the Southwest in the 1830s, recounting incidents "of pride abased; of honorable sensibilities wounded . . . of the hopes of manhood overcast; of independence dissipated." Martin Van Buren cautioned that the bank would "nourish in preference to the manly virtues that give dignity to human nature, a craving desire for luxurious enjoyment and sudden wealth." Banks produced "a sickly appetite for feminine indulgence." Western manhood would scorn the bank, Democrat Thomas Hart Benton declared: "The hunter of the West with moccasins on his feet, and a hunting shirt drawn around him, would repel with indignation the highest bribe the bank could offer him."[95]

Jackson's confrontational style ensured his success: as one friend put it, "The rock of Gibraltar could not have been more immovable. His opinions could not be changed, and the line of conduct he had marked out was fixed and unalterable. . . . No man save himself had that deep and abiding hold on the sympathies and affections of the American people, without which he would inevitably have been crushed." Jackson had little understanding of economics, but he did have his finger on the pulse of the American population. Biddle and the bank symbolized the social forces that created insecurities for the rural population. After having defeated wealthy South Carolina planters over nullification, Jackson had taken on Biddle, a man who symbolized northern capital. Emotional support for the president was overwhelming, as some voters did blindly submit to the wisdom of the president, such as Archibald Yell of Arkansas, who announced, "I am so much of a partizan that I am always for

Jackson Right or Wrong." To many, the president's power seemed threatening: Philadelphians declared, "We recognize a determination on the part of general Jackson to be the dictator of a submissive, not the president of a free people."[96] During the Bank War, the image of Jackson as a tribune of the people, not as an arbitrary "King Veto," stuck in the minds of most southern voters. In the House, P. P. Barbour emphasized Jackson's leadership, proclaiming that his "firm and fearless step" produced a "manly and independent course" that would sustain the nation.[97]

The president continued to personify the reluctant agriculturalist pulled into politics throughout his term of office. Jackson remarked that he was tired of fighting "corruption" and longed "for retirement and repose on the Hermitage."[98] The pastoral idyll at the Hermitage was, of course, marred by slavery, but Jackson seemed oblivious to that issue as either a moral or political question. Old Hickory was blissfully unaware of the paradoxical relationship between American slavery and American freedom, or the contradictions inherent in a great planter who called himself a man of the people. His fervent belief in limited government killed hopes for costly programs such as colonization of slaves to Africa. The Democrats' increasing racism in the early national period took emancipation off the political agenda. Although the influential argument for slavery as a positive good was first expounded by intellectuals such as Thomas R. Dew rather than Jacksonian Democrats, it comes as no surprise that proslavery thought dramatically emerged during Jackson's term in office.[99]

Jackson saw no contradiction because for him there was none. After all, he was still one with the yeomanry that had stood behind him as he faced down John Calhoun and Nicholas Biddle. One admiring biographer, John Frost, explained that Jackson and the people were family: "Gradually rising from the humbler walks of life to the most exalted stations on earth, he knew the wants, feelings, and sympathies of all classes, all conditions; and his countrymen were to him as the equal members of the same great family associated for the common benefit." He was, "since the maturity of his manhood[,] . . . a most exemplary specimen of human character." He could never be a "dictator" because he was a farmer. Because of Jackson's agrarian identity, one supporter proclaimed, "Jackson's principles were those which the popular interests reflected, and which his own interests, as a citizen, were identified in every respect." The president's supporters asserted that he had "administered the government on Jeffersonian principles." The *Washington Globe*, the nation's leading Jacksonian newspaper, took a vigilant stance so that "farmers" would know of plotting for tariffs "particularly at the expense of the agricultural interests."[100]

While campaign literature often cast Jackson as a popular Democrat, he did not conceive of his role within the framework of "liberal democracy." Jackson reckoned "the popular will to be an instrument of self-vindication."[101] Indeed, many of Jackson's opponents genuinely feared that he was irrational and dangerous. Some compared his ferocity to that of an animal. For example, when Henry Clay suspected that the president was weakening politically, he declared, "He still shows game, appears stout and strong; but . . . his strength is that of the buck, mortally wounded, who springs boldly forward while he is internally bleeding to death." Similarly, Nicholas Biddle described Jackson as having "all the fury of a chained panther biting the bars of his cage."[102] Daniel Webster used less colorful language but voiced the familiar warnings against Jackson's arbitrary power after the Bank Veto.[103] Webster was correct in maintaining that while Jackson fashioned himself as a tribune of the people, he was not in practice directly responsive to popular opinion. But Clay and Webster inhabited a different intellectual universe than the yeomanry did and failed to grasp the appeal of Jackson's pastoral style.

In his Farewell Address, Jackson employed his customary familial rhetoric to buttress white supremacy. After emphasizing the need for "paternal care" of Native Americans, Jackson recalled the farewell address of George Washington. The president reminded Americans that the "Father of Our Country" warned Americans against divisive issues. Without naming abolitionists, Jackson warned against their "pernicious influence." These "weak men" deserved collective "reprobation." He remarked on the bonds the "citizens of the several States bear to one another as members of one political family, mutually contributing to the happiness of each other." Therefore individuals should not raise issues that would "disturb the tranquility of their political brethren."[104] Jackson, the first president since Washington to give a farewell address, did so because, like the first president, he feared for the future of the Republic. Jackson lent such importance to quelling the slavery debate because he could not imagine an agricultural republic without the peculiar institution.

The image of the manly farmer, articulated by Jefferson and embodied by Jackson, was crucial to maintaining the coalition of slaveholders and nonslaveholders that led Democrats to electoral victories and ultimately a militant defense of slavery. The Democrats had managed to talk about politics while ignoring divisive issues of class within the white community, just as Jackson, a slaveholder, had artfully crafted an image as a defender of the people. The preservation of yeoman independence would remain a compelling theme for Democrats as Jackson spent the last years of his life warning of imminent danger from the Whigs and the banks. Jackson so feared Whig political domination and the accompanying rise of aristocracy that when Whig William Henry Harrison died shortly after taking office, Jackson gave thanks to "a kind and overruling providence" that "interfered to prolong our glorious Union and happy republican system."[105]

After Jackson left the presidency, he suffered the anxiety faced by many agriculturalists enmeshed in the market economy. As a result of his long absence in Washington, he witnessed the gradual erosion of his finances. His adopted son, Andrew Jackson Jr., found himself entangled in debt and unable to restore his credit. Jackson worked to protect his son's reputation and pay his debts, just as he had labored to free Americans from the control of the banks. Like the vicar of Wakefield, he warned his son against falling in debt for things "useless to your comfort or prosperity." He pleaded that he would "die contented in the hope that you will never again encumber yourself with debt, that may result in the poverty of yourself and little family." The former president traveled to Mississippi to find a suitable tract of land for his relatives and from there wrote to his daughter-in-law, Sarah Jackson, indicating that he had little faith in young Andrew's ability to extricate himself from debt. The importance of financial independence in Jackson's worldview cannot be overestimated, since he viewed his son's debt as an "imputation" on his own character. His son's shame was greater, although Jackson hoped that he would pay his creditors and "be once more a freeman having sustained his credit." In 1844, young Andrew's hopes still seemed uncertain as they depended on a force beyond his control, a good market price for cotton.[106]

The general left an image of the Democratic Party as the protector of rural life that would remain compelling well into the 1850s. Moreover, with his opposition to banking he had framed an issue that would become crucial for politics at the state level. In the final decade before the Civil War, pressures arising out of a modernizing economy would endanger the stability of rural society. As subsistence farmers faced economic forces endangering their way of life, the pastoral ideal continued to bind yeoman and slaveholder together in their shared identity as agriculturalists. Yet no politician was ever able to master the language of pastoral democracy as adroitly as Jackson, and his promotion of rural manhood shaped antebellum politics. While southern

Whigs actively sought women's support by 1840, the Democrats showed much greater caution in regard to allowing women to attend political meetings.[107]

Old Hickory himself had warned that electing Democrats was not enough to ensure the continuance of his principles, as he complained of "hypocracy" that "all these kind of lovers of the people are fostering, and fostered by the Banks, they are elected as Democrats but are bought in by the Banks."[108] Indeed, he informed his admirers that corruption remained a danger in a representative political system. After his death, eulogies to Jackson and biographies of the hero focused on his youth, his bravery in the face of death, and his fatherly quality as president. In praising Jackson's character, Democrats left an important question unanswered: Who, if anyone, could maintain agrarian liberty against the encroachments of aristocratic power?

2 The Approaching Storm— Southern Democrats and the Sectional Crisis

South Carolina diarist Mary Chesnut's writings bear witness to the complexity of the interaction between planters and yeomen in the Civil War era. In a famous passage in her memoir of the Civil War, Chesnut wrote of her husband, Senator James Chesnut, entertaining a barefooted member of the local citizenry. Mrs. Chesnut viewed the impoverished well digger scornfully, noting that he "was most at his ease of all. . . . He was cooler than the rest, being in his shirtsleeves, and leaned back luxuriously in his chair tilted on its two hind legs, with his naked feet up on the bannister." Mrs. Chesnut felt uncomfortable watching as her husband appeared to treat him as an equal. Possibly, she supposed, her husband accorded the man respect because "he is a near-relation, descendant, or something, of Jasper McDonald, who nailed up our colors at Fort Moultrie [during the Revolution]." But Mary Chesnut could not quite fathom her husband's courtesy to a man with "mud from the well sticking through his toes." Perhaps the reason lay simply in that McDonald was a "free white man." But Mrs. Chesnut's account suggests some ambiguity in the relationship. The fact that James Chesnut spoke with such men apparently did not stop his wife from absorbing elitist values. She described McDonald in contemptuous terms, noting that "the raggeder and more squalid the creature, the more polite and softer Mr. Chesnut grows." Paradoxically, this nonslaveholder could be viewed both as an equal "free white man" and a "squalid" social inferior with mud in his bare feet. A politician like Chesnut showed consideration to the most humble, although the courtesy stopped short of an invitation into his home. While James Chesnut's feelings about McDonald are impossible to discern, his wife's account suggests that aristocratic disdain for poor white men never disappeared.[1]

Frederick Law Olmsted, a northern Republican who wrote several travel narratives about the slave states, left a record about the uncertain relations between planters and plain folk similar to the one provided by Mary Chesnut. The writer, an extraordinarily thorough investigator, offered a barrage of detail about his explorations from which a generalized picture of an impoverished and divided society only gradually emerges. While shying away from stereotypes about southern aristocracy, Olmsted noted the plight of the landholding white majority, who "owned small farms on which they raised a little corn and rice" but were described by slaveholders as "vagabonds." He carefully traced the economic process that created nonslaveholder poverty as the prices of cotton and slaves escalated in the decade before the Civil War. Nonslaveholders, Olmsted believed, lost out to the slaveholder with "the best brute force, the best tools, the best machinery for ginning and pressing. . . . The expenses of raising and marketing cotton are in inverse ratio to the number of hands employed." While the traveler may have been affected by preconceptions he brought with him to the South, he depicted a region characterized by variety and complexity. Olmsted recognized a strain of ambivalence in master class attitudes toward the common people: he described one planter who placed nonslaveholders, at least in the abstract, "on an equality with himself" but "all the time, recognized them as a distinct and rather despicable class."[2] Like the writing of Mary Chesnut, Olmsted's work suggested that planters viewed the nonslaveholders with mixed feelings.

Both observers were astute enough to recognize the uncertainty that marked relations across class lines. Political association between whites was characterized both by solidarity based on their shared prerogatives as heads of households and by mutual suspicion founded on social inequity. As the Democrats achieved a decisive majority in the South in the late 1850s, they proved unable to forge a coherent agenda. Ordinary citizens, and even most politicians, do not study formal political theory and have the ability to hold inconsistent or even contrary beliefs. The Democrats exemplified contradictory politics, as their leaders looked hopefully to nonslaveholders as a linchpin of the slave system while worrying that they could potentially be unreliable. The uncertainty that marked connections between white men in the 1850s grew from a basic ambiguity at the core of yeoman culture. Sandwiched in the middle of society between a race of wealthy planters and a mass of chattel slaves, yeomen swung between identification with their more comfortable white counterparts as fellow property holders and resentment toward their seeming pretensions as social betters.[3] Yeoman suspicions about the slaveholders who led the political system helped shape Democratic Party politics during the decade. Slaveholder fears regarding the nonslaveholders who cast the majority of votes would also play an important role.

Alabama's Joseph Glover Baldwin wrote dismissively about the second party system, which pitted Whigs against Democrats between the 1830s and the 1850s. He declared that in light of "the exaggerated declamation, the ferocious criminations, the bustling activities and the pervasive organization of party, we feel inclined to smile as we reflect that all this machinery and excitement were occasioned by a contest about a bank, a tariff [and] a distribution of proceeds of public property."[4] To Baldwin, political conflict seemed foolish because the parties agreed on the crucial issues of private property and republican government. A hundred years later, "consensus historians" such as Richard Hofstadter, who focused on similarities between the two parties, echoed the view that they were fundamentally compatible. These historians argued that although Democratic rhetoric featured rural slogans and symbols, the party's leaders not only allowed the market to generate material change but reaped its economic rewards.[5] The consensus historians may have exaggerated the affinity between the Democrats and Whigs, but even historians who emphasize fundamental differences between the parties have noted that Democratic leaders' hostility to the market "softened" as the expanding economy propelled social change in the 1850s.[6] The evolution of Democratic attitudes toward commerce would test the party's coalition of slaveholders and nonslaveholders.

Although Whigs and Democrats did agree on the fundamentals of private property and constitutional democracy, high voter turnout and the fever pitch of political rhetoric suggest that voters believed that these contests were profoundly important. Yeoman farmers were emotionally attached to the Democrats, who, as the repository of the principles of Jefferson and Jackson, provided hope for a relatively egalitarian agricultural future. Writer Alexis de Tocqueville suggested that the very insecurity of the propertied middle class propelled its emotional response to threats to its way of life. He described the anxiety of men "still very close to poverty": "They see its privations in detail and are afraid of them. . . . The idea of giving up the smallest part of it is insufferable to them, and the thought of losing it completely strikes them as the worst of all evils."[7] Losing propertied independence seemed frightening because yeomen defined their shared identity through a "principle of exclusion" toward women, children, slaves, and propertyless white males.[8] In an era without the secret ballot, only a propertied man could fully exercise his rights as a citizen.

One Democrat illuminated the connection between the household and yeoman political traditions when he bragged, "I have raised my son to be as good a Democrat as any in North Alabama, and North Alabama can't be beat in that regard."[9] Control over the household allowed yeomen to exercise genuine political independence.

In Jackson's time, Whigs and Democrats offered starkly different policy choices. In the Whig model, government would promote economic development. Whigs favored strong banks and costly internal improvements that would increase the gap between rich and poor, and they believed the community could depend on economic growth to soften the impact of social inequality. In the Democratic Party's image of good government, state-sponsored internal improvements would remain absent. Democratic partisans hoped to maintain a virtuous yeoman's community, avoiding risky concentrations of privilege even in the face of relative poverty. This option remained attractive because of the value members of rural communities placed on holding land. Fluctuating land prices and potential taxation that would accompany Whiggish commercial schemes put farm ownership at risk.[10] Loyalty to the Democratic Party was passed down from generation to generation in upcountry districts with relatively low concentrations of slavery and commerce: John Wilson Cunningham of western North Carolina called his region "a dark place to Whigs." He proudly described battles in which "the Democracy of this gallant region" had "rolled a dark cloud over the hopes and projects" of the Whigs.[11] While slaveholders and professionals dominated the leadership of both parties, they relied on different classes for support. Whigs tended to be more urban, more involved in mercantile activity, and more likely to be large slaveholders than Democrats.[12]

Democrats maintained their ideological cohesion by redoubling their emphasis on rural manhood. In 1855, autonomy emerged as a central value when Alabama proslavery forces organized an expedition of settlers to fight in "Bleeding Kansas." After a rally in Montgomery, the state's capital, the Democratic *Montgomery Advertiser* cited the success of a Kansas slaveholder who found the country ideal "as far as the . . . profits of Negro labor are concerned." He spoke to the aspirations of men with "less capital" who reached for independence in the West. An emigrant from Eufala, Alabama, proclaimed that in Kansas, "a man can be more independent with less capital than here."[13] The stump speaker who spoke of the "independence and manliness of character" among the slave states' "humbler classes" clearly emphasized that this quality united white men regardless of social standing.[14] So did South Carolinian J. D. Ashmore, who informed the House of Representatives that "all classes, slaveholders and non-slaveholders are . . . independent as the bird which cleaves the air."[15] Ashmore's statement suggests that for some political thinkers the meaning of independence had changed, as self-sufficient farming was no longer counterposed to slave-based commercial agriculture, as it had been in Jefferson's *Notes on the State of Virginia*.

Paradoxically, praise for the proud independent farmer increased just as the expanding market economy made rural life increasingly tenuous. The specter of wage labor seemed particularly disturbing. Hard work itself was valued in the Old South, but because wage labor seemed uncomfortably similar to slavery, many saw it as dependent and demeaning.[16] William Lowndes Yancey warned that factory operatives, "bereft of individuality," would sacrifice their political autonomy and "blindly [follow] the dictates of their employer." Another speaker described workers who toiled "until disease adds them to the great heap of festering humanity."[17] This analysis contrasted markedly with northern middle-class views that wage labor was a first step toward upward mobility, and it offered Democrats a means to defend slavery without specifically discussing the power of slaveholders. Fear of wage labor helped to inject an element of hysteria into the subject of expanding slavery into territories, as young men feared they would be unable to achieve independence in the West without slavery. As land prices in states such as Mississippi grew, southerners might find it difficult to maintain their way of life.[18]

Radically democratic rhetoric increased partly because the stark distinction between the Democratic and Whig models of political economy began to blur in the 1850s. Jeffersonians had never been anticapitalist. They believed that the natural operation of the free market was intrinsically beneficial and should not be disturbed by government. But their vision of capitalism centered on the petty producer, and by the 1850s it became apparent that laissez-faire economics had unleashed forces that would undermine the ideal of the independent farmer. For many Democrats, especially the lawyers and slaveholding politicians who increasingly dominated the party's leadership, the commercial economy never seemed as dangerous as it did to the party's yeoman constituency. Indeed, the assumptions of classical economists were so widely shared that politicians such as John J. McRae of Mississippi could blithely label self-interested behavior "the natural result of the constitution of man."[19] As rising prices for cotton and slaves furnished the capital for railroad expansion and spiraling growth, the slave states had entered an era of "industrialization and urbanization."[20] Dangers loomed for the independence of rural families as a southern "modernization crisis" arrived.[21]

In the context of modernization, the credibility of the Democrats' rhetorical defense of rural life fell precipitously. The party worked to win voters by stepping up its partisan attacks on the Whigs. Conciliation was impossible, the *Mobile Daily Register* claimed, since party conflict would remain "like the strife between good and evil, to the end of the world." As long as Whig programs were oriented toward business, Democrats could portray them as threatening. For example, newspaper editor John Forsyth of Alabama claimed that "the cardinal principles of the Whig party were adopted without reference to the public good . . . and it looked only to the money power of the country to carry its measures."[22] The Democrats' tried and true formula combined such heated accusations with a clear Jacksonian program, as North Carolina's leading Democratic newspaper editor, William Woods Holden, did in calling for *"strict construction, economy in the public expenditures, opposition to a national bank and a high tariff, and approval of free suffrage."*[23] However, even rigid recitation of Democratic dogma could not allay the fears engendered by the results of modernization in the South and increasing worries over the fate of the territories.

In the 1850s, party leaders asserted that its values mattered more than "the men who are to be entrusted with . . . the process of legislation." The *Mobile Daily Register* remarked that "the principles of the Democratic Party are measures of the first importance" but did not enumerate those beliefs. Defending his party in the House in 1859, Alabama's J. L. M. Curry remarked at the "virtue, power, invincibility yet in Democratic principles," but he, too, felt no need to elaborate.[24] As the Democrats appealed to a generation that had grown up with mass politics, their pronouncements seemed increasingly egalitarian. Politicians such as Thomas Clingman charged that the Whigs "in the bottoms of their hearts do not believe the people are capable of self-government."[25] Whigs, Holden, pointed out, were known for their "disregard of popular will and popular rights."[26]

As state legislatures pressed forward with economic advancement and Democrats retreated from pastoral ideals, egalitarian symbolism became ever more important in differentiating the parties. Increasingly, voters expected politicians to be held accountable to the "vox populi." No political sin could be greater than a failure to trust the people. Democrats argued that politicians should respond directly to "the voice of the people" rather than vote on the basis of their own "individual prejudices." Curry thanked Clement Claiborne Clay, of the politically powerful Clay family of Alabama, for maintaining a degree of humility in his political style: "Let me thank you as a Democrat for not tacking "Hon" to your name on your printed speech. This love of titles is not republican."[27] These politicians understood that an honorific would contradict democratic principles in a political culture in which avowal of hierarchy had become suspect. The Democrats' fervor in promoting symbols of equality caused one aristocratic South Carolinian, William Porcher Miles, to complain about "a growing disposition to flatter" the "rudest and most illiterate laborer" as if "he had a special claim to office."[28] Miles's complaint was overstated, but he correctly noted that in every state other than his own South Carolina, many Democrats had fashioned an increasingly egalitarian style in the 1850s.

When the national Whig Party collapsed in the mid-1850s, Democrats sought out old-line Whigs for their party. In 1859, the Democratic convention in Georgia triumphantly announced, "We have conquered our enemy, and taken their generals in our ranks." But former Whigs, so long vilified, threatened to change the party. Jacksonians who had been taught that Whig principles threatened the Republic would feel uneasy to read that "we have conquered all their principles, and preserved all that was worth preserving and inscribed them on our banners."[29] The cotton boom brought an abundance of capital that, despite Democratic political predominance, encouraged the increasing prevalence of Whiggish ideals of modernity and progress among southern elites.[30] Many Democratic legislators abandoned Jackson's rural ideal, even as they paid lip service to traditional party principles.

As the Whig Party dissolved, Democrats incorporated Whig leaders such as Georgia's Alexander Stephens into their party. This process posed genuine problems. Stephens, for example, seemed a considerable asset because of his political experience, but he continued to advocate a program of economic modernization inspired by Henry Clay that was anathema to traditional Democratic values. To north Georgia yeomen anxious about railroad expansion and the encroaching market economy, Stephens's remarks that "progress and development mark everything in nature—human societies, as well as everything else" could not have been reassuring.[31] The words of a Mississippi politician who spoke "in favor of change . . . and the spirit of progress that distinguishes the age in which we live" could only seem ominous to Democratic yeomen.[32] For many poor farmers who shared an antipathy toward state-sponsored internal improvements, the words of boosters confident about the "moral and material progress" of the commercial economy must have appeared alarming, since such sentiments contradicted long-cherished ideals.[33]

With the collapse of the Know-Nothings after their disastrous campaign in 1856, Democrats in much of the South were left without meaningful political opposition. Many supporters of the party were uncomfortable with the demise of partisan competition, since many Democrats held the belief, first articulated in the 1830s by Jacksonians such as Martin Van Buren, that party politics had a genuine value in a republican system.[34] An Alabama editor worried that because "the Democratic Party is overwhelmingly a majority party; all pressure from without has been virtually removed." Many voiced the fear that the people did not control the now dominant party. Party "conventions and caucuses" were run by "cunning and unscrupulous men." By the late 1850s, Democratic partisans complained about the newspaper editors who served as power brokers. Moreover, Democratic Party dominance could intensify infighting for control of the party machinery, such as nominating conventions. In states that lacked competitive two-party elections, such conventions, composed of a fraction of the electorate, were key to power. For good reason, one Georgia activist fretted that "some of our friends fear that harmony cannot be preserved in such a large [Democratic] majority." In Mobile, Democrats complained that former Whigs had packed a party meeting, effectively stripping party veterans of their control over the nominating process.[35]

In the 1850s, political controversy increasingly focused on slavery, and unavoidably, southerners viewed the national debate through the prism of their own rapidly changing society. For decades, young men had ensured their futures as slaveholders by moving west. Now, restrictions on the extension of slavery seemed to leave them without opportunities to thrive in a slave-based community.[36] Beginning with the fragile Compromise of 1850, congressional votes on slavery broke down on sectional lines rather than on the basis of party loyalty. While the fractious nature of the party became evident in roll-call votes on the compromise, the national party showed remarkable durability as sectional hostility increased. Still, when Illinois Democratic senator and presidential hopeful Stephen Douglas condemned the proslavery Lecompton Constitution for Kansas in 1857, the national Democratic Party was all but finished. Proslavery men regarded him as "a false friend, like Benedict Arnold," trying to deny them the fruits of electoral victory in Kansas. Even Douglas allies, disillusioned with northern Democrats, informed the senator that "the Union has been lost by the apathy of Northern constitutional men + the surrender . . . to the more active + militant B. Reps."[37]

As historian Eugene Genovese has pointed out, slaveholders faced a dilemma: they needed to embrace modernity in order to retain a strong society and autonomous way of life, but in doing so they risked destroying the distinctive characteristics of their civilization. Economic booster J. D. B. De Bow pointed out the irony that southern delegates on their way to a convention meant to improve southern commercial development sat in "a railroad coach made in the North . . . [with] Yankee chairs, a Yankee table, spread with a Yankee cloth." Sole reliance on agriculture, proslavery spokesmen worried, would mean certain ruin as the soil gradually became more infertile. Only a truly diversified economy could relieve the South from a humiliating and potentially dangerous reliance on the North.[38] But a modern slaveholding economy would extend taxes, internal improvements, and commerce in ways that would threaten the agricultural civilization at the center of Democratic thought. Some proponents of modernization openly questioned the Jeffersonian rural ideal and advocated increased opportunities for white wage laborers: Alabama's Whiggish *Huntsville Southern Advocate* approvingly described "young men who [had] received the advantages of a liberal education turning their attention to mechanism." The *Sumter Democrat* promised, "The day is close at hand, when ship building will be conducted on a magnificent scale at Mobile."[39] Such pronouncements threatened the independence valued so long in Democratic rhetoric.

A few Democrats made their names by resisting the commercial orientation of the party in the 1850s, upholding the mantle of Jackson and adopting his confrontational style. These men included Alabama's John Winston, who earned the label "Veto Governor" for his readiness to take on the legislature regarding spending and internal improvements. Winston opposed what he called class legislation, which he defined as state action that favored an organized group. This elastic category ultimately included every plan for state-sponsored development in the state. Winston managed to win the enmity of both old-line Whigs and the Democratic establishment, who "did not like him much."[40] Party leaders in Alabama despised Winston, charging, "There is nothing more ridiculous than to talk about a Winston policy, when the man has never originated an idea."[41] Like Winston, Democrats such as Georgia's Joseph Brown, North Carolina's William Woods Holden, and Tennessee's Andrew Johnson gained political prominence by voicing yeoman resentments in Jacksonian language.[42]

Befuddled political leaders in Alabama struggled to make sense of the Winston phenomenon, since the governor had won popularity by opposing measures passed by a Democratic legislature. The *Montgomery Advertiser*, the semiofficial voice of the party, acknowledged the governor's popular support and found it difficult to account for the fundamental difference between the Democratic governor and legislature in a state where politicians professed to follow the popular will. The paper tried to explain the squabbling by noting, "The difficulty has been in the practical operation of our partizanship always to ascertain the opinions of the people and to give *expression* to their will."[43] Winston's Jackson-style veto messages made him a champion of traditional agrarian ideals, but the contentious politician could scarcely stall the booming economy and the modernization process that went with it.

While yeoman voters remained hostile to improvements, state legislatures prodded by business interests pushed them forward.[44] In Alabama, yeoman farmers attacked one sign of development, the telegraph. A company official contacted Winston to appeal for help because "the extraordinary superstition has got abroad that the telegraph is in some way accountable for the dry spell . . . and they have commenced tearing it down. They say . . . it scatters the clouds." The official asked for the governor's help, noting his credibility in the upcountry: "It appears to me a word from one whom all acknowledge to be a man of intelligence and a good Democrat to boot would be of infinite service to us. . . . They take it I am interested and tell them lies."[45] The perceptive developer hoped that Winston could mediate between private development interests and upcountry Democrats.

Yet despite Winston's widely acknowledged popularity, his career was eventually stymied by the power of state Democratic elites bent on commercial development. His frequent vetoes caused the legislature to deny him an open Senate seat in 1857 and again in 1859. Alabama Democrats continued to ratify state aid to internal improvements, and private enterprise picked up the slack to speed modernization. Just before the war, Alabama approved state aid to railroads, and Democratic governor A. B. Moore could happily say, "Railroads are generally penetrating the mineral regions by means of which large portions of the state . . . will become our greatest source of wealth." Democrats made increasingly frank appeals to elite opinion in favor of progress, as "the solid men upon whom rests the responsibility of fostering the interests of our fertile state," those who believed that the state needed "action."[46] With such pronouncements, tensions rose precipitously.

The test of the southern Democrats' strength came in the late 1850s. At the very time of increasing internal tension, northern attacks on slavery escalated, and Democrats stepped up the mobilization of nonslaveholder support for slavery. Despite three decades of proslavery polemics, many southern Democrats worried that the unity of white citizens would prove insufficient. Indeed, southern political rhetoric was already so full of declarations of the stake of the nonslaveholder in slavery that one wonders who politicians were trying to convince in pamphlets such as De Bow's *The Interest of the Nonslaveholder in Slavery*. De Bow's declaration that the "interest of the poorest non-slaveholder among us, [is] to make common cause with, and die in the last trenches in defense of the slave property of his more favored neighbor," reveals a preoccupation with class distinctions that belies his professed confidence in the nonslaveholders. His Whiggish promise that an independent South would "build up our towns and cities, extend our railroads, and increase our shipping" was unlikely to appeal to upcountry yeomen raised on Jackson-style rural politics.[47]

Some realized that the need for white unity in the face of the antislavery movement would require modification of liberal economic principles. Democrat William Harris of Mississippi warned that "laissez nous faire . . . would persuade you to patronize the transient abolitionist with a handful of stolen goods." He warned that the imperatives of racial consensus should outweigh those of slave-based economics, explaining that the community needed to maintain the loyalty of white mechanics, shoemakers, and blacksmiths. But such a demand for racial preferences that promoted white unity over the free market was unusual. A few proslavery visionaries, such as Virginia's Whiggish James Barbour, called for economic solidarity among white men in matters such as household debt, since a slaveholder who protected yeoman homesteads or white artisans would gain "the advantage of protection of his interests . . . at the burden of a little expense to property."[48]

Formal political equality did not bring economic democracy. Democrats resisted egalitarian measures in North Carolina, where party competition persisted the longest. In that state, Whigs appealed to nonslaveholders with a plan that would have raised taxes on slave property by assessing it at market value, while most Democrats opposed equalizing rates.[49] Jefferson Davis typified the stance of many Democratic politicians in denouncing reforms such as stay laws, which protected yeoman households against seizure of their property for debt. Davis called such measures "agrarian," condemning them as threats to the market economy.⁵⁰ Independence was so bound up with Democratic ideals that activist government measures to promote racial solidarity based on rural harmony were nearly unthinkable.

Elite southerners' proposals to build loyalty between planters and common whites required uttering the unpleasant truth that nonslaveholders might be an unreliable lower class. South Carolina's *Edgefield Advertiser* admitted that the slaveholders who neglected the interests of the nonslaveholders pursued a "short-sighted policy . . . daily and yearly sowing the seeds of disaffection." A reform-minded Mississippian spoke of the need to "expel the deadliest foe to freedom—abject want—from all classes of our people" by protecting home industry such as artisans and mechanics.⁵¹ While Cotton Belt yeomen remained loyal, the planter class had a more ambiguous relationship with upcountry whites. It may be an exaggeration to say that the upcountry yeomen "constituted a democratic threat to the slaveholding regime in the 1850's," but the difficulty in gauging opinion in the upcountry undoubtedly fed planter class anxieties.⁵²

As 1861 approached, southern ideologues voiced fears, couched in increasingly shrill terms, that antislavery ideas, abetted by northern Republicans, would spread to the nonslaveholding whites in the upcountry and border states. Such fears may well have been overstated. Nevertheless, a delegate to Virginia's secession convention warned, for example, that the state must leave the union to avoid "a shower of [Republican] public patronage" aimed at shoring up antislavery sentiment. Such money would be dangerous because each federal officer would "form a nucleus of sympathizing friends with the powers that be." Republican office holding would make the party legitimate "upon every stump." Inevitably, by exacerbating tensions between slaveholders and nonslaveholders, Republicans could turn nonslaveholders against slavery on the basis of "selfish interest." Ultimately, so-called Black Republicanism "could rivet its fetters on the South."⁵³ Under a Republican administration, planter class politicians feared, the loyalty of border states and upcountry regions could be doubtful. Although proslavery politicians praised the loyalty of the nonslaveholders, they did not want to test their allegiance under a Republican administration. Such fears would have momentous consequences, as planters began to worry about social cohesion.

De Bow, a man with unmatched knowledge of the southern economy, painted a stark picture of an economically divided society. He observed that "the non-slaveholders possess generally but very small means, and the land which they possess is almost universally poor and so sterile that a scanty subsistence is all that can be derived from its cultivation, and the more fertile soil being in the hands of the slaveholders, must ever remain out of the power of those who have none." As the price of slaves rose in the 1850s, the slave economy concentrated wealth in fewer hands. In this context, slavery continually reinforced a system of social and political privilege that seemed to discriminate against nonslaveholders.[54]

Historians have little direct evidence revealing the attitudes of antebellum nonslaveholders, but surveys of Tennessee nonslaveholders taken after the Civil War suggest that discontent simmered in the upcountry during the antebellum years. Decades after the Civil War, nonslaveholding veterans remembered resenting slaveholders. Animosity lingered despite the geographical distance between nonslaveholders and planters that characterized much of the Old South. William Baab, a farmer in Greenville, Tennessee, complained that slaveholders "moved in circle to themselves thinking themselvs on a hiar plane than the laboring man." He recalled a stigma attached to manual labor, and he believed "slaveholders led the idal life" and "thought themselves elevated above the laboring class of people." Others recalled slaveholder domination of the political system, because in elections without a secret ballot "it helped the one that owned slaves to win the contest." Not surprisingly, some Confederate veterans, including nonslaveholders, remembered the Old South with fondness. Moreover, the surveys offer only a glimpse of yeoman opinion, and it seems unlikely that historians faced with such fragmentary evidence will ever determine yeoman attitudes toward issues such as secession with much confidence. Nevertheless, the historian who has made the most thorough quantitative study of the veterans' questionnaires concluded "that the South was more a region of social seams than social seamlessness."[55]

Those seams worried planter class spokesmen. Hoping to make the economic system more fair, De Bow and South Carolina's proslavery activist Leonidas Spratt led a quixotic campaign designed to increase slave ownership rates by reopening the international slave trade.[56] Although they lacked solid data on nonslaveholder opinion, slave trade advocates believed that the concentration of slave property into fewer hands could undermine the political order. Spratt thought that the southern states had to take drastic action to ensure the incorporation of nonslaveholding yeomen into the master class by importing slaves and thereby lowering their price: "There must be no conflict of interests." With little more than his intuition to guide him, Spratt arrived at the view that "the minute you put it out of the power of the common farmer to purchase a negro man or woman . . . you make an abolitionist of him at once." De Bow favored reopening the trade specifically because of the threat posed by nonslaveholders, warning that small proprietors could "imagine that there is a tendency at present to consolidate [slaves] in fewer and fewer hands." The plan was a political nonstarter with minimal congressional support even from the South, but opponents of reopening the slave trade, such as Jefferson Davis, did acknowledge the need for "a policy which would promote the more equal distribution" of slaves already in the region.[57]

Southern antislavery activists played only a marginal role in political debate in the border states and were virtually invisible in the Deep South. Nevertheless, their presence provoked apprehension among political leaders who feared their ideas could gain wider currency as antislavery advocates tapped into existing hostility toward the wealthy. Arguing in exaggerated terms, Kentucky abolitionist Cassius Clay wrote that slavery, because it spread poverty by making land expensive and keeping wages low, condemned "five millions of non-slaveholders . . . to an almost equal servitude." Economic forces had driven nonslaveholders from their land: "This million of citizens have been expelled from the soil by inevitable and inexorable laws." The well-armed Kentuckian was able to defend himself and his newspaper from mobs, but he remained bitter about the resistance he encountered.[58]

Stretching his point more than a little, North Carolina abolitionist Hinton Rowan Helper maintained that "slavery lies at the root of all the shame, poverty, ignorance, tyranny [in the South]." New York newspaper editor Horace Greeley noted that antislavery southerners lent credibility to indictments of slavery: "as an undoubted son of the South," Helper spoke "from personal observation and experience."[59] The southern abolitionists such as Helper and Clay made few converts, but their significance went far beyond their tiny numbers. In January and February 1860, their writings provoked anger and fear, which became central to political debate. Controversy erupted over the Republican candidate for Speaker of the House, John Sherman, who had allegedly endorsed Helper's book. Debate over Sherman's nomination and Helper's book dominated proceedings in the House of Representatives for weeks, as the body deadlocked on selecting a Speaker. The frenzied attack on Sherman, a moderate who denied familiarity with Helper's writings, suggests that planter class worries about nonslaveholder allegiance, while difficult to measure, played an important role in the crisis preceding secession.[60]

By 1860, southern Democrats seemed disoriented. They maintained an abstract commitment to rural ideals, but they defended their vision with less confidence and coherence than their counterparts in the early Republic. As the proslavery argument became increasingly dominant, the Jeffersonian vision of rural virtue faded into the background. Ironically, while Jefferson had mostly ignored the existence of slavery as he imagined an agrarian world based on yeoman virtue, his self-declared heirs spent much of their energy defending human bondage. Confusion among the Democrats, who wrestled with the contradictions between Jeffersonian liberalism and slavery, left an intellectual vacuum. Therefore, the most eloquent and imaginative defenses of slavery, such as those of George Fitzhugh, came from intellectuals and theologians who were removed from the political process.[61] In a little more than a generation, the planter class had moved in retreat from Jeffersonian democracy and equality to belligerent proslavery politics.

Influential secessionist William Lowndes Yancey styled himself a Democrat when it suited his purposes. It was Yancey who engineered the walkout of southern Democrats at the 1860 Democratic convention in Charleston, which severed ties with the Douglas wing of the party. Despite his participation in Democratic politics, he complained that "the red republican spirit" of Thomas Jefferson created "the conception of abolitionism." This outburst was not typical of mainstream politicians, but such words coming from the most important Alabama secessionist exemplified the increasing political respectability of antidemocratic sentiments in the late 1850s.[62] Yancey wrote that a popular vote on secession would contradict "our system of government." His argument made clear a fundamental conflict between the secession movement and the Jacksonian ideal of a directly responsive government: "Ours is not a pure democracy—that is government by the people—although it is a government of the people. Ours is a representative government."[63] In antebellum Alabama, few politicians would have dared to counterpose representative government and democracy so sharply.

The secession crisis brought competing visions of democracy to the forefront of political debate. Those most outraged by Lincoln's election feared that popular opinion might be against them. Alabama's Curry informed Georgia leader Howell Cobb, "Alabama, in my judgement, would not agree, by popular vote, to withdraw the state from the Union." After consulting with a leading member of the Virginia secession convention, secessionist Edmund Ruffin worried "that the majority of the people of every state except S. Ca. was indisposed to the disruption of the Union." While his fears may have been overstated, Ruffin believed that a popular vote on secession would bring reconstruction.[64] Secessionists who shared a fear that disunion could not command a majority worked to keep the decision in the hands of elites. Georgia jurist T. R. R. Cobb was more frank than most when he publicly asked the legislature to "wait not till the grog-shops and cross-roads shall send up a discordant voice from a divided people."[65]

South Carolina, as the first state to leave the Union in December 1860, was in the vanguard of secession, and prominent South Carolina politicians openly questioned the value of democracy. Spratt, the radical proponent of the slave trade, believed that the country was witnessing "the contest between democracy and slavery." He completely repudiated Jacksonian democracy, noting, "Having achieved one revolution to escape democracy at the North, it must still achieve another to escape it at the South." South Carolina's uniquely conservative constitution and substantial planter class produced a society that one Virginian called an "oligarchy." South Carolina leaders consciously hurried the debate in order to manipulate popular opinion, especially in the border states such as North Carolina and Virginia. As one politician put it, "I do not believe the common people understand it, but who ever waited for the common people when a great movement was to be made. We must make the move and force them to follow."[66] Instant mobilization for secession would minimize public discussions of the move's consequences and forestall popular resistance. Secessionists, including antebellum Democratic Party leaders, appeared ready to ignore democratic processes.

Unionist Democrats framed their opposition to secession in the language of radical democracy and appealed to the memories of the party's heroes. It is unclear whether they actually represented a popular majority, but they argued that the decision for secession should be trusted to the voters. In doing so, they looked to the democratic image of Jackson and Jefferson. In January 1861, the *Huntsville Democrat* carried a strongly worded attack on secession by a writer who called himself "Andrew Jackson." A meeting of North Alabamians complained that "the refusal to submit the question to a vote of the people at the ballot box directly is . . . a violation of the fundamental principles of our government." Across the South, opponents of secession defended Andrew Jackson's stand against South Carolina in the nullification crisis three decades earlier. Unionists in Winchester, Virginia, condemned "the ignorance or deception of those self-constituted members of the Democratic Party who asserted that Old Hickory had opposed nullification, but not secession." The crowd then gave three cheers for Jackson, three for Major Robert Anderson at Fort Sumter, and three for General Winfield Scott.[67] A Mississippian exclaimed that his secessionist neighbors burned Tennessee Unionist Andrew Johnson in effigy "for saying less than Andrew Jackson has been immortalized for saying."⁶⁸ In the Virginia Secession Convention, proceedings dragged on as delegates seemed unable to resolve the issue at hand. Opponents of secession declared their allegiance to Virginia's democratic tradition: "It seems that we love the Union too well. That is our offence. . . . We learned it from your great men—your Jeffersons, your Madisons, your Monroes." A North Carolina writer, "Ballot Box," called for a popular vote on secession. He made it clear that he voiced Democratic principles when he exhorted his peers to scorn "all dictation from those who would bind you to the secession car of Yancey, Rhett, Keitt and others." These indictments of secession emphasized a conflict between secession and the Democratic Party's traditions, particularly in the nullification crisis.⁶⁹

Nevertheless, the secessionists showed superior political skills and enthusiasm. Secession activists advanced a bold political program at a time when many of their Unionist opponents hesitated and equivocated as they worked to occupy the "middle ground."⁷⁰ Secessionists did a remarkable job in rallying their supporters and overcoming the tendency that South Carolina governor William H. Gist described as "the inclination of our weak brethren to dodge the issue."⁷¹ Ultimately, secessionists overrode democratic procedures in a short campaign that featured a low voter turnout, the absence of a secret ballot, the passivity of Unionists, scattered intimidation of voters, and a change in position by many cooperationist and Unionist delegates after they were seated in convention.⁷²

Clearly, secessionist leaders such as Ruffin, Gist, and Yancey revealed a distaste for popular democracy. On the other hand, opponents of secession staked their play on the extension of democratic ideals in calling for popular referenda on disunion. Because of the difficulty in measuring popular opinion, it is impossible to know whether a popular referendum would have worked in the Unionists' favor. It is clear, however, that asking for a direct ballot was a useful rhetorical strategy that challenged the secessionists' populist bona fides. Unionists knew that secessionists were loath to experiment with extending self-rule in this time of crisis. Opponents of the secessionists could condemn them for failing to measure up to the yardstick of the radical democracy espoused by many Jacksonians in the 1850s. Yet in demanding a popular referendum, North Alabama's writer "Andrew Jackson" and North Carolina's "Ballot Box" voiced a standard of popular democracy that went far beyond the ideals of Jackson himself.

The Unionists' radical stance was the fruit of the struggles over the Democratic Party's increasing Whiggishness in the 1850s. In that decade,

Jacksonian politicians had unceasingly declared that public opinion should determine the actions of government. Throughout the 1850s, radical Democrats such as Holden, Winston, and Brown had warned the public that politicians could not be trusted. Southern citizens' experience with elite politicians who backed modernization seemed to confirm their fear that representatives could ignore the wishes of constituents. Tensions only increased when proslavery conservatives such as Spratt, Fitzhugh, and Yancey repudiated traditional democratic beliefs. The calls for direct elections in the secession crisis demonstrated the theoretical possibility of transforming Jacksonian ideals into a radical social creed. But it was possible only in theory. Poorly organized Unionists faced a smoothly operating Democratic Party, which ensured the South's secession.

Between the mid-1850s and 1861, the Democratic Party had become increasingly Whiggish, conservative, and alienated from the small farmers who constituted its traditional base of support. The transformation in the party was increasingly evident as secession and Civil War approached. A changing party provided a new political culture to which individual politicians had to adapt. The stories of five such politicians are included in the following chapters. While all of these men made adjustments to deal with the party's increasingly elitist orientation, none of them made a smooth transition. As the Civil War intensified, two of these Democrats found themselves falling out of favor. The others lost power entirely. Although each story is unique and involves the foibles of individual political personalities, they all illustrate the limitations of the Democratic Party's popular responsiveness. Elite control of the Democratic Party, which grew in the 1850s, became readily apparent as secession turned to Civil War.

3. The "Self-Analysis" of John C. Rutherfoord— Democracy and the Manhood of a Virginia Secessionist

On August 20, 1866, the white citizens of Goochland, Virginia, gathered at the county courthouse to mourn the death of their political leader, John C. Rutherfoord. A wealthy planter, successful lawyer, and Democratic Party politician, Rutherfoord was lauded in "an impressive and eloquent address" by a fellow member of the bar. Colonel J. H. Grey delivered a "lofty and thrilling eulogy upon the pure and lofty character of the lamented deceased, his worth as a public man, his accomplishments as a lawyer." That the report on the meeting used the vague and conventional term "lofty" twice in one sentence suggests a ritualistic quality to the event, which served as much to pay homage to the bygone proslavery politics Rutherfoord had represented as the man himself. A resolution declared it "our duty . . . to render tribute to the private and public character of the deceased, as an able and faithful Representative, as a citizen beyond reproach." An influential state legislator for more than a decade, Rutherfoord had been the leading figure in Goochland and a top member of the state House. In the late 1850s he headed the state's Democratic Party, and he played an important role in pushing for Virginia's secession from the Union. On one level, the leading residents of the county eulogized Rutherfoord because of his public stature. For the whites of Goochland, Rutherfoord had been the central figure in politics, the man who had bridged the gap between their world and that of the most prestigious and powerful politicians of the slaveholding South.[1]

Yet by describing Rutherfoord as an elevated figure, they also implicitly paid homage to a society that had produced such great leaders. Surely this world had been worth defending, even at a terrible cost. The cost had, indeed, been profound, as the town had been humiliated during the recent Petersburg campaign when Union cavalry under General Philip Sheridan had raided the county, destroying "enormous" amounts of tobacco and grain, breaking economically crucial locks along the James River, burning a gristmill, a sawmill, and a warehouse, and freeing Union soldiers imprisoned in the town jail.[2] By extolling a leader's qualities, the county's residents could help revive memories of better days. Indeed, the speeches to honor their representative helped symbolically reclaim an important public place, the Goochland Court House. Before the war, Rutherfoord had practiced law there and delivered numerous political speeches near its steps.

Rutherfoord would have been gratified that Goochland County's residents praised him for his "manly fortitude."[3] Indeed, the public resolutions signaled that "manliness" was, like "lofty" character, crucial to public life in this community outside Richmond and key to the success of a leading citizen such as Rutherfoord. He had confirmed his self-worth by becoming a leader of men and zealously sought, like many of his contemporaries, to gain public recognition. Unlike most of his peers, however, he recorded his rigorous exertions to gain political influence. This Democrat's personal and political philosophy emerges in his remarkable collection of diaries and commonplace books in which he performed a "self-analysis" designed to bring "personal improvement" to increase his fitness to exercise power. Rutherfoord's industrious documenting of his interior life, which focused on his struggle to achieve self-discipline and power, lasted with sporadic interruptions from his college years in the 1840s until his death in 1866. His writing depicts a man who wielded power in both public and private life and yet always wanted more power. The relationship between Rutherfoord's self-scrutiny, in which he sought to "turn the mind's eye back upon itself," and his public actions in a decade-long political career illuminates the interwoven themes of political supremacy and masculine authority.[4]

Rutherfoord's diaries and commonplace books, in which he diligently recorded thoughts he never would have revealed to the public, have been neglected by historians, who have mined them only for their reports on political intrigue. Yet his story can offer much more: the intersection between the inner world of a leading man and the public realm of politicians. Despite a recent increase in interest in gender relations in southern history, historians' knowledge of the ways antebellum and Civil War politicians conceived their identities as men is limited. Thus far, initial studies of political culture and manhood have focused on states such as South Carolina, where leaders most openly defended hierarchical, deferential politics.[5] Despite the fact that most southern political historiography has focused on Jacksonian politics of white egalitarianism, the relationship between the ideas of "herrenvolk democracy" and manhood has yet to be explored.[6] Historians have been slow to grasp something the citizens of Goochland recognized in their resolution, the link between "public and private character." The story of Rutherfoord, as an exponent of Democratic principles and leading Virginia secessionist, can help us better understand the relationship between southern democracy, manhood, and planter power.

Rutherfoord's career exemplified an adherence to Democratic Party orthodoxy, as he opposed state-granted privileges for bankers, embraced laissez-faire economics, and doubted the wisdom of government-funded internal improvements, which he denounced with Jacksonian rhetoric. Yet he was a paradoxical man. While publicly committed to an egalitarian, even agrarian, creed, he became increasingly conservative in his private writings, until his personal opinions sharply contradicted his democratic public pronouncements. This longtime Jeffersonian Democrat would, on the day Virginia seceded from the Union, reject in his diary the central ideal of Thomas Jefferson, the political hero of his young manhood: that all men, or even men of the white race, were created equal. His writings illustrate the link between the struggle for internalized self-discipline he called "self-mastery" and the political assertiveness he referred to as "mastery over others." Rutherfoord needed reserves of self-control to pursue his law practice, run his plantation of eighty slaves, and act as head of a private household. He drew on the same resources to establish the "command over others" he wished to achieve in public life.[7] His fashioning of an identity as a planter-politician clarifies the power dynamics of Virginia Democratic politics, in which egalitarian rhetoric coexisted with slaveholder leadership in the political system.[8]

John C. Rutherfoord's youth showed an emphasis on work as the route to independence and manhood, which would be prerequisites for leadership. His need to labor for success reflected the changing social climate of antebellum Virginia. The sons of the post-Revolutionary gentry had, to many observers, been extraordinarily susceptible to habits historian Jan Lewis has described as those of "indolence." Many never outgrew the youthful folly associated with the notorious laziness of young men at the University of Virginia. An observer of early republican Virginia described his frustration at having only slothful gentlemen of leisure as political candidates: one was "an indolent, and almost useless member of any deliberative political body. . . . His talents are lost to the public from a total want of energy." And this aspiring politician's opponent was little better.[9] Young Virginia gentry of the post-

Revolutionary generation seemed mired in inertia and witnessed declining fortunes. Part of the problem, agricultural reformer John Taylor of Caroline noted, was "apparent to the most superficial observers. . . . Our land has diminished in fertility." Nevertheless, the Virginia gentry of this period suffered in comparison with their heroic Revolutionary fathers, who had not only won independence but also maintained and increased fortunes through tobacco farming, commerce, and land speculation.[10]

Jackson-era Americans were swept up in a market revolution that witnessed increased commerce and the psychological internalization of a vigorous work ethic. Sons of the Virginia gentry were very much part of the process, since by the early nineteenth century it had become clear that an inherited estate benefited its owner only if he successfully managed it for the market.[11] By the 1820s, elite Virginians understood that they needed to work hard in order to succeed. Increasingly, a public-spirited culture of civic virtue gave way to a political economy that valued the pursuit of individual self-interest through systematic effort. Steady work was necessary to avoid crippling debt, dependence on merchants, and the ultimate fear for slaveholders in an increasingly dynamic economy: slipping into the ranks of the nonslaveholding or even landless class. One Virginia tobacco manufacturer later described the effect the market economy had on the children of the gentry: "Many are constantly passing from one [class] to another as changes occur in their circumstances and fortunes. . . . There are many imbeciles now in the mire who can easily trace their ancestry back to aristocracy."[12] Upward mobility has been stressed by many historians, but with the declining soil of antebellum Virginia, downward movement and the loss of cherished personal independence were just as real a possibility. By the time Rutherfoord was becoming an adult, the influential writings of agricultural reformer and southern-rights activist Edmund Ruffin were reaching a receptive audience. He pointed out the difficulties faced by young Virginians, many of whom were forced by economic pressures to leave the state.[13]

Numerous southern historians in the past twenty years have emphasized the centrality of personal independence for white southern men, but only recently has it been recognized that independence overlapped with masculine identity. Antebellum Virginians certainly connected manhood, agrarian economic independence, and the work ethic. Taylor, a noted Democratic theorist as well as an agricultural reformer, contrasted independent farmers with the "idle classes" and perceived the positive effects of agricultural labor, both manual and managerial, on personal character and masculinity. Taylor wrote that agriculture brought a "thorough knowledge of the real affairs of life, with a necessity for investigating the arcana of nature, and the strongest invitations to the practice of morality." He credited slave-based agriculture as an ideal environment for raising the well-rounded statesman and defended the "public and private character" of young slaveholders, whose experience on the plantation suited them for public service.[14]

Taylor's ideas remained influential in the antebellum South, and other slaveholders made the link between independence, work, and manliness. Autonomy remained the overarching value that defined white southerners as men throughout the antebellum period. Thus the political implications of independence were crucial, as Richmond writer Joseph Hodgson attested when he wrote that "it requires no political foresight to observe that the liberty of a nation springs from the noble, God-like sentiment of personal independence." As in slaveholding Greek democracy, it was "private autonomy as masters of households on which . . . participation in public life depended." Independence is a difficult term to pin down and hardly a precise description of the political economy of planters and yeomen in Virginia. Planters depended on slaves, nonslaveholders on the labor of women and children, and both farmers and planters worried about the fluctuations in the price of agricultural staples they grew for the market. While a secure freehold, which was difficult for many to maintain with Virginia's declining agriculture, defined an antebellum Virginian's manhood, independence was rarely absolute as portrayed in Jacksonian rhetoric. Moreover, discussion of the shared independence of slaveholders and nonslaveholders could mask real inequality in power and prestige. Independence was a necessary prerequisite for manhood but did not imply equality: some men were more powerful than others.[15]

Rutherfoord had to work to gain the personal independence slaveholders associated with manliness. His struggle to gain financial autonomy never faded from his mind, even after he built a successful law practice, remodeled his grandfather's luxurious estate in Goochland County, and acquired several dozen slaves. As he grew into maturity, his grandfather, Thomas Rutherfoord, was a strong influence pushing him in the direction of work discipline. Thomas exemplified the social mobility that characterized the Old South, including Virginia. A Scots-Irish immigrant, he scratched his way to personal influence and an immense fortune through tobacco trading and land speculation during the post-Revolutionary years and subsequently became a leading resident of Richmond, exerting considerable influence on the development of the city. As the owner of fifteen thousand acres in Kentucky and Ohio and a luxurious house in Richmond, Thomas Rutherfoord felt his life was such a success story that he advised his grandchildren on how work would help them maintain a place in the gentry in a didactic autobiography he wrote in the 1840s.[16]

In a book that resembles Benjamin Franklin's *Autobiography*, Rutherfoord described his achievements for the benefit of his descendants. His dream of "independence" was tied to his strong work ethic, which he developed as a member of the merchant capitalist class that linked the tobacco economy to the world market. He set off for America to avoid an extended apprenticeship in the mercantile trade and a consequent "dependence on others." Indeed, his chief desire was "doing something for myself." The young man sailed at the age of eighteen from Scotland to Virginia with a cargo of goods worth ten thousand pounds sterling for sale in Virginia. Thomas Rutherfoord possessed both mercantile savvy and "honor and reputation" for honesty and diligence. He pointed out that he rose in society and business because of his standing as a hard worker, emphasizing that other merchants arrived in Richmond at the same time that he did but failed. Although "some of them were highly respectable," they lost money because "many of them were greatly dissipated and given to all manner of vices, so that in a few years, perhaps two-thirds of them disappeared from the ranks of decent society."

Eventually, Thomas Rutherfoord's hard work helped him win independence. As the size of his holdings grew and his habits remained steady, in all his "various transactions, almost uniform success had attended" him. He so disciplined himself to work that even financial success would not quell his need to earn and speculate. During the United States' embargo against England and the War of 1812, Rutherfoord poured his resources into undeveloped land, which would eventually pay handsomely. Moreover, his son John married into the well-regarded Coles family, and his daughter married the affluent William B. Randolph, cementing the clan's place in the Virginia gentry with respectable marital alliances. Nevertheless, the lack of work meant that "withdrawn at once from all active operations of business . . . [he] was not very happy at this period." Rutherfoord eagerly sought at the close of the war to return to the pursuit of happiness, which for him lay in the "pursuit of business." His love of work caused him to continue in a variety of business ventures even after it was "seemingly in [his] power to have retired from mercantile business." He was hooked on deal making, even as investments began to go sour in the declining Virginia economy of the 1830s. He lost money on sales of tobacco and because of falling land prices in Virginia. Yet even as he retrenched, Rutherfoord emphasized to his descendants, he continued to work. Labor that "contributed very little to our support" was still worthy because "idle men fall into habits of dissipation and expense." With "steady perseverance" he had "nearly weathered the storm under which many have fallen victims." Ultimately, his independence and reputation remained intact because he worked hard, even if his businesses were no longer turning a profit.[17]

Thomas Rutherfoord left his grandchildren with advice that blended the centrality of personal industry and the attainment of independence with the prospect of social distinction. Before a young man could marry, and hence attain manhood, he must be sure that "his prospects are such as to induce him to believe that he will be enabled to maintain his accustomed rank in society." This notion of independence, which would strongly influence the young Rutherfoord, sharply differed from the egalitarian ideals espoused by Jacksonians. Although the aging grandfather understood that many young men failed to succeed because of the stagnating Virginia economy in the 1830s and 1840s, he warned his descendants that "much of the misery we witness arises from our own vices, sloth, prodigality, etc."[18] Rutherfoord gave advice on dealing with the "pressures of self-reliance" in a market economy based on the declining tobacco crop. His injunctions toward caution resemble Jefferson's lectures to the younger generation of his family "on the value of self-control," and he shared the assumption running through Taylor's work on agricultural reform that an individual farmer through intelligence and hard work could shape his own destiny. Rutherfoord's work ethic was typical of the slaveholder who began his career as a businessman: "It was the rare master who ceased his quest for more land and slaves." As scholar Drew McCoy has noted, few in early republican Virginia's ruling class countenanced "idleness."[19]

Gentry fathers such as Jefferson believed that moral qualities such as self-control could be "transmissible in a certain degree from father to son."[20] Thomas Rutherfoord's son John raised John C. Rutherfoord at his plantation in Goochland. John Rutherfoord left few personal papers but clearly played an important role in passing down to his son the internalized discipline exemplified in Thomas Rutherfoord's *Autobiography*. Apparently, he sometimes did so in a cruel manner, leading John C. to recall that his father had always told him he was a "very bad child." Nevertheless, he led the way for his son to become involved in politics. After serving as acting governor of Virginia in the early 1840s, he became a friend and political ally of former president John Tyler. Although he began his political career as a Whig, John Rutherfoord was a Democrat at the time he served as acting governor and remained in that party for the rest of his life. John Rutherfoord's political opinions apparently remained important to his son, who wrote to his father for advice during the party jockeying of the mid-1850s.

For a gentry son to follow his father into politics was the rule. Thomas Nelson Page noted in his nostalgic *Social Life in Old Virginia before the War* that "politics took the place of honor among the gentlemen": "'My father's' opinion was quoted as conclusive authority on . . . all points." John C. Rutherfoord lived with his father when the legislature met in Richmond after his election to the body in 1852. John Rutherfoord continued to foster discipline in his son even after he reached adulthood. The younger Rutherfoord noted that his father's residence shielded him from the "dissipations" of hotels. Like so many slaveholding Virginians described by Page, John C. Rutherfoord had learned responsibility and "gravity from his father and grandfather."[21]

Hard work and self-discipline were essential for men who aspired to leadership in Virginia, and leaders hoped those virtues would be developed through education. Jeffersonian democracy had depended on the notion of a "natural aristocracy" of the most talented and virtuous rising to political leadership. When Jefferson recommended that each year twenty boys "be raked from the rubbish" of Virginia society and educated for a higher place in the community at state expense, he meant to improve, not subvert, a hierarchical order by incorporating the most talented sons of the less prosperous into the elite. Yet even his modest proposal for educating the needy at public expense was rejected by a gentry that, Jefferson noted, hesitated "to educate the poor at the expense of the rich." While he celebrated yeoman virtue and yearned for an aristocracy of talent, he understood that Virginia would continue to practice deferential politics in a stratified society composed of

> aristocrats (the great planters), half-breeds (yeomen who had married into aristocratic families), pretenders (men of wealth not belonging to established families), a solid, independent yeomanry, looking askance at those above, yet not venturing to jostle them, and last and lowest, a seculum of beings called overseers.[22]

In the context of financial conservatism that limited access to higher education to the sons of the gentry, schooling would provide hereditary class distinctions in Virginia society with a meritocratic gloss. The majority of young men should be trained to read and write in order to conduct business, to know a citizen's rights and duties, and "to observe with intelligence and faithfulness all the social relations under which he shall be placed." An elite with the intelligence, work ethic, and financial resources to pursue university education would, Jefferson planned, "form the statesmen, legislators, and judges, on whom public prosperity and individual happiness are so much to depend."

Yet the seeds for disaster lay in this vision for Virginia's future. The founding father worried that during their plantation childhood Virginia's young men had formed habits of "despotism" inappropriate for leaders in a democracy. In a famous passage in the *Notes on the State of Virginia*, he criticized slavery because it would produce young men raised in habits of domination. Jefferson hoped to alleviate the problem through education. Part of training statesmen involved inculcating ideas, but just as important was creating a strict university environment apart from the indulgence of childhood on the plantation, one conducive to "morals, to order, and to uninterrupted study."[23] He hoped education could vitiate the corrupting influence of slavery on the democratic ethic.

If Jefferson and Thomas Rutherfoord believed that work and self-control were necessary conditions of manhood and leadership, few University of Virginia students in the early 1840s, when John C. Rutherfoord attended, had achieved this ideal. The sons of the gentry gained notoriety for their gambling, drinking, and womanizing at the university. Many such young men had embraced a cavalier ideal that included college as a time of entertainment rather than an ascetic preparation for leadership. At Charlottesville, students were famous for their alcoholic consumption: Matthew Singleton wrote home that the "greatest pleasure they have is to get drunk."[24] John C. Rutherfoord, like other students at the University, enjoyed the revelry yet took his chance to gain an education and self-discipline seriously. While publicly posing as an apathetic student, after evenings at parties he secretly studied into the night and eventually gained academic distinction. As a young man, it was with some pride that he recalled, "I had not only attained the highest academic honors . . . I had the reputation of being wild and dissipated." But his ambivalence about study later turned to regret that he had not worked harder. In a passage written more in remorse than self-congratulation, he recalled, "It was after being drunk the whole of the preceding night that I stood with distinction [in examinations]."[25]

The highlight of Rutherfoord's university career, and the beginning of his political career, was his selection to deliver the address commemorating the centenary of Jefferson's birth. His performance so impressed the audience that the university's Jefferson Society published his work. The speech shows

Rutherfoord's youthful commitment to egalitarianism. "Jefferson," he remarked, "labored to build up the sovereignty of the great people." The student claimed that in Virginia elitism had become outmoded because "the people have suddenly risen into respect." Jefferson had devoted himself totally to "the democratic principle." The leader's Enlightenment creed drove out irrationality and the aristocratic spirit, because "the same spirit has, in every age, cried out against reform and improvement." The former president left a legacy of democracy and "unbiased reason." The two principles were intertwined, since "unbiased reason rebels against the divine right of kings." Rutherfoord unapologetically hailed the French Revolution in his address. In denouncing "aristocracy," he echoed Jacksonian Democrats and opponents of "artificial" privilege such as John Taylor of Caroline. In the speech, he praised Jefferson as the author of the vigorous democracy of the antebellum United States. It is by no means certain that Jefferson would have been comfortable with the contentious popular democracy American politicians trumpeted in 1843, but Rutherfoord framed the former president's legacy as the founder of Jacksonian democracy.[26]

The "Jefferson Day" tribute shows an idealistic young man's commitment to reason and democracy. Rutherfoord's regard for Jefferson's Enlightenment heritage was sincere, and his commitment to "reason," however vaguely he defined the term, would continue throughout his life. While his address promoted the "democratic principle," unlike most Jacksonians, Rutherfoord seemed a bit complacent about the state of democracy in America. Rutherfoord described "philosophers, poets, historians, orators, and statesmen" who exerted all their powers to "advance [the people's] interests and gain their applause." His rhetoric sounded like an approving description of a racially exclusive egalitarian democracy, a society in which white men exercised ultimate control over political and intellectual life. Yet Rutherfoord knew that antebellum Virginia was hardly a bastion of radicalism. His recognition of this truth is apparent in the handwritten text of a speech he delivered in Goochland several years later, in which he declared, "I have been ever in favor of the prominent measures which are supported by the ~~Democratic~~ Republican party." That he crossed out Democratic, which implied the party of Jackson, and used the word Republican, which suggested representative rule by informed leaders, indicates an understanding that the Virginia power brokers who could advance his career were not comfortable with "agrarian" democracy. The distinction between the appellations "Democratic" and "Republican" for the party of Jefferson and Jackson was crucial to antebellum southerners. South Carolina's archconservative John Calhoun, for example, insisted on using the term "Republican" to describe the group popularly known as the Democratic Party.[27]

A political career would have to wait until Rutherfoord achieved his financial independence and owned a plantation, and that required work. The ambivalence about intellectual work that led Rutherfoord to pose as dissipated while studying feverishly continued to haunt him soon after he left school. While he embarked on a successful law practice, three years after college he resolved to occupy no more of his days "in sowing wild oats": "It is time for me to commence a life of study, if I am to succeed in the world." Rutherfoord's desire for personal transformation and increased self-discipline coincided with an organized effort in Virginia to change the university, where the school's reputation as a center of immorality had been exacerbated by several riots and a mysterious murder. Rutherfoord was part of the university reform effort. Four years after graduation, he complained that the incidents at the university revealed "a legitimate fruit of the shocking immorality + recklessness and insubordination which characterized the body of the students." He condemned the decadent student culture and proposed to the administration a stricter code of discipline, although still "nothing would be demanded which would not be required . . . of a polite and accomplished gentleman."[28] One of the prerequisites of gentility was learning. Therefore, he emphasized the need to value the university's role in teaching proslavery values to the future leaders of the state.

Rutherfoord's involvement in reforming the University of Virginia represented part of a larger movement for constructing a proslavery intellectual culture within the universities. The 1840s witnessed increased activity to improve southern higher education, diminish increasingly suspect northern influence, and increase the moral and political weight of the university curriculum. That movement was bound up with fears that northerners would otherwise intellectually dominate and feminize the South's young men. As North Carolina Democrat Thomas Clingman noted, abolitionists targeted "women . . . and professors." The efforts to improve proslavery education soon bore fruit at the University of Virginia. In 1851, three years after the move to reform the school, it boasted one of the first campus southern-rights clubs. Given his militant proslavery politics, Rutherfoord was undoubtedly pleased by its call for "firm . . . united action."[29]

Pioneering southern sociologist Daniel Hundley, who attended the University of Virginia in 1851, wrote of the southern gentlemen he encountered there in his influential *Social Relations in Our Southern States*. In delineating the character of the "Southern Gentleman," Hundley described young men as restrained from "dissipations" by considerations of "family pride." Indeed, he noted, "in no one place in the South is the truth of the above observation illustrated with greater force and clearness than at the University of Virginia," where the vast majority of young men diligently applied themselves to their studies. Hundley's description of university life may be too idealized to be fully credited, but clearly he had learned the ideals of southern gentility that Rutherfoord wanted young Virginians to absorb at the university. Like Rutherfoord, Hundley drew on the Jeffersonian tradition to link manhood and work, declaring that "the innovations of Mr. Jefferson made it necessary for the Gentlemen of the South ... to struggle to maintain their position, else to be pushed aside by the thrifty middle classes." Work was crucial to maintain social position.[30] While the university perhaps never became the ideal bastion of the work ethic, the relaxed atmosphere became more serious. The school developed as a stronghold for what the *Richmond Enquirer* called the "intellectual defense" of the South and slavery. Virginia became one of many southern colleges and universities at the center of a sophisticated proslavery intellectual culture.[31]

Despite his ideals of self-discipline, Rutherfoord found himself torn between pursuing the legal career and planting duties needed to win his financial independence while in his twenties and his desire to pursue the less disciplined lifestyle of so many of his college classmates. He quickly passed the bar and built a successful practice in Goochland County and the surrounding judicial circuit. Yet he had not fully achieved autonomy, as limited financial resources forced him to live on his father's estate until he was nearly thirty. He had to work hard, later recalling, "For the law, I have a distaste, but can not afford to abandon it." Several years after passing the bar, he did briefly escape for a trip to Europe. Hundley had noted, "The Southern gentleman ... if his means be ample ... gives his education a finishing polish by making the tour of Europe."[32] Rutherfoord had to raise the money himself but still felt the trip was essential to making him a man of the world. Even then, the work ethic inculcated by his family shaped his tour. He carried a letter of introduction from his grandfather, who still maintained contacts in Britain. The young lawyer, who hoped for a leisurely exploration of the Continent, must have been disappointed to read his grandfather's note suggesting he must soon return to work: "My grandson has commenced the practice of law at those counties in the neighborhood of his Father's estate from which I do not think he can afford to be long absent.... He cannot call his time his own, think he will be necessarily hurried back, without having enjoyed all the gratification he expected."³³ The young lawyer stretched his time as far as he could but did have to return sooner than he wished. His notes on the tour reflect an admiration of the British monarchy unbecoming to a young democrat but fitting for a man who wished to achieve the status of a gentleman with more polish than the simple yeomen of Virginia.

Shortly after his homecoming, an event occurred that transformed his life and that he never referred to in his diaries or commonplace books. John C. Rutherfoord's father left the Goochland County estate he shared with his young son and took up residence in the Richmond home of the ailing Thomas Rutherfoord. That move left the youngest Rutherfoord as an independent lawyer and planter with his own estate. In one sense, his grandfather's illness and subsequent death, along with his inheritance of the estate at Goochland, must have been a liberating experience for the young man, as he became the master of a plantation. Perhaps ambivalence about the event, in which he indirectly benefited from the demise of his grandfather, explains his lack of comment on this extraordinary change in his life. As a symbol of his new autonomy, he redesigned the household's grounds, drawing on architectural and gardening ideas he had picked up during his trip to Europe. In 1922, his daughter, Nannie Rutherfoord Johnson, in a description of the elaborate gardens and renovations Rutherfoord constructed, observed "he had traveled extensively in Europe and was a keen observer of architecture and of landscape gardening."³⁴ Rutherfoord himself did not exult in his new independence, however. Instead he questioned his own commitment to actively mastering the estate's economic affairs and hence his power as a slaveholder. In his diary, he confessed to the feminine activity of "reading novel after novel" and later described himself as "debauched by novel reading" during this period. He even questioned the improvements to the estate, which he renamed Rock Castle for the stone he used to decorate the facade. Although he was proud of Rock Castle, he also feared that he "weakened [his] mind by castle-building of the wildest kind." The aesthetic improvements could not allay Rutherfoord's sense of guilt over his lack of productivity.³⁵ Even with his architecture, he signaled his growing fondness for European aristocracy by remodeling his home as a tribute to castles.

The plantation household has attracted attention in recent years as both the linchpin of the slave-based economy and as a smaller world in which white men exercised power over not only slaves but also white women and children.

As in so many plantation households, rule within the Rutherfoord plantation depended on a systematic relationship of paternalistic obligations between master and slave. He believed himself to be the benevolent guardian of the slaves, firing an overseer because the slaves made allegations of improper treatment. Although finding a good replacement overseer would be difficult, he explained, "I shall have to discharge my overseer, if what the negroes tell me of his treatment of Little Nancy be true."[36] Rutherfoord felt it necessary to defend his slaves because it was his responsibility as a master, which equaled his duties as a citizen. He wrote of his wish to "unshrinkingly do my whole duty . . . to my god, to my country—to my family, to my servants."[37] His view of the sheer unpleasantness of plantation life was shared by many of his Virginia contemporaries, who saw slavery as an unrewarding "duty and a burden." Virginia's R. L. Dabney remarked, "There could be no greater curse inflicted on us than to be compelled to manage a parcel of Negroes."[38] Rutherfoord would have agreed.

The plantation left Rutherfoord dissatisfied, and he believed his position as head of the household to be an onerous responsibility. He preserved energy for action off the plantation by resolving "never to discuss mere questions of household + domestic economy." Rutherfoord's ambitions were far different from those of his more avaricious grandfather; he declared, "More money would be made from farming doubtless if I gave my attention to nothing else." Yet politics, not planting, would dominate his ambitions, because, as he explained, "to make money is not the main object of my life."[39] He wanted what he called political "reputation," which he distinguished from "wealth and glory." Rutherfoord thus followed the career path that Hundley described as typical of the southern gentleman. On achieving a prosperous and independent estate, such a man "turns his attention to politics, and runs for the State Legislature." Mere wealth and power could not match Rutherfoord's lofty political goal of achieving historical importance. Therefore, while still a young man, he spoke of his desire for "posthumous distinction."[40]

Before he entered the political world and began his struggle to discipline himself as a leader of other white men, Rutherfoord suffered from periodic bouts of "nervous depression" and "despondency." By 1852, Rutherfoord had become a successful planter and respected lawyer, but he found life on the plantation frustrating: "I find myself without ambition! Without an ideal! almost without an object! Indifferent to life and indifferent to death." Politics helped cure his despair by providing a focus for his active intellect. In his most hotly contested legislative race in 1855, he discovered "practically exemplified in [himself] what a powerful motion . . . may do in developing mind and character." Political life, Rutherfoord discovered, offered a sense of personal satisfaction that he could not obtain from his life as a country lawyer and planter. For Rutherfoord, returning home to Rock Castle after the legislature closed and the political excitement ended meant the unappealing prospect of "complete rural solitude." Away from Richmond, he experienced a feeling of "ennui."[41] That feeling did not diminish after his marriage to Anne Bruce, which he did not write about until nearly two years after the event. Nevertheless, he described it as a "change for the better," which gave him "strong additional incentives in [his] moral nature from the chilling influence of solitude." But even this fleeting reference focused only on himself and his self-improvement and tells us little about his feelings for his wife.[42]

Why did Rutherfoord show little satisfaction with his life as a planter and scarcely enjoy the "independence" he had worked so hard to achieve? Historian Kenneth Greenberg has located part of the problem for planters such as Rutherfoord in the dynamics of the relation between master and slave. Influenced by Hegel, Greenberg has argued that masters could not be satisfied with the domination of a subordinate slave population and that therefore each master "depended on community opinion to confirm his status." If the master were to rely on the recognition of the slave, one writer has argued, he would "seek to be recognized by someone he does not recognize. And this is what is insufficient—what is tragic—in his situation." Even the most benevolent and paternalistic master could gain little satisfaction from his relation with slaves, because he viewed them as mere dependents. For example, the slight passing concern that Rutherfoord evinced for his slave "Little Nancy" who was abused by the overseer indicates that his benevolence had distinct limitations. In general he viewed protecting slaves from overseers as a nuisance that wasted his time.[43]

While Greenberg's argument helps explain why planters such as Rutherfoord sought community approbation outside the plantation, it is incomplete because the abstract model of the master-slave relationship on which it is based ignores the family. Even if slaves could not satisfy the master's desire for recognition, one wonders why his relationship to Anne Rutherfoord could not afford him more satisfaction. Rutherfoord's personal writing betrays a distinct lack of interest in his wife compared with fixation on his self-discipline and self-improvement. At least part of the problem lay in the political culture of Virginia. The Jeffersonian ideals in which Rutherfoord shared as he grew to maturity not only asserted the primacy of reason but gave the ideal of rational enquiry a distinctly masculine twist. The dominant strain in Enlightenment thought, especially as it developed in France during the Revolution—the touchstone of Jefferson's and Rutherfoord's measure of political progress—excluded women from political deliberation: they were dependents whose "functions of child-bearing, child-rearing and maintaining the household" were deemed to "correspond to their unreason." Women were "viewed as inferior to the male-dominated 'public' world of civil society and culture, property, social power, reason and freedom." The elimination of women from political life continued in antebellum times as the Jacksonians defined the public in terms "perhaps more inveterately masculine than ever." Rutherfoord could not receive the recognition he craved from a dependent, but only from his fellow white men. Moreover, he felt driven to succeed according to the standards of his father and grandfather. In his commitment to public achievement even at the expense of family life, he resembles men from Loudoun County, Virginia, who historian Brenda Stevenson has argued could not understand the needs and perspectives of their spouses.[44] Rutherfoord needed to make his mark in the world of men.

The greatest excitement of Rutherfoord's career in the House of Delegates came when he stood for Democratic principles and against elites in struggles over the Jacksonian issues of opposition to banks and state-funded internal improvements. Rutherfoord attacked "log-rolling" maneuvers to fund railroads and other spending. He criticized omnibus measures because they denied the people a chance to judge individual bills on their merits. His ultimate aim in politics was to "secure the hard-earned deposits of the working classes" and stop projects that brought a "burden of debt and taxation." Rutherfoord was a self-declared advocate for "the great body of farmers and mechanics," modeling himself after "the example of Jackson in his war on the national bank."[45] He declared that American democracy relied on the increasing power of the people: "In the nineteenth century, it is public opinion that is king, making and unmaking the laws."[46] Rutherfoord's public remarks meshed with the agrarian rhetoric of the founders of the Democratic tradition. He described himself as a follower of the "great men of Virginia" such as "Jefferson and John Taylor of Caroline."[47] Rutherfoord's pronouncements were typical of a Democratic political culture that assumed the freedom of all white men was based on the slavery of blacks to do the menial labor.[48]

Rutherfoord's personal thoughts on politics appear dramatically different from his public declarations, and the divergence between his public and private views creates a problem for the historian. Generally, writers on political culture take the utterances of statesmen seriously, presuming that they are sincere except when specific evidence creates doubt.[49] There is good reason for this approach, since historians who casually dismiss the statements of their subjects would be in danger of condescending to historical actors and projecting the values of our politically cynical times on the past. In the case of Rutherfoord, however, there are ample signs suggesting the need to examine his self-proclaimed democratic faith critically. Since he headed the Democratic Party in a politically crucial southern state during most of the 1850s, his private writings pose a significant problem. For example, the antebellum period was a time of fierce party fighting, and Rutherfoord styled himself a consistent, principled Democrat. Yet this partisan warrior, while serving as head of his state's Democratic Party, matter-of-factly recorded sentiments sharply at odds with his political pronouncements, noting, in the midst of fighting between the Democrats and the Whigs in the early 1850s, that "there is no great difference between the two parties in the House of Delegates."[50] Southern politicians and many historians have portrayed the Democrats as defenders of "agrarian values" against Whig activism that could bring "aristocracy." Rutherfoord's speeches lend credence to such an interpretation, as he seems a clear opponent of elitism. However, his private notes indicate that he understood his public portrayals of principled differences between parties were exaggerated.[51]

Despite public declarations in which he defended Jacksonian antibank principles and fought a rear-guard action against internal improvements such as railroads, Rutherfoord's personal writings about the politics of progress were surprisingly optimistic and Whiggish. They bear little resemblance to the reaction against modernity some historians have associated with the Democratic Party. His worldview was derived from Enlightenment optimism about the progress of ideas that pervaded the intellectual culture of the Old South: Eugene Genovese has observed that "Southern intellectuals, political leaders, and ordinary slaveholders, as their numerous diaries and personal papers attest, regarded themselves as progressive men."[52] Rutherfoord's enthusiasm for modernity is most evident in his excitement about a British historian he discovered in the 1850s: Henry Thomas Buckle, who wrote the Whiggish *History of Civilization in England*. In 1856, Anne Rutherfoord wrote to a friend that she and her husband were reading Buckle. Several years later, her husband remarked, in an assessment that seems quite inflated in retrospect, "No book of the nineteenth century has made as deep an impression upon my mind . . . probably the most valuable contribution to English literature since the novum organum of Bacon." Buckle's thesis that "intellectual truths have been the cause of progress" fascinated the Virginian.[53]

Buckle's claim that ideas, especially the truths of political economy, were more important than moral truths for advancing progress in society appealed to the politician. Buckle's faith in the advance of reason dovetailed with Rutherfoord's self-professed position as a moral "latitudinarian," as both men believed that interference with the natural workings of the political economy would retard human advancement. Rutherfoord's faith that activist government could not stand up to rational examination is apparent in an 1854 public declaration on banking that "errors will guide us to the truth. We will find it, if we seek it, free from bias, in a spirit of cold and candid enquiry."[54] Similarly, Buckle discussed the rapid progress of the truths of political economy until it reached "those parts of society where habits of thought are not very frequent." Indeed, Buckle linked the American and French Revolutions as results of the rise of enlightened thought on economics and even inaccurately suggested that Jefferson led the French Third Estate to "proclaim itself the national assembly and thus set the crown at open defiance."[55] Buckle's ideas appealed to Rutherfoord's interest in equality of rights, laissez-faire economics, separation of church and state, and small government.

Yet for all his admiration for Buckle's optimistic view of history, doubts gnawed at Rutherfoord, and they increased as the sectional crisis intensified. Buckle's optimistic rationalism contradicted the planter-politician's personal experience of Virginia government, which suggested to him that reasonable men did not always hold sway as securely as they should. Privately, he complained that stump speakers "have generally endeavored rather to excite the prejudices than to convince the reason of the people." Indeed, the nativist Know-Nothing movement, organized by many of Rutherfoord's Whig opponents in the mid-1850s, achieved successes that diminished his faith that enlightened men would prevail. The rise of the secret nativist organization struck Rutherfoord as an attempt to subvert discussion with a secret conspiratorial organization. He feared the Know-Nothings would bypass rational political debate and foster a return to European-style despotism. As a friend wrote to Rutherfoord, the Know-Nothings were potential autocrats: "The 'Secret Police' of Russia is not worse."[56] Some feared that without voice voting, which allowed planter scrutiny of voter behavior, "the whole South . . . would be groaning under the weight of Know-Nothingism." Rutherfoord feared that Know-Nothingism could ultimately undermine slaveholder support for slavery and the master class, since the party's appeal to white Union sentiment was "bitter and unscrupulous, appealing to the lowest prejudices + class feelings."[57] In his opinion, the Know-Nothings had been successful in appealing to nonslaveholder class hostility against the slaveholders. Whether or not this characterization of the Know-Nothing movement was accurate, the party's disconcerting, if short-lived, success contradicted the Enlightenment optimism of Jefferson and Buckle.

Rutherfoord's faith in reason and in Virginia politics gradually declined in the 1850s. Despite his faith in democracy, he privately worried that "the problem still remains to be solved whether the American government is too good for the American people. . . . The age of our government is not sufficient to determine that the people of the United States are fully qualified to possess the dangerous powers confided to their hands." Many times he returned to his Enlightenment rationalism, declaring solemnly in 1855 that democracy could survive if based on the virtue of the gentry: "It is a solemn duty resting upon the educated classes to labor for the removal of error and the diffusion of truth."[58] Rutherfoord's belief in the viability of democracy seemed to waver and change from day to day during his career. But gradually a trend emerged. His faith in democracy eroded while he witnessed the success of untrustworthy men in politics.

After his election to the legislature, Rutherfoord's private writings on politics came increasingly to suggest that personal success would depend on the domination of other men. Here, the implications of his growth into independence as a master became evident. Rutherfoord, who had worked so hard to attain the self-discipline that prepared him for independence, began to envision himself as one who could attain mastery over other white men. As he mused in the mid-1850s, "By pushing steadily, nine hundred and ninety nine people in a thousand will yield to you. Only command . . . and you may be sure a good number will obey." Politics involved dominating white men and was integrally bound to his sense of manhood, as he wished for more power in "commanding and controlling men."[59] His political philosophy, with its celebration of ambition and desire for glory as the natural attributes to man, drew on the "profoundly gendered" writings of Machiavelli.[60] For Rutherfoord, habits of command would be the key to political success. Success in mastery, on the plantation or in politics, was tied up with the desire for self-control he learned as a youth, which produced his incessant private exhortations to increase his "self-command" in order to increase his ability to "control others."[61]

Rutherfoord's skepticism toward democracy revealed itself in questions he raised about Buckle's optimistic view of political and intellectual progress. As secession approached in 1861, Rutherfoord hoped that decisive action by political leaders such as himself would lead Virginia out of the Union and end its wavering. He increasingly longed not for the progress of ideas but for the arrival of a great man to lead the South. He spoke admiringly of Louis Bonaparte's 1851 liquidation of French democracy, praising the ruler's dispersal of the French parliament and restoration of "order" amid political repression. Of course, Bonaparte ruled in direct contradiction to Jefferson's and Buckle's ideal of the pursuit of truth through reasoned inquiry. Bonaparte controlled France, as one contemporary put it, not through ideas but through wielding "force without phrases" to stifle "the force of phrases." Yet by 1861, Rutherfoord praised the French dictator because he led by commanding: "When a great, wise man finds himself placed in such a position as Louis Napoleon, may he not—the one man—by his knowledge . . . thus materially influence the course of civilization? Has not this already been done by Louis Napoleon, himself?" Rutherfoord represented a seemingly paradoxical philosophy—an admixture of Jeffersonianism and Bonapartism. His private pronouncements hailing the gravedigger of French republicanism reveal a startling departure from his earlier public creed. Despite the significance of this change from Jeffersonian democracy to reactionary absolutism, a common thread emerges. Rutherfoord admired the great men he believed made history, the kind of man he longed to become.

Rutherfoord's changing views on leadership mirrored those of many in the planter class who steadily lost faith in democracy.[62] The House leader feared the state's nonslaveholders could prove politically unreliable as the secession crisis approached. Across the South, defenders of slavery linked the threat posed by the John Brown raid with the revolutionary appeals to nonslaveholders made by white southern abolitionist Hinton Rowan Helper, whose book *The Impending Crisis of the South and How to Meet It* sparked controversy in the late 1850s. When Brown raided Harpers Ferry, Virginia, in 1859, he initiated a wave of fear that secessionists such as Rutherfoord used for political capital. Historian Peter Wallenstein has argued that in Virginia, with a large nonslaveholding population, Helper's appeal to disaffected whites created fear in the slaveholders. Rutherfoord understood that the status of slaveholders as a minority within Virginia society made them vulnerable because they could not be sure of their hegemony over slaves and nonslaveholders. Therefore, he linked northern "admirers of Brown and endorsers of Helper" as a dual threat to southern order. He realized that slaveholding families, as less than 20 percent of Virginia's population, had reason to be concerned about their position.[63] He understood that slavery could only be preserved if nonslaveholders followed their traditional leaders, men who had proved themselves by their success in the universities, professions, and plantation economy.

The secession crisis marked the high point of Rutherfoord's career as a public figure, as he played a key role as a secession leader. He believed that because "the people" seemed "irresolute and undecided as to their course" they needed guidance. Therefore, he made a crucial speech in favor of secession in February 1860, when the idea was still the province of extremists. Leadership would determine the outcome of the crisis, he explained: northern abolitionists showed the power of a determined few, as "the sway which a minority violently uncompromising and sleeplessly working, never fails to exercise . . . over the lifeless mass of a dormant [northern] majority." The attacks of the abolitionists made secession the only honorable course for Virginia. The publication of the speech marked Rutherfoord as a key secessionist leader.[64]

While historians have rightfully noted the crucial role of Henry Wise in leading Virginia to secession, it is also important to recognize the role of southern-rights agitators such as Rutherfoord who held the former governor's feet to the fire. Historian Henry Shanks, author of the most thorough study of Virginia secession, argues that Rutherfoord and O. M. Crutchfield "marshalled secessionist forces" in the House of Delegates and exercised effective control of the mostly Democratic body until the secession convention met. The Goochland leader opposed Wise's "scheme of fighting in the Union" after the election of Lincoln, instead supporting South Carolina and secession. This was in sharp contrast to the "shiftiness and evasions" of Wise and the caution of Governor John Letcher, who enjoyed the support of western Virginia.[65] Rutherfoord was most proud of his ability to win over the people of Goochland County to a secessionist stance ahead of the rest of the state. There, in the fall of 1860, he convinced the electorate to back both himself and his secessionist agenda.[66]

The story of Virginia's secession, from the state's election of a pro-Union secession convention to its exit after South Carolina attacked Fort Sumter, has been told many times. Months of political jockeying were required by resolute secessionists in order to lead Virginia out of the Union. This mission was advanced when a mob nearly overthrew the convention in early April.

Leading secessionists forced the convention's and the governor's hand on April 16 by seizing federal forts before the state had seceded.[67] Rutherfoord helped map out the secessionists' seizure of power, noting the importance of sending troops into West Virginia. The convention was thus presented with what Rutherfoord called a "fait accompli" that overwhelmed the democratic process of rational deliberation.[68]

Rutherfoord reveled in his role in the vanguard of secession. In late March, his father and Edmund Ruffin were honored by the Confederacy by being taken for a tour of the Charleston batteries with members of the South Carolina secession convention. Their imminent exit from the Union brought excitement for the delegates and their guests. Appropriately, it was on April Fool's Day that a journalist with the pro-secession *Charleston Mercury* reported on the festive occasion, exulting that "the champagne corks popped one after another . . . a fair premonition, on a small scale, of the fire of shells from the heavy mortars, soon to begin."[69] Secession and the impending attack on the enemy occupying Fort Sumter were cause for celebration. On the fateful day of April 16, when secessionists forced the issue in Virginia by seizing the forts, Rutherfoord proudly noted that from the beginning he was "one of the precipitationists. . . . We found ourselves in a minority." His role won him praise, as *Richmond Examiner* editor John M. Daniel, also an important player in secessionist politics, offered to secure him the Speakership of the House of Delegates. While too ill to take on the Speakership, in 1861 Rutherfoord was at the pinnacle of his career, serving as a Speaker pro tempore and deciding "nice points of order."[70]

The secession crisis illuminated the manner in which the Virginia ruling elite jettisoned democracy to prepare for the war to defend slavery. Rutherfoord had by now completely repudiated the egalitarianism once interwoven with his public ideology, declaring that "nature never intended either that there should be equality among races of men or among individuals of the same race. This inequality was part of the scheme of divine government." This extraordinary rejection of white men's democracy was scarcely unique. A backlash against popular rule occurred in the state's secession convention, which remained in session after the state left the Union. The movements of the body against democracy have been well documented and included arguments for preserving the voice vote, the linchpin of planter scrutiny over their social inferiors and informal control over popular politics. Indeed, one delegate guessed that two-thirds of the members of the secession convention privately wished to make the governor's office appointive and were deterred only by the danger of angering nonslaveholders in the midst of war.[71] In the logical culmination of his evolution from Jeffersonian democrat to would-be autocrat, Rutherfoord linked the conservative movement within the secession body to an ideal of government by the dominant men in society: "It was necessary for the people, in such times, to act through their representatives and it was necessary for their representatives to be *men*, + take the responsibility which belonged to their position" (emphasis in original).[72]

Opponents of secession understood that Rutherfoord and his allies, such as Wise, had effectively abandoned Democratic Party ideals, and they therefore leaped to the defense of the party of Jackson. Some from the West charged that the legislature was filled with slaveholders who "are the most wealthy and most influential persons in the various counties in which they lived. . . . They control the Legislation of the Commonwealth." Such control by the wealthy was hardly in keeping with Democratic principles. Indeed, many Unionists protested that their Democratic faith had nothing to do with the stance of Democrats who proposed secession. One delegate fondly recalled "the iron logic of General Jackson, and the inexorable decree of the great Democratic party put their heel on it [secession] . . . and it never recovered from the defeat until very recently." Like Rutherfoord, these politicians understood the conflict between Democratic traditions and the emerging secessionist politics of Virginia's slaveholding leaders. Unionists believed that the argument was not a regional one between East and West or a party fight between Whigs and Democrats but an "irrepressible conflict . . . between the laboring man and the slaveowner."[73] White men's democracy, in this view, had been overwhelmed by the slaveholders' struggle to win secession of their state.

In keeping with his admiration for Louis Napoleon, Rutherfoord wished for a great man to lead the Confederacy to independence. He hoped that Jefferson Davis would be the powerful man to change the course of history. Early in the administration, Rutherfoord remarked that Davis in Richmond "looked the hero—the great man." Like Rutherfoord, Davis represented a heritage of Jeffersonian democracy tinged with an admixture of elitism. Davis's father had been a devotee of Jefferson during the revolution of 1800, and his sons maintained their Democratic Party loyalty even as they became one of the wealthiest families in Mississippi.[74] This aristocratic politician often sounded egalitarian, as when he emphasized in his farewell address to the U.S. Senate in 1861 his belief that "all men were created equal." Yet Davis also was ambivalent about democracy, as his inaugural address denounced the "despotism of numbers."[75] But the South never got the Napoleon that

Rutherfoord wished for. Despite the calls for martial law from some quarters, especially from Rutherfoord's friends at the *Richmond Examiner*, no strong man on horseback appeared to rescue the South.[76]

Davis never became a great man, though he did emphasize manhood in the war effort. In mobilizing support, Davis repeatedly warned of the threat of "subjugation." The word suggested not just military defeat but social humiliation, a peeling away of the privileges that the masters of households shared. Indeed, manhood permeated the rhetoric of the war, as Davis constantly complained of attacks on women and children that came because the Union was "invading our home." Confederate men must therefore defend their heritage as free men "purchased by the blood of [their] revolutionary sires."[77] For Virginians, as for men across the country, fighting in the Civil War became a test of masculinity.[78]

While the Civil War could have offered Rutherfoord an opportunity to prove his masculinity, it instead exposed his weaknesses. As a result of ill health and depression that he had struggled with throughout the 1850s, Rutherfoord found himself incapacitated and "on [his] back, helpless and powerless" as his state prepared for war. In a state of despair, he wished that he could be "well enough to go with them." If he failed to go, he certainly would be perceived as less virile, by both men and women. On April 25, 1861, only nine days after helping to engineer the secession of his state, Rutherfoord recorded a painful scene as one man's wife declared:

> He must set out with the Goochland troop. . . . She would march in the ranks . . . herself before Virginia should be conquered. Gave my uniform, sabre + all my equipment to William Hart.[79]

In this striking juxtaposition, Rutherfoord appears to associate the humiliation of one of his fellow citizens with his own shame as he gave away his military equipment. Feeling "dejected," he slunk away to "visit in a watering place, in the midst of a bloody war in which my state is invaded," in an effort to recover his health. Despondent, he decided to "think no more of public life."[80]

Rutherfoord did eventually muster the strength to return to the House of Delegates, but politics no longer held any satisfaction for him. Proceedings were a "cause of depression" as most members, comfortable in Richmond, demonstrated "apathy" even as McClellan advanced during the Peninsula campaign of 1862. Dissatisfied with public life, he spent his time at Rock Castle overseeing his domestic affairs. He resolved "to leave behind . . . my ambition" and "content myself with honestly striving to discharge my duties in the humble sphere of private life, and seek no other distinction." But for a man accustomed to leading men, domestic life held few rewards. Gradually the former leader became unhinged. He planned but then dropped the idea of writing a historical novel and sunk into a depression so deep that he engaged in "self-imposed punishment" to correct such moral lapses as having "completely lost my temper and self-control" with an overseer. Plantation life held no satisfaction for a depressed man who had sought public approbation and posthumous distinction.[81]

John C. Rutherfoord had one last hope for salvaging some meaning from his life and his identity as a man. He hoped to succeed in raising his son, who was born in 1862. To do so meant that he must be a strong father and hide his "depression and despondency . . . to avoid speaking of my bodily feelings and suffering even to my wife . . . cultivating fortitude and concealing pain." He and Anne Rutherfoord extensively discussed child-rearing philosophy and concerned themselves with the "formation of character." Rutherfoord had recorded no interest in the development of his daughter, but he thought deeply about his son, writing that "the nature of his education from infancy to manhood was with [him and his wife] a favorite subject of conversation." He emphasized "the importance of early impressions . . . early lessons in morality." Even as the Civil War effort, and with it his plantation life, collapsed, he determined that "the ruin of my future by the war renders my daily labor necessary for the subsistence of my family. The rest of my life must be devoted to the rule of feeding, clothing, + educating my children. I must abandon my dreams . . . living for my wife and children rather than myself." It was no doubt with such considerations in mind that the former politician involved himself in proceedings to "regulate relations between the white man + the negro laborer" after the war. Even following the "humiliation" of talking the oath of loyalty to the United States, Rutherfoord drew a sharp distinction between the white "man" and his "laborer."[82]

Rutherfoord's Virginia contemporary Edmund Ruffin has been emblematic of the secessionist who could not accept the outcome of the war. Ruffin shot himself on June 17, 1865, writing in the final entry in his diary, "I here repeat and willingly declare my unmitigated hatred to Yankee rule."[83] Rutherfoord was perhaps as deeply depressed by the overthrow of the planter's world, but his determination to raise a son to carry on his name kept him at work. He continued to battle despair after the war, despite his resolutions to devote himself to duty. Then, on June 9, 1866, Rutherfoord's three-year-old son died, and the event was recorded in another hand.[84] No entries in his diary followed, and Rutherfoord died several months later. His fate gave a special poignancy to a poem written by a supporter in the 1850s:

> I hope at the next session . . .
> you may immortalise your name
> may you die a happy death and
> when that time is by and gone
> and in your grave be stood
> I hope you'll leave behind a son
> named John C. Rutherfoord.[85]

The Virginian never achieved the greatness he hoped for as a young man; nor did he even have the satisfaction of continuing the family name. Following the collapse of slave society, his political career, and his family life, he had little reason to live. Some planters adjusted to the New South, but Rutherfoord's attachment to the old order made such an outcome impossible for him.

This man deserves historians' attention, even if he did not rise to national prominence or achieve historical greatness. History has long ago ceased to be concerned solely with the progress of great men and their ideas, the focus that drew Buckle to study the past. Scholars in the past several decades have offered us close examinations of the lives of women, slaves, the yeomanry, free blacks, and poor whites. Yet only a few planter-politicians could emerge as dominant figures, and we know remarkably little about the great majority of southern leaders—those who did not rise to the heights of power. Many, like Rutherfoord, would fill important roles and wield influence, hoping to gain recognition and distinction, but inevitably only a few could become great statesmen. Planters carried their culture of mastery from the plantation to the political world, but only a few could achieve the deference from other leaders that they received in the household or the county as their due. Certainly, Rutherfoord was not typical of his class; of antebellum planter-politicians only South Carolina's James Henry Hammond was nearly as copious in his self-examination. Yet none could escape Rutherfoord's central problem: the respect they commanded in the household was unsatisfying because it came from dependents. Rarely, if ever, was such respect matched in a political arena. If Rutherfoord's self-documentation was unusual, the problem he faced in achieving recognition as a public leader was not.

Rutherfoord's analysis of his progress toward manhood raises questions about the limits of antebellum southern democracy. While his public declarations could sound like Jacksonian egalitarianism, his private writings belied such ideals. No simple model in which politicians follow the will of their constituents will account for the dialectic between Rutherfoord's Democratic heritage and increasingly authoritarian views. One historian has recently described antebellum Virginia as a place where both "Democrats and Whigs gave Herrenvolk democracy their solid support" and where the secession "process was an exceedingly democratic one." Caution about such conclusions is in order. Indeed, the argument that the "1861 constitutional convention that ended with a declaration of secession was a product of the new democracy of the 1850s" is misleading. After all, the declaration of secession did not end the convention. Instead, the body stayed in session and wrangled over the limits of democracy as it discussed suffrage limitations and ending the direct election of the governor. The fight over the viability of popular rule in a proslavery republic would not have surprised Rutherfoord. The convention fight over the uses and dangers of democracy eerily reflected his personal struggle to come to grips with the meaning of leadership in a slave-based society.[86]

Attention to the relationship between mastery, independence, and manhood suggests the need for greater skepticism about the popular responsiveness of the Democratic Party. Men instilled with strict self-discipline that enabled them to compete effectively in an economy based on the domination of slaves would learn to rule over less successful white men. Jefferson had worried that "the man must be a prodigy" who could retain his democratic habits in a plantation society. Rutherfoord was, like so many of his class, no such prodigy. Southern politics can be better understood if historians examine the relationship between the public professions of politicians and the psychological underpinnings of their energetic competition for power that marked Democratic politics. Rutherfoord's strength of will, and hence manhood, scarcely measured up to that of Andrew Jackson or even Wise. Yet his attention to manliness helps to explain their political world.

4 An Ambiguous Democrat— Joseph Brown, Secession, and the Confederacy

Few figures in Confederate history remain as enigmatic as Governor Joseph Brown. Brown's contradictory history involved wild swings between affection and animosity for the planter class throughout the Civil War era. Journalist J. Henley Smith spoke for many when he wrote, "I can't understand what the man means unless it is to be contrary."[1] Part of the frustration about Brown stems from a seeming paradox: the leader of upcountry yeomen led the drive to secession, only to spend four years squabbling with Jefferson Davis. The notion that Brown fought with Davis because of his insurgent upcountry politics has often been repeated. The portrait of Brown as a north Georgia radical originated with the governor himself, who described his readiness to defend the plain folk with a "sort of Jackson like stubbornness." A pioneering writer on Georgia politics would, several decades after the Civil War, call Brown's election a "a shock to the aristocratic regime in Georgia" because it placed a leader of "the sturdy yeomanry" in office.[2]

Although Brown effectively and enduringly portrayed himself as a radical agrarian fighting with plantation aristocrats, his real position was more ambiguous. He was born in the upcountry, but he was also a slaveholder, judge, and Yale law graduate.[3] Far from being a shock to aristocracy, his rise to power in the gubernatorial campaign of 1857 was managed by elite Democratic operatives. Brown, torn between the yeoman constituents who made up his base of support and the Democratic kingpins who brought him to power, manufactured a contradictory set of politics. The Georgia leader often denounced aristocracy but in a pinch could throw his support to the state's Whiggish Democratic leadership. Brown's career did feature Jackson-style wrangling over contentious antebellum issues. Moreover, when viewed in light of the Civil War, the Georgia governor did not operate like an agrarian radical. He played a crucial role in ensuring that the state seceded, and despite his occasional denunciations of the Confederacy's central government, he helped secure Georgia's cooperation with Jefferson Davis.

Brown's emergence as Georgia's governor must be analyzed in the context of the contentious class-based politics that shaped the Democratic Party in the Old South. Democrats in Georgia, as elsewhere in the South, had to manage tensions between slaveholders who led the party and nonslaveholders who made up the party's most reliable base of support. As the 1850s progressed, southern Whigs such as Alexander Stephens found their national party "in ruins" as it split on the slavery issue.[4] Democrats such as Robert Toombs gloated that the Whigs would dissolve in the South as "the whole Whig party" moved "into the extreme antislavery position of Seward."[5] Many Whigs did jump ship and joined the Democrats. Yet the Democrats' traditional leadership in the upcountry was endangered by their very success, as leaders worried that the entry of leading Whigs into the Democratic Party could alienate nonslaveholding voters. One old-style Jacksonian Democrat described an increasingly Whiggish party:

> I have been battling for the Democracy in Bibb County 25 years ago—a quarter of a century, when each and one of them was doing good service exactly on the other side.... We primitive folk never heard of ... great men amongst us (they had all come in, or found the party since) to tell us who to send to conventions.[6]

This Democrat harkened back to an earlier age of popular control over the Democratic machinery, at least in the upcountry. The domination of the Democratic Party by the so-called triumvirate of Stephens, Toombs, and Howell Cobb ultimately threatened the Democrats' image as the agrarian party with its traditional upcountry bastion of support.

Democratic leaders in 1856 feared that the secretive, nativist Know-Nothing Party could compete successfully against Democrats in their upcountry home turf. The explosive growth of the Know-Nothings in the early 1850s shocked political operatives. Leading Democrats' correspondence contained hushed warnings that the Know-Nothings could win power in the upcountry by cashing in on widespread frustration with Democratic leaders. The Know-Nothings could make advances by exploiting popular disenchantment with the close links between Cobb and the unpopular Buchanan administration. Stalked by the worry that they were more closely linked with Cobb than traditional agrarian radicalism, Democrats feared that the Know-Nothings were everywhere: one Georgia Democrat confessed to Cobb,

"You and [Herschel V.] Johnson are the only men I feel *perfectly certain* [do not belong]."[7]

Across the South, Democrats worried that the Know-Nothings wished to stir up class conflict by "appealing to the lowest prejudices and class feelings" on the part of nonslaveholders.[8] Johnson was concerned for northern friends of slavery in the face of former Whigs bound in a "masked battery of secrecy." He guessed that "there are not fifty men in the state who know anything about the working of it, the balance are literally Know-Nothings." Georgia power brokers such as Toombs feared Know-Nothingism in the upcountry as the entering wedge of antislavery radicalism. He demanded:

> merciless warfare ... the equality + safety + liberties of the South are indissolubly bound up in the defeat of Fremont and Fillmore + considering the fact of the state of parties in the South it is more important to defeat and crush Fillmore and his friends. We can unite against Fillmore even to the sword—his friends aim to divide and betray us.

He asked that the party be "put under the ban of Southern opinion" because of its hostility to the fugitive slave clause of 1850.[9]

Of course, some of the denunciations of the Know-Nothings resemble the hyperbole that for years had dominated the politics of slavery. But private correspondence indicates that among leading Democrats there was a genuine concern that the Know-Nothings could break up the traditional Democratic alliance of planters and yeomen. Democrat E. A. Barclay warned Cobb about increased Know-Nothing support in the upcountry, writing, "In the Mountain signals Know-Nothingism is making inroads upon us.... The people seem to be mad. The devil is in the doctrine and he is about like a roaring lion." Another upcountry Democrat wrote to Cobb of Know-Nothings who "here all take ground against the Georgia platform and call it a disunion measure ... with the view to injure us." They genuinely feared its rise to power on the strength of the upcountry: Toombs informed Stephens that Democrats would "be fighting to carry the state in one month."[10]

Brown's political ascent to the governor's chair in 1857 has been portrayed as a "mysterious stroke of fortune."[11] However, the fear of upcountry dissent, expressed as Know-Nothing support, helps explain his selection as the Democratic nominee. The convention deadlocked because of its need to accomplish two tasks simultaneously: to distance the party from Cobb and the Buchanan administration, and to maintain Democratic support in the upcountry. Cobb's candidate, John Henry Lumpkin of the upcountry, was rejected by a Democratic Party convention that worried about Cobb's close links to the president, whose mixed signals on slavery and popular sovereignty in the Kansas Territory led Georgia's Thomas W. Thomas to call him a "free soil . . . traitor."[12] What followed has often been misunderstood. The traditional account has Brown plucked from a mountain obscurity so extreme that Toombs responded to the nomination with the words "who in the devil is Joe Brown?"[13] In fact, most leading Georgia Democrats knew and trusted Brown, who had served as a judge and state legislator. Under the leadership of former Whig Alexander Stephens, Democrats chose Brown to provide balance with the elite men, including Stephens, who dominated the party. Linton Stephens, Alexander's brother, suggested Brown's name in a closed-door session and then led the move for ratification of the choice by the convention. Linton Stephens wrote to his brother that Brown "was poor but borrowed money and graduated at Yale College. He stands high in the upcountry and deserves it. He is more of a *gentleman* in his bearing and manners than any man in that country" (emphasis in original).[14] Unwilling to take a chance on Lumpkin, Democrats believed Brown could win upcountry nonslaveholders and stop the Know-Nothing "demagogues" who threatened the very fabric of the Republic.[15]

Far from being selected as an upcountry radical, Brown became the choice of the Stephens brothers to meet the real upcountry political enemy, Benjamin Hill. Hill, the Know-Nothing candidate, and Alexander Stephens had nearly fought a duel over their political debates in 1856. Indeed, Stephens accused Hill of "the most unscrupulous lies that were ever uttered by the most abandoned and profligate scoundrel on earth." Stephens was not alone in thinking that preventing Hill from a rise to power was a life or death matter. Stephens's confidant Thomas W. Thomas worried about a Hill administration, remarking that if "we go down, such knaves as Ben Hill & Co. will rule during the present generation." Even Cobb, whom the Democrats snubbed in choosing Brown, knew the nominee and grudgingly accepted him as a reasonably reliable candidate. He informed Stephens, "I know Judge Brown very well and he will conform to the judgement of his friends, but if left to his own may blunder. This canvass is deep water and it requires prudence . . . to conduct it successfully."[16]

Those characterizing Brown as an antebellum radical have focused on his fight with the state's banks. Yet his radicalism had its limits: he opposed specific abuses of corporate power associated with the banks, not the entire system of modernization sweeping the Georgia upcountry. In Brown's first inaugural address, he announced his plan to strip banks of their charters for suspending specie payments. Bankers had broken a solemn legal promise to repay their debts, he complained, halting payments in "the midst of a high state of commercial prosperity." Even worse, legislative tolerance for failed banks had made bankers a favored class, contradicting the spirit of democratic institutions. His attack on the banks embodied a symbolic assault on state and corporate power rooted in Jacksonian political culture. The banks represented the forces of privilege and state-driven development that had become increasingly threatening to the yeomanry in Georgia and elsewhere. But the radicalism of his stance should not be exaggerated. Bank suspension was opposed not just by upcountry Jacksonians but by Alexander Stephens, whom Brown thanked for his "approval of [Brown's] course in vetoing the bank suspension bill."[17]

On issues other than the banks, Brown proved remarkably accommodating to Whiggish development plans and their elite backers. For many upcountry farmers, the railroad "loomed as a disrupter of customary relations and values." Nevertheless, Brown praised Georgia's "railroad enterprises being pushed forward with rapidity, connecting the different sections of the state together." Although conflict simmered among yeomen who opposed railroad development in upcountry Georgia, the governor openly campaigned for state-sponsored railroads, using language that embraced Whiggish doctrines of progress. Brown, who himself held railway stock, lobbied for railroads as the first step toward an ambitious education program. He declared, "I wish to see every free white child in the whole state educated.... The road in a few years should be made to pay the entire public debt of the state and increase the educational fund." Indeed, in a marked departure from upcountry radicalism, he called for Georgia to imitate New England and his alma mater. He pointed out that New England's policy of financial "liberality to Yale College ... greatly enlarged their wealth at home." Just as important, Brown admiringly noted that New England colleges instilled into "youthful minds ... many of their own peculiar notions of religion and government."[18] Brown shows the difficulty in inferring the opinions of nonslaveholders from the policy positions of their putative representatives. His war with the banks was but a single episode in a career that included both conflict and collaboration with the planter class. His flexibility explains why the slaveholder-dominated Democratic convention of 1859 renominated Brown, who told Alexander Stephens he was "proud of the unanimous endorsement of a convention so large and composed of such respectable material."[19]

Brown's background and the bank war gave him genuine, if not unchallenged, political power in the upcountry. He used that power to play a prominent role in the secession crisis by consistently articulating the case for disunion at a time when the secession of the state was by no means assured. Secessionists had to overcome the backers of 1860 pro-Union candidates Stephen Douglas and John Bell, who had together gained a majority of presidential votes in the state. Unionist Herschel V. Johnson later commented that only the political cohesion and energy of the secessionists accounted for Georgia's exit from the Union, and Brown was certainly key to that secessionist agitation.[20] It is only a slight exaggeration to say that Brown had been "the moving figure in public matters" in the Civil War era. The stakes were high, because if Georgia had followed the lead of Unionists such as Johnson and Hill, the Confederacy might have been stillborn.[21]

Indeed, he proved crucial to winning nonslaveholder support for Georgia's secession. As one commentator noted during the secession winter: "Gov. Brown is out in a very important letter. It advocates secession, and embraces an appeal to the poor men of the mountains well calculated to arouse them, and to fortify their minds against the appeals of demagogues . . . which array the poor against the wealthy—The non-slaveholder against the slaveholder."[22] The writer's emphasis on Brown's appeal to "poor men" was astute: only a Democrat of Brown's populist credentials could play such a key role in mobilizing support for secession. During the secession crisis, the man who had denounced "aristocracy" in 1857 flatly denied the very existence of social inequity. Now, he argued that slaveholders and white laborers alike maintained an interest in keeping the cost of labor high and that slavery promoted harmony between capital and labor. It followed that Georgia's social system was "one of perfect homogeneity of interest, where every class in society is interested in sustaining the other class."[23] As he argued for secession, Brown abandoned his antebellum rhetoric of class conflict.

Yet Brown's actions belied his denial of class divisions among whites. The governor quietly channeled aid and equipment to his state's mountain counties to help check early Union sentiment and mobilize support for secession. His political organizing made a difference when many Georgia secessionists could only "fear the result in North Georgia" and worry about Unionism among yeomen. Brown's influence proved crucial in securing nonslaveholder votes critical to achieving secession by a "paper thin" margin.[24] Brown, an expert at taking the political pulse of the upcountry, warned Unionist slaveholders such as Alexander Stephens that Republican control of the national government could touch off opposition to slavery on the part of nonslaveholding whites. He feared the influence of southern abolitionists such as Hinton Rowan Helper. Even though Helper's incendiary book *The Impending Crisis of the South and How to Meet It* was not widely circulated in the South, it disturbed southern politicians such as Brown because it "appealed to class divisions between slaveholding and nonslaveholding whites."[25] Helper's book seemed threatening because it raised the possibility that a Republican administration would organize upcountry whites against slavery, using "inflammatory abolition documents" that appealed to nonslaveholders' resentments of the master class. Brown alerted his fellow slaveholders that if Lincoln was elected, the selection of a Republican ticket in the South, which would pose the danger of opening the door to further criticism of slavery, would be a real possibility by 1864. His concerns about the upcountry, along with elite Georgians' anxieties about the supposed link between Know-Nothingism and Republicanism, contradict the notion that "the last years of the 1850's do not yield any evidence that the established politicians doubted the nonslaveowners' 'loyalty.'" Although few said so in public, many shared the fear of Toombs that the Republicans "would abolitionize Maryland in a year, raise a powerful abolition party in Va., Kentucky and Missouri in two years, and foster and rear up a free labour party in the whole South in four years." Indeed, Toombs even noted the danger in communicating about the yeomanry's unreliability: "I did not press these views in my speech, for reasons which you will readily perceive."[26]

Brown's influence with the yeomanry helps account for the confidence of Georgia secessionists and the apparent passivity of Georgia's significant Unionist population. Moreover, Brown's decisive action in seizing Fort Pulaski two weeks before secession was motivated by a desire to preempt the democratic process and hasten secession by presenting the state with a fait accompli.[27] While contemporaries worried about the loyalty of the upcountry, by the time the election of a secession convention occurred, counties with few slaves elected nearly as many secessionist delegates as the Black Belt. His political strength with "the poor man of the mountains" helps to explain the political management that made disunion possible.[28] The most important act of Brown's public life, his campaign for secession, rested not on agrarianism but on the disavowal of class conflict. Ultimately, slaveholders shaped the terms of debate—after all, every participant in the famous secession debates at Milledgeville owned slave property—but elite secessionists could not have carried the upcountry alone. That they had to depend on upcountry leaders, especially an unpredictable and ambivalent politician such as Brown, reminds us that secession was far from certain, even after the election of Lincoln.

Brown was too complicated a creature, and too entwined with the state's elites, to be easily characterized either as an upcountry radical or as a Calhoun-like paternalist. Brown embodied what historian Charles Sellers has called "ambiguous democracy." His politics are only comprehensible in light of his full career of political vacillation, which would lead him not only from the Bank War into secessionism but from secessionism to near defeatism during the war, then to postwar Republicanism, and finally back into the Democratic Party. Brown's inconsistent course reflected his awkward position as a slaveholding lawyer following a path between his upcountry supporters and the Democratic leaders who brought him to power. Although Brown had yeoman roots, he operated in a "slaveholder's democracy" that had selected him for his party's nomination. The ability of a democratic system to assimilate leaders like Brown strengthened the slaveholding class. Indeed, symbolic jousting over issues such as banks had "muffled the contradiction" between a growing market society and democracy and helped construct a mythology of pure democracy in which "the people" ruled through ostensibly radical politicians. Brown was not unique. Yeoman-oriented Democrats such as Andrew Johnson of Tennessee and William Woods Holden of North Carolina also made radical changes in political course in the Civil War era and, like Brown, gained the enmity of many contemporaries and historians. W. E. B. Du Bois understood these yeoman-based politicians well when he described their worldview as one of "unconscious paradox and contradiction."[29]

Brown's contradictory politics were an integral part of his appeal to the nonslaveholding whites. Although nonslaveholders resented wealthy planter-aristocrats, they also identified with them and wished to protect their households against the slave majority. Brown's politics resemble that of the rural petite bourgeoisie so ably described by Karl Marx and Frederick Engels in their writings on revolutionary Europe. The salient feature of the small property holders lay in their simultaneous resentment of the wealthy and hatred of the poor. The end product was political vacillation; indeed, the poor farmers of France were described as "a living contradiction." Tossed between their hopes of entering the wealthy class and their fear of falling into the ranks of the propertyless, this class was "extremely vacillating in its views."[30] In Georgia, of course, slaves and abolitionists stood in for urban workers as a threat to the sanctity of property and the rural household. But like the

European peasantry, the yeoman class of Georgia resented the rich and despised the propertyless. The chameleonlike Brown embodied the contradictions of this class.

Brown recognized the anxiety of small property holders and exploited it to his political advantage during the Civil War. He would attack the wealthy and the Confederate government in Richmond, engaging in harsh polemic with Jefferson Davis. He understood the fear felt by small property holders during the conflict and gained their approbation by attacking aristocracy. But Brown most effectively played on popular anxiety in warning that slaves posed a threat to yeoman households. He therefore would spend the Civil War veering between criticism of the Confederacy and warning of the danger posed by slaves. Ultimately, fear of emancipation ensured Brown's loyalty to the Confederate cause, in spite of his cantankerous denunciations of the manner in which Davis pursued the war effort.

Despite Brown's role in secession, his name is synonymous with the political squabbling that tore through the Confederacy. Yet his prickly personality and his political squabbling with the central government should not obscure the fact that the logic of his middle-class politics pushed him toward genuine loyalty to the Confederate cause. And while combativeness was central to his political identity, his popularity with Georgia voters, who twice reelected Brown during the Civil War, suggests that he was no mere eccentric.

Although Brown's anger toward Jefferson Davis grew exponentially in the wake of the president's 1862 call for conscription, he usually "balked at stirring class resentments" during the Civil War.[31] His continued attempts to build class solidarity are evident in the months after the war began. Abolitionism, Brown argued, endangered the intertwined institutions of family and property. Northern abolition armies threatened both to incite slaves to insurrection and to "inflict . . . the most outrageous wrongs upon our wives and daughters." It seems unlikely that, as Brown declared, Republicans used the battle cry of "beauty and booty" to recruit soldiers in northern cities. The slogan instead represented the worries of Georgia's property holders, who saw their property rights linked to their control over the family. Brown declared that "the poor, honest laborers of Georgia" would "never submit to abolition rule." Even as the war dragged on and increasing numbers of Confederates became disenchanted, he defended the South's economy as one that offered the yeoman social mobility: "Under our form of government, wealth and honors are the exclusive prerogatives of no family. Like the waves of the ocean they are constantly changing place."³² The equality, property ownership, and manhood of Brown's constituency prepared them to protect their rights in battle.

Brown was "as anxious for her [victory] as any man can be," reckoned Confederate vice president Alexander Stephens, "but for the sake of harmony he can never surrender principles."³³ Yet while Brown worked to promote the war effort in Georgia, the conduct of the Civil War government at Richmond genuinely shocked and concerned him. He worried about threats to "principles which lie at the very foundation of our system" as the war produced a revolutionized social life. He especially resented conscription and centralized military control.³⁴ In damning such measures in his state, Brown embodied not disloyalty to the Confederacy but discomfort with the centralized way Jefferson Davis conducted the war. Brown fought against a nationalistic war effort, denying the claim of "necessity" from which it was born. Such pleas, he argued, only paved the way for "French-style military despotism."³⁵ By 1862, the course of Confederate mobilization clashed with Brown's heritage of Jacksonian democracy. If the banking system in antebellum Georgia represented an unacceptable concentration of centralized power, the Confederacy's national war effort seemed unsuitable for a politician so publicly concerned with maintaining the independence of the yeomanry.

Brown saw defense of his state as his primary responsibility. Like other Confederate states such as North and South Carolina, Georgia contributed to the national war effort while worrying about Union depredations along the Atlantic coast. The conflicting priorities of state and national defense left Brown vulnerable to criticism at the outset of the war, as the governor had to defend himself against charges that he neglected the seacoast.³⁶ He also worried about the potential for slave insurrection as soldiers left the state to fight for the Confederacy. Such concerns were far too touchy to mention in public, but the governor told one correspondent, "There are now troubles with the negroes in some parts of the state and I must put some arms at the most exposed points."³⁷ Moreover, although Brown had garnered significant upcountry support for secession, he had reason to worry that some counties would resist disunion. One citizen confidently informed him, "We the people of Walker Co. . . . do not intend to submit to secession . . . which has been taken out of the hands of the people and has fallen into the hands of demagogues and office seekers, pickpockets and vagrants." Finally, Brown feared that few in the state legislature were able to grasp "the magnitude of the crisis" in home defense. He publicly chided the state's lawmakers for exposing "the people of Camden and the ladies of Saint Mary's" to "the mercy of negro invaders, who may insult and plunder them at pleasure."[38]

Concern about the security of Confederate Georgia motivated Brown's many requests to Richmond for improved local defense, and states' rights provided the ideological rationale for such appeals. Some historians, most notably Frank Owsley, have argued that adherence to states' rights doctrines damaged the Confederate war effort.[39] But in Brown's view, the war effort and states' rights went hand in hand. States' rights doctrine represented a way of protecting personal freedom for Brown's constituency, the property holders of Georgia. He often invoked the trinity of "states rights . . . constitutional liberty, [and] personal rights." He believed that elites would control the power demanded by an active national government. Brown claimed to trust Jefferson Davis but, like a good lawyer, worried about "a precedent that in the future may be used" to defend centralization. He emphasized that Confederate practice contradicted Democratic principles, comparing the government with "Webster, Story, or any other statesman or jurist of the Federal School . . . not the doctrine of the republican party of 1798, as set forth in the Virginia and Kentucky resolutions." Before the war, states' rights was a slogan of planters who resisted Union interference with slavery. Now it was a rallying cry against the impositions of a government that sought to preserve slavery. Little wonder, then, that Alabama's William Lowndes Yancey sarcastically called Brown's doctrine a "new phase of State Rights."[40]

As early as November 1861, Brown perceived few checks against a government that could "become uncontrollable master instead of useful servant to the states." The war-making power of the Confederate government made the banks that he squabbled with in the antebellum period look puny. If banks conjured up images of financial aristocracy, Confederate power evoked even darker pictures of usurpers and patronage. Brown denounced Davis for leading a "Confederate Star Chamber" in Richmond.[41] He struck a chord with voters whose conception of democracy included responsiveness to the citizenry when he denounced the Confederate Congress's practice of meeting in closed session.[42]

Confederate soldiers elected their officers at the outset of the war, a practice that reflected the traditional democratic ideal of the militia. Elite opinion, echoed in the pages of the *Richmond Enquirer* and *Charleston Mercury*, suggested that elections damaged unit cohesion by allowing soldiers to express their "dissatisfaction with . . . military discipline."[43] When the practice of electing officers virtually died out in 1863, Brown feared that the Confederacy could use its power to appoint officers to undermine state sovereignty. He spoke of an unwritten "contract" that existed between the state and its volunteers, giving troops the right to select their own officers. Brown's objection to Confederate appointment of officers should not be confused with lack of enthusiasm for the cause: the governor believed such elections boosted morale in the volunteer military. Soldiers needed to have "confidence" and share "fellow feeling" with their officers.[44] But while Brown worried that use of military appointment power could strengthen the centralizing tendencies of the Confederacy, he quickly bowed to Richmond's demands that the War Department organize the armed forces, including brigades from Georgia.[45]

Brown's hostility to conscription can only be understood in the context of his support for a volunteer war effort and his interest in a guerrilla defense strategy. He believed volunteer spirit was the key to maintaining the war effort under a republican government: "Our people will have the intelligence . . . and the patriotism and the valor to prompt them to respond by voluntary enlistment. . . . To doubt this would seem to be to doubt the intelligence and patriotism of the people." Brown's ideal was the force of "brave, generous, high-toned freemen, who have left their homes at the call of their state." Such an army could keep two hundred thousand men in the woods, mountains, and fields, resisting the Union for twenty years if necessary.[46] His plan called for reliance on militia forces rather than a regular army. Such a fighting body could "defy the combined federal forces for years to come." It would work like a guerrilla force, able to "fly rapidly from point to point as an army of attack."[47] George Washington's and Andrew Jackson's military successes made belief in the militia a key part of Democratic thought, and at the outset of the war, numerous loyal Confederates supported a strategy of home defense that could make the South "as military as the Swiss, who are all soldiers, yet few . . . regulars."[48]

With the aim of strengthening the Confederate cause, the governor complained that some planters failed to support the war effort sufficiently. Brown announced that the "man who because he has the means, indulges in luxuriant abundance is guilty of a crime against society . . . when there is not a plentiful supply for all." Such individuals owed sustenance to the soldiers, who fought for "the wealth of the whole state." Brown asserted that the planters "are dependent upon our white laborers in the field of battle, for the protection of their property . . . and their families are dependent upon the slaveholders for a support while thus we are engaged. The obligation is mutual and reciprocal." His proposed solution to the problem of collective interdependence showed him willing to go further in advancing the war effort than many planters: "Private property and private rights must yield to the great public interests now at stake."[49] Elite Georgians claimed to agree on the necessity for "universal self-sacrifice," but many, like planter-politician Toombs, defied Confederate authority by growing lucrative cotton crops instead of corn. Brown took action against the squandering of grain by whiskey manufacturers, and this move to bolster supplies for the troops met "an overwhelming endorsement of the whole people." His approach differed markedly from that of Georgia planters who were unwilling to make sacrifices for the war.[50]

Brown associated faithful military service with an ideal of manliness. When he wrangled with the Confederacy over distilling whiskey for the army, he demanded that surplus grain go instead to indigent families. Such a move relied on the will of "a soldier who is a man." Brown criticized Richmond's organization of the military, not only because he feared central authority but because he worried about "our women and children . . . left at home almost entirely without protection" against slaves. Similarly, he appealed for stay laws against property confiscation on the grounds that without them there would be "an immense amount of suffering among helpless women and children."[51]

In Brown's ideal Confederate army, women played an important role in encouraging the troops. He doubted that his state would ever fall short of troops because "the noble women of the State, who have done so much for the cause, would not tolerate such delinquency." He repeatedly invoked the "patriotic daughters of Georgia" who would "mark with perpetual reproach . . . every man who . . . has not the courage and the manliness to take up arms." In this view, a man waiting to be drafted before serving in the army merited contempt, since the enemy wished to "insult and cruelly injure his wife and his daughters." The shirker should "fear lest he be marked as disloyal." Brown played on men's deepest anxieties as he tried to motivate them for the war effort: "Let the last man in the Confederacy die nobly at the point of the bayonet, and let our wives and children and all the property we possess, perish together on one common funeral pile. . . . We lived freemen and died freemen."[52]

Whatever qualms Brown had about the Confederacy, his ideal of independence left no room for conciliation with Unionism. He therefore remained a loyal Confederate. Despite his verbal tangles with Richmond, he accurately pointed out that his state "always furnished more men than the President has asked, without a single case of exception."[53] Even Davis had to praise Brown's commitment to the Confederate cause, writing of the "determination of Georgia to prosecute the present war with the utmost rigor and energy.... This reaffirmation is a gratifying proof of their true appreciation of the magnitude of the struggle in which we are engaged."[54] For Brown, rebellion against Confederate tyranny never involved accommodation to northern rule. His politically astute stance of criticizing the Confederacy while providing military support increased his popularity as governor. His enemies such as Howell Cobb could only impotently declare that "honest and good people were still deluded" and that Brown's perceived popularity "is to me a source of excruciating indignation."[55]

Although relations between Davis and Brown were hostile, the two men remained close enough on the political spectrum that Brown could say, "In the main, I have cordially approved of your official course, and have always accorded to you high administrative ability and lofty patriotism."[56] Whatever his complaints, Brown cooperated with the Confederacy. He would have vehemently objected to Cobb's claim that it mattered little for troops "if they fight under the flag of Georgia or under that of the Confederate States."[57] But because Brown's conflict with the Confederacy remained confined to rhetoric, he allowed the national government to have the upper hand in determining policy. Paradoxically, he may even have helped to strengthen Georgia's war effort by acting as a safety valve for loyal opposition. Discontent in north Georgia was relatively limited in comparison with other disaffected yeoman strongholds such as western North Carolina, east Tennessee, and northern Alabama. Among Confederate states, only South Carolina witnessed fewer defectors to the Union army than Georgia.[58]

Brown promoted state militia organization as a means to secure southern independence. His enthusiasm for the abilities of Georgia's troops led him to endorse a strategy more like a national guerrilla struggle than the Confederacy's largely conventional military approach. Brown's faith in the militia led him to imagine his state's plain folk taking up six-foot pikes against their better-armed opponents in order to defend home and hearth. "Let them move in double quick time," Brown declared, "and rush with terrible impetuosity ... till each man has hewed down at least one of his adversaries." His advocacy of the pike was inspired by a romantic ideal of Spanish resistance to Napoleon—he cited "the terrible slaughter of the French troops by the Spanish mountaineers" using pikes.[59] Brown's strategic ideas may seem reckless, but they must be understood in the context of Democratic political culture, which had celebrated the invincibility of the militia.

Brown's hopes for a guerrilla strategy made good sense if the goal of the Confederacy was simply to hold off federal conquest. Other thoughtful Georgians contemplated guerrilla war, as did Herschel V. Johnson, who never criticized Davis in public. Johnson admitted that he did not expect success in the conventional strategy of the Confederacy because its territory was too extensive to be defended: "We have not the men to protect our immense border lines." Brown worried during George McClellan's 1862 Peninsula campaign that "the picture looks dark" for the Confederacy. He therefore confided to Johnson that he envisioned a climactic battle for the survival of Georgia: "My present inclinations are . . . if the worst comes to the worst find an honorable grave in the last battle on the soil of the state."[60] Brown's vision of a guerrilla-based strategy relied on some wishful thinking, but it was not manifestly absurd. Ultimately, Jefferson Davis would contemplate a similar path in 1865.[61] Many historians have criticized Davis and Lee for their single-minded emphasis on defending Richmond, and some have suggested that the Union probably would have lost the war "if the Confederacy had decided to wage it as a guerilla war." But although Brown's strategy had widespread appeal, it was unworkable, since the certain chaos of guerrilla war might require the South to accept the end of slavery.[62]

Early in the war the central government adopted high-handed tactics against Brown's complaints on such issues as officer elections and brigade organization. In 1861, Confederate secretary of war Leroy Pope Walker issued a veiled threat to Brown, warning the governor that if he was not more forthcoming with brigades, "you will regret it." Brown's reply— "I deprecate any thing like conflict between State & Confederate authority"—stretched the truth only a little.[63] Brown, who remained confident of his political support within Georgia, knew the Confederacy lacked the power to coerce him into silence or submission. Yet he took an ambivalent position toward Richmond, delivering troops to the Confederacy while complaining that Confederate impositions were undermining self-government for Georgia's "unborn posterity."[64]

The governor's complaints against the Confederate government left him open to the charge that he was responsible for the disenchantment of thousands of Georgians.[65] Yet Brown knew more about the weakness of Georgia's internal defense than his critics: in some cases hundreds of slaves were supervised by only two white overseers.[66] A number of leading Georgians stifled criticism of the Davis administration because of their fear of giving aid and comfort to the Union. Alexander Stephens remarked that many

Confederates "yielded" to Davis "against their better judgement to avoid greater apprehended evils." Georgia's B. H. Hill, who underestimated the governor's political popularity, told Davis that Brown was part of a minority of agitators, spurned by the people, who lacked "principle and patriotism." Yet Brown's alienation from Davis did not create frustrations among Georgians as much as it reflected them. Many of Georgia's Democrats were just as angry at the Confederacy as Brown, although leaders such as Johnson refrained from publicizing their opposition to conscription and suspension of habeas corpus in the interests of wartime "harmony."[67]

Brown appealed at first to Georgians to fight "subjugation" at the hands of the North; later, he worried about "subordination" to the Confederate military. The complaints bore a family resemblance that went deep into the Confederate psyche. Before the war, secessionists had warned of the Union enslaving a defeated South. After the advent of conscription in 1862, Brown complained about the power of enrolling officers to "drag conscripts, like slaves, in chains."[68] Many leading Georgians shared Brown's fear of being reduced to slavery. Fellow Democrat Johnson would later declare that the Confederacy "enslaved [men] on the pretext of making them free."[69] Johnson's rhetoric revealed a fear of subordination, crucial to Democratic politics, that Brown managed to tap into with his fights against centralized power such as banks and the Confederate government.

Brown's contempt for the Confederacy grew as the war drew to a close. The governor had portrayed antebellum society as one with equality of opportunity, but now class antagonism rose to the surface. He complained that the armed forces could grow by 50 percent if they conscripted the "countless swarms of young, able-bodied officers, who are to be seen . . . in all our hotels." His charges betrayed growing alienation but not defeatism. Ironically, his rhetoric near the close of the war resembled that of his rhetorical foil, Davis. Like Davis, Brown exhorted all Confederates to make greater sacrifices, and both expressed frustration that many planters failed to do their share, particularly in regard to slave impressment.[70] Confederate men and women who had embraced self-sacrifice in 1861 began to see the war as endless and self-denial without any purpose.[71]

As late as November 1864, after Sherman had wreaked havoc on Georgia and dealt a death blow to the Confederacy, Brown still chose to criticize the government in Richmond. Near the end of the war, he began to increase his attacks on the idle rich, as he complained about "the advocates of a strong central power, both in the United States and the Confederate States" who wore gold lace and drove fancy horse carriages.[72] As the Confederate military unraveled in 1865, Brown's fears of Confederate despotism became irrelevant. Still, he claimed that the real problem in the Confederacy was the "breaking of the spirits of our people by unwise laws, unjust taxation, and a departure from the principles which are dear to them." He complained sadly in private that "state sovereignty only exists in name, and that the Government at Richmond has usurped as absolute power as can exist in the hands of a government hard pressed by a powerful enemy."[73] He stubbornly refused to acknowledge that such power was negligible in light of Sherman's march. Apparently, and incredibly, he still hoped for the continuation of some version of popular warfare.

Sherman attempted, through Brown, to detach Georgia from the Confederacy. The northern general based his efforts on the faulty assumption that Brown's hostility to Davis meant that the governor could be friendly to Unionism. As Alexander Stephens explained, "Sherman acted under the idea that Brown was disaffected" enough to "oppose the cause."[74] Sherman's strategy of total war rested on the assumption that "the poorer and industrious classes" could be made sick of fighting and abandon their slaveholding allies. Despite ample opportunity, however, Brown did not take Georgia out of the war or propose a reconstruction convention. Sherman's hopes to "arouse the latent enmity of Georgia to Davis" through Brown foundered because of the governor's unwillingness to enter into formal negotiations. Brown's actions as his state fell were contradictory. He allowed the militia to return home to harvest crops after the fall of Atlanta, but he fled the state capital at Milledgeville rather than surrender to the hated Union. Much to their commander's amusement, an informal party of Sherman's men constituted themselves the legislature of Georgia, elected a Speaker, and repealed the state's ordinance of secession. Rebuffed in requests for negotiations with Brown, Sherman expressed disgust with a governor who "ignominiously fled" Milledgeville.[75]

The South faced a paradoxical situation in the late 1850s. In light of increasing northern power, the region feared political domination by the North and its dynamic politics. The only alternative to northern domination was a collective southern military effort that forced the region to take on many characteristics of its opponent. In standing up to centralization and strong government in both the North and the South throughout the war, Brown acted as the last truly Jacksonian politician. He continued to try throughout the war to pay obeisance to two increasingly incompatible Jacksonian principles, the independence of the yeomanry and the defense of slavery. Brown was an ambivalent Confederate, backing the Confederacy but unwilling to stand for the measures needed to establish southern nationhood. Unable to choose between defending slavery and white independence, Brown seemed without a compass as the two imperatives collided.

5. The Price of Moderation—Francis W. Pickens and the Factionalism of South Carolina

Antebellum South Carolina politicians, educated in the ideas of John Calhoun, took extraordinary pride in their meticulous adherence to the Constitution. Raised in a "Constitutionally fundamentalist" political culture, South Carolinians viewed themselves as devoted defenders of constitutional rights and dogged opponents of centralized power.[1] Yet after taking South Carolina out of the Union in December 1860, the state's secession convention refused to dissolve itself and strengthened the authority of Governor Francis Pickens. Pickens was allowed to appoint an Executive Council of advisers and given greater control over state functions such as the militia. Then, in November 1861, the sovereign convention stripped the legislature and Governor Pickens of power, establishing a new Executive Council of five men with dictatorial control over the state. One observer aptly described the new authority as a "five-headed dictatorship."[2] This council took the reins of a government granted broad new prerogatives and established absolute control over the economy, society, and politics.[3] The rise of the second Executive Council vividly illustrates the potential ruthlessness of secessionist politicians, who were willing to overturn democratic processes that they claimed to revere.

The radical action of the secession convention in creating the all-powerful Executive Council might appear baffling, as it seemingly contradicts the stated values of many leading South Carolinians, who followed John Calhoun's belief in popular sovereignty. Moreover, the emergence of a Civil War dictatorship is striking given that antebellum South Carolina, with its large slaveholding population, witnessed unparalleled unity among white men on the issues of slavery and republican government.[4] While South Carolina's political system did unite white men who agreed about the benefits of slavery, political grudges originating in the antebellum period simmered within the Democratic Party.

The rise of the council occurred because these schisms, manageable during peacetime, intensified because of the onset of war. Bitter conflict over antebellum issues such as legislative apportionment and South Carolina's relationship to the national Democratic Party divided the state's politicians. Throughout the 1850s, South Carolina politicians squabbled over the proper relationship between South Carolina and the national Democratic Party, which few forgot was the party of Jackson, the man who crushed the state's nullification movement in the 1830s. Hostility between Pickens, a so-called National Democrat, and South Carolina's states' rights vanguard was exacerbated by conflict over how Pickens handled the crisis at Fort Sumter in early 1861. Antebellum tensions, heightened by the approaching war, served as a backdrop for the council's Civil War dictatorship.

A common explanation for the secession convention's action in establishing the Executive Council lay in the supposed incompetence of Governor Pickens.[5] Yet it seems unlikely that he lacked the ability to govern South Carolina. Pickens, who held a variety of public offices during a long career in politics, was at least as knowledgeable, experienced, and fit for the job as any of his contemporaries.[6] The fact that South Carolina's leaders bypassed normal procedures for removal of a governor by impeachment and instead adopted institutions that broke with the state's constitutional heritage highlights the fact that more than Pickens's fitness to rule was at stake. Defenders of the convention argued that its sovereignty gave it the right to alter the government, including the right to diminish the strength of both the governor's office and the legislature. But such rationalizations of the convention's actions did not obscure the radical nature of its repudiation of mixed government limited by constitutional procedures.[7]

When he entered office in November 1860, Pickens predicted, "If we fail . . . the public mind will despondingly turn to the strong and more fixed [governmental] forms of the old world."[8] His forecast seemed confirmed when, only a year later, he was virtually stripped of power. As the state's secession convention called itself back into session and established the Executive Council in November 1861, it stipulated that this five-man body would oversee all state functions, including the touchy issues of conscription and impressment of slave property. Since a majority of the five were needed for the state to act, authority effectively lay in the hands of the three members appointed by the convention— James Chesnut, Isaac W. Hayne, and William H. Gist. The establishment of the council effectively ended Pickens's authority as the governor. Pickens, who had been delegated greater responsibility than previous executives by the convention at the time of secession, now sat on the council as a minority voice.

The Executive Council, an organization unique in the Confederacy, can best be understood in the context of the rivalries engendered by South Carolina's distinctive antebellum political system. When Pickens lost his gubernatorial powers, it was the culmination of tensions between two fiercely competitive political factions in the state. In South Carolina's one-party system, politicians generally adopted a stance of public unity, but behind the scenes sharp divisions developed without the machinery of a two-party system to manage political disagreement.[9] States' Rights Democrats, disproportionately but not exclusively representing the planter class in the coastal low country, jockeyed for power with National Democrats drawn primarily but not entirely from the state's up-country.[10] The best-known National Democrats, James Orr of Anderson and Benjamin Perry of Greenville, espoused racially exclusive democratic politics and emulated the political rhetoric of white male equality that many Democrats voiced across the South. These leaders, who remained steadfast nationalists, represented the legacy of Thomas Jefferson and Andrew Jackson, and their political ideals resembled those of many rank-and-file southern Democrats.[11]

The States' Rights Democrats opposed the National Democrats and defended the state's constitution of 1808, which gave greater political influence to the low country than its white population warranted. They wished that the state would distance itself from the national Democratic Party, since involvement with the party could endanger the state's political independence. The national Democratic Party could potentially corrupt South Carolina's politics by using the spoils system to gain power within the state; indeed, Calhoun wrote that "the only cohesive principle which binds together the party rallied under the name of General Jackson, is official patronage."[12] States' Rights Democrats believed that they alone upheld Calhoun's ideas, which were necessary to maintain slavery. While the factions within the Democratic Party never hardened into a permanent two-party system, they shaped the direction of policy and controlled access to political power. Despite South Carolina's reputation for sectional militancy, for most of the 1850s the National Democrats were ascendant. Only in 1860, with the impending election of Lincoln, did the States' Rights group grab the initiative in state politics.[13] The secession of South Carolina was the culmination of years of effort by States' Rights forces. To achieve popular unity, States' Rights Democrats needed the help of politicians who had been National Democrats before secession, but they also distrusted their traditional opponents.

The historical significance of slavery, the issue that united white South Carolinians in the antebellum period, should not obscure disagreement over two other issues that citizens believed crucial to the future of their state. First, politicians clashed over the state's archaic political system, which gave extraordinary legislative influence to low-country parishes and placed the selection of officers such as the governor and presidential electors in the legislature's hands.[14] Under the state's constitutional reform of 1808, representation in the nearly all-powerful legislature was slanted toward the interests of planters. The Senate was elected according to districts drawn in 1790, which gave equal representation to tiny low-country parishes and large up-country districts. As time went on and population spread to the up-country, this fixed scheme of representation increasingly favored the wealthy low-country parishes. Because representation in the House of Representatives was based equally on population and property taxes, the wealthy parishes with the highest rates of slave ownership also enjoyed an advantage in that body. An early historian of South Carolina scarcely exaggerated when he said that "there never was a time until the reconstruction days that the black belt, or the greater low country did not absolutely control the government."[15]

South Carolinians in the 1850s also disagreed about what kind of stance the state should adopt regarding the national Democratic Party. On the one hand, National Democrats, including Pickens, believed that active participation in the party of Jackson could secure South Carolina's interests, especially regarding slavery. On the other hand, States' Rights Democrats such as Gist and Robert Barnwell Rhett Jr. hoped that South Carolina would remain apart from national parties and maintain its distinctive brand of conservative politics.[16] In the minds of most South Carolinians, these two issues, proportional representation and participation in the national Democratic Party, were linked. National Democrats, who wished their state party would unite with other Democrats across the United States, also favored expanding democracy in the state through abrogating the 1808 compromise and allocating power on a one-man, one-vote basis. States' Rights men, who distrusted affiliation with the national Democratic Party, feared increased electoral democracy in the state. They wished to prevent reform of South Carolina's uniquely hierarchical system of representation. With sharp ideological differences between camps and the resulting factional maneuvering, one writer exclaimed, "No living man's pen is competent to portray the conspiracies of our public men one against the other."[17]

The antebellum split between States' Rights Democrats and National Democrats, extending back to the controversy over nullification in the 1830s, has been dismissed as a "tactical dispute between two groups of Southerners" over how best to defend slavery.[18] But it was much more. Politicians understood that the factions disagreed over key principles of republican government, as the ongoing controversy over political representation brought fundamental issues of political philosophy to the forefront. Indeed, South Carolina became the only state to maintain the "virtual representation" characteristic of eighteenth-century colonial rule into the nineteenth century.[19] Those who questioned the system risked upsetting the order of this uniquely conservative state.

The epithets used in the debate over democracy indicate the emotional fervor surrounding the arguments about political change. Perry complained that reformers "have been denounced as 'red republicans,' 'levellers,' 'revolutionists,' 'demagogues,' &c." Yet while nationalists such as Perry disavowed radicalism, they affirmed that they led a fight between "two antagonistic principles . . . the one an aristocratic principle . . . the other a Democratic principle." Proponents of the status quo saw the conflict in apocalyptic terms. In 1860, planter and politician James Henry Hammond condemned democratic reforms, bemoaning the "little great men who would seek notoriety by proposing to elect Judges, Senators and Representatives . . . by universal suffrage." He feared "demagogues at home more than enemies abroad" and warned of democracy bringing "the guillotine at work upon good men" in South Carolina.[20] Democracy, even limited to white men, appeared threatening to many elite South Carolinians.

Residents of Edgefield County, the home of Pickens, were especially dissatisfied with the state's system of legislative apportionment. Edgefield, a county that was economically centered on the cotton economy, found it difficult to attract commercial development, even when high cotton prices drove South Carolina's booming economy during the 1850s. Edgefield's pro-commerce business and political leaders blamed their district's failure to win more railroad development on the inadequate efforts of the legislature to attract capital. County leaders, especially George Tillman, argued that the up-country's growing railroad network neglected Edgefield because the region lacked political clout. As the decade progressed, Tillman joined with

Perry, the up-country National Democrat and self-appointed spokesman for the yeomanry. Although Edgefield County's economy resembled many counties of the cotton south and its politics was dominated by slaveholders, a sense of grievance against the low country grew there as the Civil War approached.[21]

Not surprisingly, those who desired white equality resented the fact that South Carolina's electoral system favored the established planters of the low country. In this system, small low-country parishes along the coast held political power that equaled the Piedmont and up-country districts, which had a greater white population.[22] Even defenders of the 1808 representation system admitted that it discriminated not only by region but by class, as it gave more weight to planters than yeomen. As the *Edgefield Advertiser* explained, in the parishes and middle districts "wealth or taxable property is large, and white population small," whereas "in the mountain districts white population is numerous and taxable property comparatively small."[23] The low country could "absolutely control the government of the state," and the extreme imbalance between sections brought anger and agitation throughout the antebellum period.[24]

To proponents of reform, including Pickens, change in territorial representation seemed a modest and necessary step. The future Civil War governor hoped electoral reform would reduce the potential for class antagonisms in the state: "To settle the question now would be to take a subject of agitation out of the hands of demagogues, who will always keep it up to affect local results and make party divisions in our state, where we should have none. If not given to the people now, it . . . may lead to other far more levelling and serious changes."[25] In his reference to the danger of "levelling" and "more serious changes," he hinted that slavery would be safer if South Carolina relied on universal white male suffrage and proportional representation. Advocates of reform wished that South Carolina could imitate states such as Georgia and Alabama, where egalitarian constitutions coexisted with vigorous proslavery politics.

Opponents of reform adamantly resisted change. They denounced reapportionment in heated terms that reveal genuine fear of even limited political innovation. A writer from the middle country warned that "from the numerical strength and homogenous interests of the mountain Districts," the controlling party would produce "wild fanaticism" with all its consequences, including abolition. Constitutional reform would bring "in the state almost a new North and a new South."[26] Although such concerns may have been overstated, opponents of electoral reform worried that South Carolina risked losing its status as an independent representative republic. With reform, the state would resemble other states where "'democracy' of course degenerated into all that is vulgar and disreputable" bringing "desecration of the elective franchise."[27] Such comments underscore historian Stephanie McCurry's contention that South Carolina planters distrusted yeoman democracy.[28]

Equally divisive was the issue of South Carolina and the national Democratic Party, as Calhoun could brag that South Carolina's political autonomy meant that "party organization, party discipline, party proscription—and their offspring, *the spoils principle*, have been unknown."[29] Calhoun's followers believed that spoils would undermine the independence, and therefore the trustworthiness, of politicians. Controversy arose in 1856 when National Democrats proposed sending a South Carolina delegation to the Democratic National Convention in Cincinnati. They argued that because of misguided principles against political parties, the state had stood aloof from the presidential nominating process for far too long by not sending delegates. The pleas for national participation underlined the way in which involvement with the National Democrats dovetailed with local electoral reform. Orr linked proposals to draw closer to the Democratic Party with the democratic vision that underpinned state-level electoral reform. He believed the Democratic Party arose under Andrew Jackson when "men saw the importance of making an election by the people. . . . Conventions are in the judgement of the people of all the other states the safest and fairest means of ascertaining and concentrating the popular will."[30]

The Jacksonian tinge to Orr's appeal, evident in his reference to "the popular will," did not sit well with States' Rights Democrats. They argued that involvement with the National Democrats would inexorably shift power to Democrats outside the state, who would use party patronage to control the state's politics by manipulating it to benefit national officeholders. Lowcountry politicians' fears of South Carolina entering a national Jacksonian party intensified as the election of 1860 approached. National Democrats, they worried, would capitalize on the state's internal divisions and diminish the state's resolve to defend slavery: States' Rights politician William Porcher Miles received a letter urging him, "We have too many Yankees among us, and unfortunately they have enough influence to keep us divided and distracted on collateral issues, when we ought to stand as one man." Political spoils, in other words, could threaten South Carolina's solid political consensus.[31] States' Rights politicians asserted that only South Carolina's constitution, and isolation from the national Democratic Party, preserved the founding fathers' republican legacy. Links to a national party could veil "demagogues" as they manipulated rank-and-file members, or as they bowed too quickly to the whims of the "multitude."[32] Such politicians agreed that links to the national Democratic Party would blunt the edge of sectional unity: Rhett pointed to Georgia as an example of what could go wrong when scheming politicians put party interests ahead of the South. He condemned Howell Cobb, Robert Toombs, and Alexander Stephens of Georgia for a "base betrayal" of the South regarding the territorial conflict in Kansas. The Georgia Democrats had plotted, at the behest of party leaders, a plan "perpetuated to relieve the Democratic Party and [Buchanan] administration" by abandoning proslavery forces in Kansas.[33]

Despite South Carolina's reputation as a bastion of aristocracy, National Democrats generally outmaneuvered the States' Rights men for much of the 1850s. South Carolina did send delegates to the Cincinnati Democratic convention in 1856 and helped secure a strong proslavery platform and a candidate, James Buchanan, who was very friendly to the South. In fact, Buchanan and Pickens maintained a long-standing friendship. National Democrats believed that they had strengthened slavery by promoting both constitutional reform and the Democratic Party. Still they faced the anger of States' Rights opponents, partly because of disagreements on sectional issues during the previous thirty years. On several occasions in the antebellum period, most notably during the nullification crisis, South Carolina skated near the edge of secession. States' Rights advocates such as Rhett claimed that the state submitted to Democrats like Andrew Jackson because the political system was plagued by "spoilsmen" more loyal to national powers than to their state interest. Open participation in party conventions, such as in 1856, could only worsen matters as politicians would seek patronage and "all of our ambitious men . . . must necessarily court the favor of the North" and therefore undermine southern rights.[34] Moreover, States' Rights men claimed, other southern states vacillated on southern rights because of their ties to the national party. States' Rights men drew the lesson that South Carolina, if it was to maintain its rights, must stand aloof from the Democrats and maintain its independence.

The differences became clearer in the 1850s because of the lack of authoritative leadership after Calhoun's death. Tensions between National Democrats and States' Rights Democrats became increasingly public. In 1858, former Speaker of the U.S. House of Representatives and National

Democrat Orr coveted a Senate seat, which would require his selection by the legislature. Despite his considerable credentials, he was brushed aside because of his unpopularity with politicians representing States' Rights interests in the parishes. As Pickens observed, "With the present parish interest + feeling, it seems to me, it would be very difficult to elect [him]." Pickens feared the election "would turn on local points [that] we do not desire to bring into full agitation for the present." An aggressive movement by Orr supporters would, Pickens argued, produce "local division of parties" between up-country and low country, a result that would lead to Orr's defeat because of the low country's predominance in the legislature.[35] Although politicians' personal letters provide evidence of sectional tensions, such problems were downplayed by everyone concerned and almost never publicly expressed in newspaper articles or stump speeches. Nevertheless, political operatives such as Pickens knew they could ignore the state's divisions only at their own peril.

In the context of heated factionalism, Pickens became the target for much of the anger of the States' Rights politicians, because they despised him for abandoning the southern cause. Pickens, a cousin of Calhoun's, had worked closely with the great leader in congressional battles over slavery, Mexico, and the congressional gag rule in the 1830s and 1840s. Nevertheless, he ultimately defected to the National Democrats, most notably in supporting the proposal for a South Carolina delegation to the 1856 Democratic National Convention. Pickens never wavered in his support of slavery but believed that the unity of the national party offered the best way to preserve the peculiar institution: "Ultraism under existing circumstances would lead to division + division will prove our ruin." He was astonished that his loyalty to the national party led to accusations that he was "not true to So Ca + slavery!!! They say I desire federal office."[36] In this context, the former congressman knew that his name was "distasteful to those who control[led] the state." Therefore, he "never openly allowed [his] friends to run [him] for anything in the state."[37] In Pickens's view, factional divisions left him adrift in state politics, unable to gain the legislative support needed to win high office.

Pickens's weak political position meant that if he wanted to remain in public life, he could do so only through obtaining a national political office, the sort of position that States' Rights men condemned as spoils. The election of Buchanan as president in 1856 provided him with an opportunity. Buchanan and Pickens had long been friends, and Pickens wanted a post in the administration, believing that only through the national government could "our wise institutions" such as slavery be saved. Pickens's loyalty to Buchanan, a northern friend of slavery, was consistent with his principles. Like the other prominent National Democrats in South Carolina, he linked Unionism with the cause of democratic reforms, favoring the state "giving the election to the people."[38] In his mind, democracy on the state level was connected to Unionism on the national level. The Democratic Party would protect slavery because "under existing circumstances we have practically the Gov't under our control."[39] Pickens's support of a strong Democratic Party and electoral reforms meant that he was as close as a South Carolina politician could come to claiming the mantle of Jacksonian Democracy. Of course, for States' Rights politicians, his ties to the national party were far too close.

He accepted the position of ambassador to Russia under Buchanan, a post that temporarily kept him out of political controversy in South Carolina. He remained abroad for most of 1860, when Stephen Douglas was the northern favorite for the Democratic nomination. To the States' Rights faction, Douglas's politics represented the dangers of national unity on Democratic Party lines. When northern Republican opponents such as Abraham Lincoln forced Douglas to clarify his stance on the Dred Scott decision and the territorial disputes of the 1850s, his views on slavery in the territories proved unacceptable to many southern Democrats. South Carolina's National Democrats therefore favored the selection of a southerner such as Robert M. T. Hunter or John Breckenridge to head the Democratic ticket, while States' Rights advocates entirely opposed attending the convention. As South Carolina politicians squabbled, Pickens was fortunate to be out of the country, because his absence put him above the political fray.

Events in 1860 exacerbated the rancor in South Carolina politics. Chaos reigned at the state Democratic convention. As witness Isaac Hayne noted, "madness ruled the convention" as National Democrats and States' Rights men fought in an atmosphere of "suspicion" and "distrust." States' Rights politicians feared that National Democrats would back Douglas because "this is a spoils party."[40] Through the allegations made about gaining patronage, support for the national party became equated with corruption. Rhett feared that after "outside pressure" southern Democrats in the convention would strike a sectional deal. William Henry Trescot thought that Douglas would gain the loyalty of South Carolinians "who want[ed] his ear and his patronage."[41] States' Rights men feared that distribution of lucrative offices by Douglas would limit the independence of South Carolina politicians and place them under the control of a northerner with dubious credentials on the slavery issue. Extreme southern-rights advocates incorrectly forecast that

Douglas would win the Democratic nomination in 1860, with disastrous consequences for slavery. Instead, the convention culminated in a southern walkout that split the party.

The dire forecasts by States' Rights men misread the intentions of South Carolina's National Democrats. Virtually all of them opposed Douglas, even as they worked to avoid a sectional Democratic Party split.[42] Although they agreed on the preservation of slavery and the right of secession, by 1860 South Carolinians split along the lines that would polarize the South as a whole: radical fire-eaters wanted immediate state secession, while National Democrats wanted cooperative activity with the national party or, failing that, cooperation with other southern states.[43] The decision over whether to precipitate disunion by independent action inevitably overlapped with ongoing debates in South Carolina between National Democrats and their States' Rights counterparts. As the election of Lincoln seemed imminent, controversy raged over whether South Carolina should focus on independence for its uniquely militant state or wait for cooperation with other states, especially Georgia.

Pickens remained the ambassador to Russia, and his distance from South Carolina allowed him to stay out of this argument. He remained a believer in the national Democratic Party, noting to a friend, "If our extreme men North and South . . . could witness the state of things here [Europe] they would yield all minor points to sustain and strengthen our Federal Union."[44] When the National Democrats seemed in control in South Carolina prior to 1860, he, as a member of the Buchanan administration, sided with them from abroad. He told Unionist Perry, "I rejoice to see in our state more wise + reasonable councils prevailing than for years."[45] He declared his "personal esteem" for President Buchanan and linked his loyalty to Buchanan with his "desire to save the constitution + the Union of our common country." He still hoped for reform of the electoral system in South Carolina.[46] Pickens's political friends, who believed that he could succeed Buchanan as a moderate able to unite the camps of Breckenridge and Douglas, tried to promote him for the presidency in 1860.[47] As 1860 began, Pickens looked like a National Democrat who would embrace secession only in the most dire circumstances. His Unionism seemed strong when he wrote in May 1860, "My heart sickens when I think of our Union falling to pieces," but he cautiously avoided public pronouncements on the sectional crisis. He proposed cooperation with other southern states and expressed hope that secession would not occur until Buchanan left office.[48]

Yet when Pickens returned to South Carolina in the fall, secession was imminent. The split between the Douglas and Breckenridge factions in the Democratic Party's 1860 national convention virtually assured the election of Lincoln with a northern majority. In this context, virtually all of South Carolina's National Democrats had become eleventh-hour advocates of secession. Pickens, who had been away from the state and its factionalism, seemed an ideal choice for governor after he belatedly and opportunistically embraced immediate secession in November 1860, just before the gubernatorial election in the state legislature. His new secession stance endeared him to the fire-eaters while his history as a National Democrat gave him credibility with that faction. His selection by the legislature, designed to ensure unity, was not well received by everyone in the parishes. Yet even many of Pickens's enemies believed his election was necessary to maintain "the greatest spirit of conciliation and harmony, with a view to united action" between political factions. As the low-country power broker Trescot put it, South Carolina needed a governor who would "conciliate as well as give confidence to all of the men in the state."[49]

Pickens's last-minute support of secession failed to endear him to old political opponents, especially as it became clear that he differed with most immediate secessionists about how to lead the state as it entered the Confederacy. As a former member of the federal administration, he wished to avoid conflict while Buchanan remained in office. Moreover, he hoped gradually to persuade border states, especially Virginia, to enter the Confederacy. He therefore differed with South Carolina hotheads, represented by the *Charleston Mercury*, who demanded war with the federal government in the hope of pushing the border states out of the Union. His problems worsened when U.S. troops under Major Robert Anderson slipped out of the vulnerable Fort Moultrie to the more commanding Fort Sumter in January. Pickens had been assured by his state's unofficial representative in Washington, Trescot, that the federal troops would not move. When they did, critics ridiculed the governor for his failure to take Moultrie.[50] While some blamed the fiasco on his incompetence, the angry reaction in South Carolina intensified primarily because of his close relationship with Buchanan and his continued hope for reconciliation through the national Democratic Party—positions anathema to the newly ascendant States' Rights faction.

Pickens felt pressured by the demands of States' Rights forces that he should move quickly to take Fort Sumter. Fire-eaters such as Rhett distrusted his attempts to negotiate a settlement regarding the fort with Buchanan. Rhett complained of "the mixed folly and cowardice of our Governor" in pursuing negotiations. He questioned Pickens's secessionist credentials, accusing him of seeking a reconstruction of the Union through a compromise fostered by the border states, and argued that "no cooperationist could beg more humbly for aid than our Governor now does." He claimed that Fort Sumter's resistance and the governor's inaction meant "we in the state are disgraced already."[51] Extremists pushed the governor to act immediately. Anderson, the Union commander of Fort Sumter, noted accurately that Rhett's newspaper, the *Charleston Mercury*, "publishes everything that is calculated to bring on a collision."[52] The controversy boiled down to an issue that had already split the state's antebellum factions: whether South Carolina should pursue an independent course or align with Democrats outside the state.

Pickens, who felt that independent action by South Carolina would be doomed, found himself sharply at odds with the agitators of Charleston regarding the struggle for Sumter. While he favored a moderate course, his opponents advocated war. Many South Carolinians agreed with J. L. Pugh that "there is another way of avoiding the calamity of reconstruction and that is war . . . taking Fort Sumter at any cost." Pugh warned that border states would accept sectional compromise unless South Carolina forced the issue.[53] A few extremists went even further, favoring immediate action without regard to states such as Virginia, Tennessee, and Kentucky because the Confederacy would be better off without these states, which were not sufficiently proslavery and would ultimately prove "too powerful" in the Confederacy.[54] Pickens, who sharply disagreed with the demands to move toward secession without the border states and while Buchanan still held power, bore the brunt of demands to attack Fort Sumter. In the feverish atmosphere in Charleston in late 1860 and early 1861, few publicly opposed Rhett and other advocates of immediate action; proponents of "delay" were "not strong enough to speak out."[55]

Among those afraid to speak out was Pickens. Yet the governor was determined to avoid rash actions, and the nascent Confederate government instructed him to hold off attacking Sumter in early 1861. In January, state emissary Isaac W. Hayne told the governor that leaders such as Jefferson Davis and Virginia's R. M. T. Hunter "all concur on the policy of procrastination" in regard to Sumter. The senators of the other seceding states hoped for "an amicable adjustment of the matter of differences" rather than an attack on the fort.[56] Pickens pinned his hopes on the Confederate government, believing that the new government would be free of the "vulgar influences" and "demagoguism" that prevailed in South Carolina. He thought that moderates outside South Carolina could secure a negotiated peace with the Union—a position that put him sharply at odds with local militants. He opposed attack on Sumter because "it would involve our new Govt at the very moment when their negotiations were in actual progress."[57] But fire-eaters wanted to preempt moves toward peace by the Confederacy, and many South Carolinians suspected that Jefferson Davis might favor reunion.[58]

While tensions mounted over Sumter, the suspicion grew among fire-eaters that the central government was dragging out negotiations in the hope of reaching a settlement to reconstruct the Union. Former States' Rights men, conditioned by years of hostility to National Democrats, focused their suspicion on both the Confederate government and Pickens, who was perceived as its supporter. The governor believed, as he indicated to Davis, that "moderate and wise councils" were necessary to ensure the secession of the border states. To Pickens's opponents, who for years had talked of an independent South Carolina, such moderation was anathema. His reputation also declined because he could not publicly discuss another, crucial reason for delaying the attack on Fort Sumter. South Carolina was in a state of administrative confusion and lacked military supplies.[59]

Pickens therefore had the unhappy task of restraining Charleston residents from the "very strong inclination to seize Fort Sumter and Castle Pinckney in advance of any negotiation."[60] Federal officers on Fort Sumter assessed the situation realistically, noting the difficulty Pickens had in controlling "the temper of the common people" of Charleston in early 1861. Shifting from a "high pitch of excitement . . . to a suddenly conciliatory course, the reasons for which they [did] not perceive," was a political disaster. The result was that the "temper of the people of this state [was] becoming every day more bitter."[61] Things got so bad that Pickens feared South Carolina troops would fire on Sumter in defiance of their officers. In February, he cut his losses by passing off the responsibility for the Sumter affair to the new provisional Confederate government, but not before he had sustained serious political damage.[62] The man who gave the fiery secessionist speech just before the gubernatorial election had seemingly disappeared, and extremists doubtless believed that the old Pickens, the National Democrat who had split from Calhoun, had reemerged. This combined with the perception that Pickens favored the up-country over the low country in appointments also helped to rekindle old divisions between the factions.[63]

The governor's star fell even further after Union forces successfully encroached upon the South Carolina coastline and took Port Royal in the fall of

1861. For numerous Carolinians, especially in the besieged low country, morale collapsed: "The spirit of the low country is depressed . . . the confusions resulting in the sudden breakdown of a most unfortunate and overweening confidence . . . in the next place we have no head. Even [Robert E.] Lee does not know the country or the peculiarities of its people." Lee, then commanding Confederate forces in the low country, dismissed the wishes of planters who wanted to defend their homes. He rejected, as one observer noted, "that small sort of partisan fighting which does not commend itself to his longer and cooler military judgement."[64] Further, Lee had to contend with a "general attitude of resistance" to central authority by low-country South Carolinians, which greatly complicated coastal defense.[65] The failure of the Confederacy to protect coastal South Carolina also stemmed from its strategy of concentrating many troops in northern Virginia. The results proved disastrous, as "slave refugees came behind civilian lines at rates without precedent."[66]

Sectional tensions in the state played a role in undermining Pickens, as the up-country remained immune to the threat faced by coastal parishes. In the fall of 1861, the *Edgefield Advertiser* recommended that the government stop asking for more up-country men to defend Charleston, because Edgefield had already raised more volunteers than had Charleston itself.[67] Such callousness to the plight of the low country could not reflect well on Pickens. Indeed, the governor played no part in the Confederate decision to deemphasize defense of the South Carolina low country and to allocate key resources to northern Virginia, which was bitterly resented in the wake of Port Royal. Pickens privately protested the lack of resources for South Carolina, threatening "to look rather more to [his] own state and her local interests."[68] Yet he refused to criticize the Confederacy in public and therefore still received a good share of the blame for the disaster along the coast.

After November, the secession convention replaced the weak Executive Council controlled by Pickens with the stronger council dominated by Hayne, Gist, and Chesnut. Secessionists needed a rationale for such a bold stroke against representative government. They found it in Calhoun's theory of the sovereignty of the people gathered in convention. According to Calhoun, constitutional conventions when in session were not just representatives of the people; they literally were the people in their sovereign capacity empowered to make organic law. If a convention chose to do away with the separation of powers, it had that authority as a sovereign body. Aware of his tenuous political position, Pickens acquiesced in the council scheme, though not without expressing some reservations about its legality. He privately questioned "the legitimate power of the Convention" to establish the council. The governor believed that once the convention transferred the state to the Confederacy, its power should have ended, making it impossible for the convention to adopt "a total change of our internal government."[69]

At first, the extraordinary action of the council received remarkably little attention in the press. Typical of the muted reaction to such a remarkable event was the brief announcement of the formation of the council tucked in a corner of the *Columbia Guardian*, which noted discreetly, "We cannot approve of the action of the Convention in this matter." The lack of protest or even public discussion about the council resulted not from unity but, as Hammond made clear, because of fear. According to Hammond, former sectional conciliators were subject to a "Reign of Terror." The intense fervor in the state created such intense anxiety that Hammond, who was normally accustomed to speaking his mind, became "afraid of going to Columbia." He complained that "common sense is now gibbeted."[70] Pickens, who presumably understood the balance of forces, cooperated with the council, waiting for an opportune moment to regain his power.

As the immediate military emergency that accompanied the creation of the council passed, citizens grumbled about the council's power grab and its constitutional implications. Hammond, who stayed out of the fray, privately attacked the reasoning behind the Executive Council: "The theory is about a convention of the whole people *assembled*" rather than of representatives. Therefore, political theorists, especially Calhoun, had left the state with "a sort of sham . . . an imaginary 'social compact.'"[71] Pickens's old allies, the National Democrats, began in late 1861 and early 1862 tentatively to criticize the Executive Council and to support him. The *Charleston Courier*, a formerly Unionist newspaper, printed a short and restrained article defending Pickens two months after the council took power: "It is said to be leaking out that the Convention means its recent action as a slur upon the Governor. . . . If such was the Convention's purpose we confidently say that it has not truly reflected the feelings and wishes of the people of South Carolina." Despite Pickens's public silence regarding the convention, his old political friends had no illusions about the fact that his "enemies" created the council.[72]

As criticism of the council increased in late 1862, its proponents had to defend the necessity of the dictatorship. The *Charleston Mercury* justified the council on the grounds that the sovereign convention had the constitutional power to make such changes. Moreover, the newspaper insinuated that

Pickens was inept: "The Convention had not absolute confidence in the competency of the Executive to fulfill the duties in the emergencies of the State." Most important, the formation of the council could be traced to the conflict within South Carolina over how to deal with Union troops in Charleston's harbor. The *Mercury* wrote, "If Major Anderson had been prevented from getting into Fort Sumter—as might have been done with great ease, and as was much pressed upon Governor Pickens, all of our troubles to get it back would have been unnecessary, with all the after consequences. . . . Lincoln's secret war preparations might never have been made. . . . Our hesitancy and delay gave Lincoln great advantage, if it did not encourage and inaugurate the war."[73] To blame Pickens for Sumter, and by extension the whole war, was more than a bit of a stretch. Yet the *Mercury* insisted that Pickens's policy of negotiating with Buchanan in 1861 proved the need for the council. The editorial confirms that the conflict between those who had wanted independent action against the Union and those who had desired cooperation with the border states, such as Pickens, still had great resonance with the state's politicians.

Pickens, while meekly cooperating with the council and keeping a low political profile, warned his opponents that the council could worsen political "dissension" in the up-country. He was right. The council took its first major misstep in January, when it created political patronage offices and advertised them only in the Charleston newspapers, which incensed citizens outside the city. Many suspected that the council members showed favoritism in screening applicants for these jobs in order to keep their friends out of the army. Privately, Pickens complained about preferential treatment for the low country, noting that "the upcountry [had] sent nearly all her men into service."[74]

In the summer of 1862, amid rising complaints about the council, Pickens publicly distanced himself from the body. His gambit proved remarkably effective in shaking the confidence of his opponents. The *Mercury* was indignant, denouncing "efforts which have been made to divide the people of the state." Meanwhile, the council found that it needed Pickens's help in appealing to up-country slaveholders who vigorously opposed the impressment of their slaves to build fortifications in the low country. On behalf of the council majority, Gist asked Pickens to help quell "disaffection and the spirit of resistance to lawful authority" in several up-country districts. Fearing that it was becoming politically isolated in the midst of a dangerous war, the council resolved to "state to His Excellency that it would be more satisfactory in the emergency that the Council should act in conjunction with the Governor."[75]

Growing dissatisfaction had diminished the council's prestige and strengthened Pickens's hand.

As the summer of 1862 progressed, Pickens's disaffection with the council became increasingly known, and attacks against it grew. Public protest confirmed the return of factionalism. Chesnut, a council member and low-country aristocrat, leveled an ill-timed attack on up-country opponents of the council, accusing them of "disaffection" and "prospective treason." William Gilmore Simms worried that the end result of the council could be more conflict between the two factions. He believed that the war had initially restrained "intrigue," which, having now openly appeared, could get worse.[76] Council records are conspicuously silent on political issues, but it could not have escaped council members that dissension caused by their power grab could prove singularly dangerous to the war effort.

The council's demands for slave impressment to build low-country fortifications backfired, leading disgruntled up-country planters to seeks its abolition. Public meetings in Edgefield, Marion, and Richland called for the abolition of the council, and the *Charleston Courier* stepped up its campaign against the body in the late summer of 1862. The *Charleston Mercury*, an early supporter of the council, became noticeably silent on matters relating to its continued existence.[77] James Henry Hammond bemoaned the fact that popular pressure meant authorities were "forced to recall the [Secession] Convention" so that it could consider the continuation of rule by the council. When Orr filed a petition for the recall of the convention, abolition of the council became a certainty. The council majority saw the handwriting on the wall, and only Isaac Hayne defended the body's legality or fought against its dissolution. As Hammond put it, the council "was an intrigue which failed and is now shirked by the same" men who created it.[78]

The conciliatory stance of Pickens, who alone seemed able to quell up-country dissent, helps explain the passivity and silence of the council. As the council experiment drew increasing fire, his hometown newspaper, the *Edgefield Advertiser*, diplomatically suggested that the council could be relieved of power "without giving moral aid to Lincoln." In his first speech after the abolition of the council by the secession convention, Pickens did point out his disagreement with the council in principle, calling it the "very essence of despotism." But the governor made policy recommendations designed to move the war effort forward and raise popular morale. He called for increased funding to relieve hardship among the families of soldiers. He urged unity behind the Confederate war, asking citizens to "withhold nothing, and make no complaint calculated to weaken the hands of Confederate authorities in particular."[79] When the legislature reconvened, Pickens extended the olive branch to low-country conservatives by denouncing "the extremes of democracy." Aware that his term was nearing its close, he also asked for legislation extending the governor's term in office from two years to four. The legislature, still apportioned in favor of the low country, ignored his request.[80]

Although Pickens's first legislative address after his return to gubernatorial office was conciliatory toward his opponents, his return to power represented a setback for the low country.[81] Low-country members of both the council and convention stood "no chance," observers believed, of choosing the next governor, since the legislature needed to assuage discontented up-country citizens. Indeed, Simms feared that the choice of a new governor could result in "large steps . . . towards anarchy." He described the possibility of a gubernatorial deadlock between up-country and low-country factions. Rumor had it that if Pickens's supporters could not elect former National Democrat Orr, they would stalemate the legislature by casting blank ballots, leaving Pickens with de facto control.[82] The low country still did have a legislative majority, and Pickens's term was running out. Nevertheless, the National Democrats had new leverage because of the need for wartime unity and popular disillusionment with the council.

When Pickens's term expired, he could not succeed himself because governors were limited to one term. So by December 1862, some Carolinians, even in the low country, were speculating about something that would have been unthinkable in 1861: electing Jacksonian Democrat and Unionist Perry to the governor's chair. As one of Perry's friends noted, "The next Governor must be from the upper country first because it is better at this time [of war] that it should be so." Perry's friend was correct to note that at least some power had shifted to the up-country despite the long-standing "clannishness of the parish people."[83] But Pickens was much too cautious a man to promote the career of a radical such as Perry. Instead, he convinced the legislature to install his close but colorless ally, Milledge L. Bonham, in his place, and neither Pickens nor Bonham ever tried to settle scores with those who had promoted the council. Both men were deeply committed to the preservation of slavery, and they strove to prosecute the war effort as efficiently as possible. Low-country radicals continued to grumble about the conduct of the war, but if the pages of the *Charleston Mercury* are any indication, their attention shifted to the shortcomings of President Jefferson Davis.

After it collapsed, Perry offered an incisive critique of the council that underscored the way that issues of section, faction, and democracy were intertwined in South Carolina. He argued that the council manifested "party spirit and faction." He said "[the convention] took good care . . . to elect themselves. . . . . Not one was from the Western part of the state, or the upcountry." While aristocrats shirked the draft and sought exemptions, the "nonslaveholders . . . who opposed secession" went to the front "without a murmur." The solution to sectional grievances raised by the usurpation of the council, Perry suggested, was greater democracy. Calling the Executive Council "arbitrary, tyrannical, and despotic," he argued that "a convention is the representative of the people, not the people themselves." He suggested that "the right and proper course sanctioned by Democratic principles" would be to submit decisions of the convention to the people for ratification or rejection.[84] To Perry, people should make decisions through radically democratic measures such as a popular referendum, rather than having decisions taken behind closed doors by the convention and council. In articulating his faith in radical democracy, Perry went well beyond traditional Jacksonian principles. In unambiguous language, he condemned the undemocratic nature of South Carolina politics.

The story of the Executive Council provides a reminder of the way that politicians viewed Civil War politics through the prism of antebellum squabbles. Despite the overwhelming agreement among South Carolina's white men about slavery, factional animosity, rooted in antebellum dissension, underpinned the development of a Civil War dictatorship in South Carolina. While antebellum infighting over the state's unequal legislative apportionment and its relationship to the national Democratic Party was an ongoing irritant, factional conflict remained contained by the rule of law. That South Carolina's secession convention was willing to overthrow that law for a year indicates the seriousness of divisions within the state. While the council's leaders eventually were prudent enough to cede power, their disregard for democratic procedure remains breathtaking, even by the limited standards of the Confederacy.

6 Curing the "Sir Walter Disease"—The Politics and Fiction of Jeremiah Clemens

Historians have argued about the causes of the Civil War for generations, but none have advanced such a provocative explanation as Mark Twain. Twain remarked that "Sir Walter Scott had so large a hand in making southern character, as it existed before the war, that he is in great measure responsible for the war." The "grotesque chivalry" of Scott captivated the southern mind, spreading a vicious "Sir Walter disease" that inflicted a profound sensitivity to slights against honor. Twain's disdain for Scott derived from his personal experience with the cult of chivalry. Before he deserted from the Missouri-based Confederate partisan band "The Marion Rangers," he encountered men who were typical of the Old South, being "young . . . full of romance, and given to reading chivalric novels."[1] Although Twain's assertion that Scott helped cause the Civil War was surely tongue in cheek, he made a larger, more serious point: southern honor, which dovetailed with the chivalric themes of Scott's novels, had enormous destructive consequences.[2]

Ironically, the ordeal of Mark Twain's second cousin, Alabama's Jeremiah Clemens, demonstrated the damage that the cult of chivalry and honor could do to southerners. For such a remarkable figure, Clemens has received surprisingly little recent scholarly attention.[3] Born in Huntsville, he seemed destined for greatness as a young man. He practiced law, served in the state legislature, and fought in both the Texas Revolution and the Mexican War. In 1849, Alabama's legislature elected Clemens, then a Democrat, to the U.S. Senate, making him the youngest senator in Washington at the time. His life is remarkable not only because of his early promise but also because of later frustrations. In the early 1850s, Clemens was attacked by political opponents for his actions in the Senate. His political career went adrift, and he retreated to his plantation to write novels. In 1861, Clemens briefly returned to politics, leading the opposition to Alabama secession. Although he opposed dismantling the Union, Clemens initially remained loyal to his state and joined the Alabama militia following secession. In 1862, he crossed over to Union lines and because of his political prominence became a symbol of Alabama Unionism loathed by the state's Confederates.

Clemens's novels provide a unique resource for those seeking to understand the workings of southern culture. As a troubled politician who wrote fiction, he connected through his work the political and literary worlds of the mid-nineteenth century. Clemens's last and best novel, *Tobias Wilson* (1865), provides a blistering indictment of the Confederacy and southern honor that foreshadows the critique made by his better-known cousin decades later. Because sectional and slavery issues were closely linked to honor, men calculated the impact that their political actions would have on their reputations as independent men. Clemens's case shows the ways in which southern honor circumscribed the actions of politicians. In Alabama, one of the most democratic states in the Old South, Clemens faced political difficulties posed by aspersions cast upon his honor. His problems reveal ambivalence among Alabama Democrats regarding the role of political representatives. Many espoused radically egalitarian political principles in declaring that politicians should follow the will of the electorate; Alabama politicians would fail if they lacked a close "rapport with the people's will."[4] However, Democratic precepts coexisted with a code of honor that valued politicians' autonomy and independence of judgment. Southern honor militated against pandering to voters: if politicians blatantly styled their views to correspond to popular opinion, they risked losing the reputation for independence critical to a man of honor.

In recent years, several writers have explored the idea of southern honor that Twain decried with his attacks on the "Sir Walter disease." Honor, historian Bertram Wyatt-Brown has explained, "lies in the evaluation of the public." Honor shaped the individual's awareness of his identity and place in the social order. The community determined that order, as reputations rose and fell through rituals of assertion and deference, most notably dueling. It resembled the values of Walter Scott's *Ivanhoe*, in which "honor . . . meant reputation and self-sufficiency."[5] Kenneth Greenberg has emphasized the importance of southern honor for the region's political culture, the world that Jeremiah Clemens inhabited for much of his adult life. Greenberg argues that the ideal politician asserted his honor and manhood through independence from both popular influence and personal ambition. Such an independent man found that "in a society steeped in . . . traditions of honor, election to public office was one of the major ways a man's status and reputation could be publicly confirmed." Yet the honors of office could only go to men who voiced disinterest in public acclaim.[6] In this culture politicians held positions of honor, buttressing them with assertions of their autonomy. Southern honor coexisted and competed with Christianity as the foremost arbiter of ethics. In political culture, honor was a crucial source of values and a guide for public behavior.[7]

Honor was bound up with two key concepts for southerners: independence and manhood. Andrew Jackson had become the most popular politician of the antebellum South because he exemplified the values of honor and independent judgment.[8] In disclaiming any political designs or ambitions, Clemens affirmed ideas central to Alabama's political culture. Alabama politicians believed in personal autonomy. A Dayton man testified to the connection between the independent household and power in Democratic political culture when he declared, "I . . . found another *member* added to my household, in the person of a fine looking daughter—this makes 6 Democrats under my control—4 of which will be voters in the course of time."[9]

In the antebellum South households were the common unit of both production and reproduction. Households varied from great plantations to small farms, but their centrality in antebellum slave society "reinforced traditional gender constraints." The household shaped political culture, as a "principle of exclusion" of women, children, slaves, and propertyless white males defined the independence of farmers in the 1850s. The independence of white men, bound up with both slavery and the subordination of family members, had significant consequences for the political culture because only heads of households participated in the political arena.[10] One Democrat illuminated the link between paternal authority and Alabama's up-country political culture when he bragged, "I have raised my son to be as good a Democrat as any in North Ala and North Ala you know can't be beat in that line."[11] In contrast, as the market economy spread in the early-nineteenth-century North, gender relations were undergoing a process of transformation. As middle-class men increasingly worked outside the home, northern families shifted from a system of absolute "patriarchal authority" to one of "maternal affection" as women took on the role of moral leaders in the family.[12] The South's masculine political culture of honor contrasted with the growth of evangelical ideals of self-discipline that dominated the northern states.

The importance of honor and the intertwined value of independent manhood to antebellum southern political culture has received increasing attention in recent years. In slave societies, historical sociologist Orlando Patterson has argued, the slave is denied honor. Mastery, in this view, is bound up with honor. Historians writing about southern honor have associated it with independent manhood, which was crucial to republican political discourse.[13] Joseph Glover Baldwin, an acute contemporary observer of antebellum Alabama, argued that southern politics were shaped by the desire of the voters "to side with the strong." Martial values played a central role, as "whoever has observed much of the conduct of the masses, knows that the hero of the crowd is a representative of the sterner qualities, rather than the softer." Baldwin affirmed that political status was bound up with a public desire to "honor" great men. Andrew Jackson was at the center of the Democratic Party's cult of manhood and honor because he "could forgive an enemy, but the enemy must first surrender at discretion."[14]

Jackson's struggle against the Second Bank of the United States had long-term repercussions in Alabama. To yeomen, the bank seemed dangerous because it undermined men's independence, which was so closely bound up with yeoman conceptions of masculinity. Paper currency and a moneyed aristocracy, many Democrats feared, could endanger the autonomy of farmers.[15] Baldwin explained the dangers of credit to the autonomy of the yeomen in his *Flush Times in Alabama and Mississippi*, which lampooned a freewheeling frontier economy built on bad credit and "money got without work." Many Alabamians shared the sentiments of a Virginia congressman who argued that the "firm and fearless step" of Jackson produced a "manly and independent course" that would sustain the nation against the bank.[16] After the Bank War, Democrats presented themselves to the public as opponents of centralized power.

As a young man, Jeremiah Clemens must have seemed the epitome of a chivalrous and honorable man. In the state legislature, he proved his independence from corporate power by systematically combating privileges for Alabama's banks. His service as a volunteer in Texas and Mexico also elevated him in public esteem. Society belles viewed him as handsome and desirable: one young woman in the 1840s called him a "quondam knight" and "gallant cavalier."[17] Clemens's star rose so quickly that he was elected to the U.S. Senate in 1849 at the age of thirty-five. He quickly earned acclaim for his highly visible denunciation of California's admission to the Union as a free state. He became a prominent opponent of the Compromise of 1850, which was designed to heal sectional tensions between North and South.[18]

While southerners drew on both the value of honor and Christian ethics in the antebellum years, ideas of honor played the more central role for Clemens. His dedication to the code of honor became apparent in his opposition to the Compromise of 1850. Matters concerning slavery inevitably proved central to southern strength, honor, and ideals. Submission to northern insults, states' rights leaders argued, would be both dishonorable and dangerous.[19] Under Clemens's leadership, the Alabama congressional delegation sent a petition to Governor H. W. Collier that argued the compromise, and particularly the admission of California, represented a conspiracy "against the interests and honor of the slaveholding states." Clemens declared that Alabama could not "submit" to the federal exclusion of slavery from the territory won in the Mexican War. Collier affirmed Clemens's position, noting the "universal sentiment of our state in favor of such measures as will maintain our honor." He urged Alabama's congressmen to avoid "degradation" that would come with submitting to free soil forces.[20] Because slavery issues were bound up with honor, many Alabamians saw the compromise as dishonorable and unchivalrous. For example, the *Huntsville Southern Advocate*, Clemens's hometown paper, reprinted a South Carolina paper's congratulations to Clemens for his "consuming and burning zeal for the rights of the South." During floor debate on slavery, he aggressively defended the "faults" of his section, including fights over honor with "pistol and bowie knife," as vices that "have a touch of manliness in them."[21] He declared his devotion to southern rights, saying he would not turn "traitor to [his] convictions of duty" because he would want no "national reputation purchased at such a price."[22]

Despite Clemens's efforts, the compromise passed. To his surprise, it proved popular in Alabama, especially in the northern part of the state. When Unionism prevailed among the north Alabama yeomanry, Clemens became a convert to sectional conciliation by backing the compromise in its entirety. In a startling political turnabout, he worked to win acceptance of the compromise in his state. But Clemens overreached in his attempt to adapt to popular sentiment. His too rapid change of opinion damaged his reputation for independent judgment, as he appeared to be an opportunist, reversing his views for the sake of political gain. Clemens's opponents soon capitalized on his apparent inconsistency. Southern-rights newspapers went on the attack, arguing that his stance on the compromise meant dishonor: it involved "the timorous, obsequious, obedient, submissive, humble and negative qualities of nature generally." Clemens's rapid shift from confrontation to conciliation made him appear weak and calculating. The *Huntsville Democrat* reflected the anger of southern-rights activists by charging him with weakness:

"You preferred to stand, like a rampant lion, at the gate of the edifice of Southern liberty, and roar defiance.... You then crouched and roared greatly as a sucking dove—'Union! Glorious Union!'"[23]

Just as important, he fell victim to the revenge of southern-rights politicians whose accusations undermined his standing as an independent public man. Unionists predicted that despite the popularity of the compromise, "there will be an unscrupulous and systematic effort made, by aspiring demagogues, to destroy Col. Clemens . . . but the masses, the substantial yeomanry of the country upon whom the burden of dissolution would fall . . . sympathize most heartily with him."[24] Other politicians prospered after supporting the compromise, but Clemens's sudden reversal left him open to charges that political expediency overrode his independent judgment. He was more vulnerable than many other contemporaries who backed the compromise, partly because of the vehemence with which he had initially opposed it.

Southern-rights politicians launched a campaign to discredit Clemens, which focused on the propriety of his election to the Senate. The legislature's choice of Clemens had raised suspicions because he had received critical votes from the Whig minority. In 1851, after he reversed himself on the compromise, several southern-rights Whigs charged that Clemens made a corrupt bargain with their party's legislative caucus to support Whig president Zachary Taylor in exchange for the votes that would make him a senator. Jefferson Buford and Paul McCall, members of the Whig caucus in the Alabama legislature, charged in writing that Clemens had secretly "pledged himself if elected, to support the administration of General Taylor." South Carolina's Robert Barnwell Rhett aired the charges in the Senate, alleging that Clemens had struck a deal to secure office. Clemens stood accused of sacrificing the personal independence essential to a man worthy of political honor.[25] The charges seem credible because they were made in writing by such prominent individuals. These men testified that they had not only heard of Clemens's initial verbal pledge but had seen a written promise made by Clemens to support the administration of Taylor. Clemens never held high office again, primarily because of the damage to his personal reputation. As historian J. Mills Thornton has argued, Clemens "emerged from the ordeal a broken man."[26]

Clemens may not have been completely broken, but the allegations of political chicanery threw his independence and honor into question. He vigorously denied the charges, labeling them "invective, abuse, and systematical misrepresentation." He noted that he opposed Taylor on California statehood and awkwardly blamed Buford and McCall for not bringing the charges forward until he switched his opinion on the compromise.[27] A few loyalists, most notably the editors of the *Huntsville Southern Advocate*, continued to support Clemens. In fact, the paper asserted that his position in support of the compromise won substantial approval in the up-country.[28] But to continue in the Senate, Clemens needed the backing of the state's Democratic power brokers in the legislature, which he undoubtedly lost. The party never nominated him for high office again. While it is difficult to tell how many politically active Alabamians believed the charges against Clemens, the rapid decline of his political fortunes suggests that Alabama Democrats, and probably most Alabamians, considered the accusations true.

The charge of bargaining with the Whigs to secure office was especially damaging because it undermined Clemens's standing as an independent man. If he owed his office to the Whigs, then he lacked the personal autonomy that was a prerequisite to honor. His stock fell further when he did not challenge his accusers to a duel. South Carolina novelist William Gilmore Simms noted the importance of a man's willingness to risk death, arguing that the duelist "fights to maintain his position in society, to silence insult, to check brutality, prevent encroachment, avenge a wrong of some sort, and in obedience to fierce passions that will not let him sleep under the sense of injury and annoyance." Men fought duels over insults much less significant than those Clemens endured.[29] But Clemens did not challenge any of his Alabama opponents to combat. He maintained a specious distinction between insults made directly in his presence, which he would not allow, and those made at a distance, which he ignored. Without such a rationale he would have been in a precarious position because of the sheer number of his accusers. In July 1851 forty-three Alabamians signed a public letter accusing Clemens of an "outrage" in "pledging himself secretly" to the Whigs, noting it was a "grave charge."[30]

Clemens insisted that he would defend his honor and "look for no repose until the last hope of doing me an injury is extinguished." He denied the charges of bargaining with the Whigs, calling them "a foul lie, unmitigated and unredeemed by the slightest regard for the truth."[31] But few could believe that he exemplified the independence that marked the successful politician. His rapid turnabout on the compromise, when combined with the evidence that he struck a bargain with the Whig opposition to gain power, meant that his independence—and honor—had been thrown into question. In the face of charges made by the well-known Senator Rhett, who was backed by two members of the Alabama Whig caucus, Clemens's standing as an independent man was endangered. Because the charges were made in writing and aired on the floor of the Senate, their importance was greatly magnified.

Clemens's failure to challenge any of his accusers to a duel only undermined his attempts to defend himself through the pursuit of public office. The *Huntsville Democrat* declared, "It may surprise the public that you should now appear jealous of your honor," and Clemens's career as a Democrat collapsed. He failed to win the legislature's approval to return to the Senate and lost an 1855 bid for Congress as a Know-Nothing candidate. To Democrats, this attempt to regain political power seemed dishonest because the Know-Nothings represented only "the new-fangled dirty Whiggery under the alias of Know-Nothingism."[32] Clemens hoped for nomination to a cabinet office in the Pierce administration, but he had gained too many enemies to get a position. Rumors of public drunkenness further lowered Clemens's standing in public opinion: at one point he informed states' rights leader William Lowndes Yancey that he had to get drunk to bring his "genius down to your level." Clement Comer Clay, a former senator and governor, summed up elite feeling toward Clemens when he told his son: "I have maintained that it was impossible that a man who had betrayed his party and gotten into the Senate by private pledges to the Whigs—to say nothing of his bad moral habits and principles—could receive . . . confidence and trust."[33] Taking the stump in north Alabama in 1856, Clemens attacked the Democrats and attempted to rehabilitate his languishing political reputation. His efforts failed in the face of unfavorable comparisons to Yancey and to his own speeches from before his flirtation with Know-Nothingism.[34]

The destruction of Clemens's reputation epitomized the workings of a system in which party leaders used their power to enforce party discipline and set the terms of political debate. Alabama politicians noted that the domination of the party press was so strong that "if the Democratic Party were slaves and the Editor their legally constituted overseer, he could not speak in terms of more mandatory authority." Clemens had been cast out of a Democratic Party controlled by a relatively small core of activists. Gubernatorial nominating conventions could be "controlled by cliques and factions." Politicians continued to calculate that the key to political success lay in influencing "those who at the different precincts are the *working men* at elections, and who control their little coteries of county politicians."[35] The charges against Clemens especially damaged his reputation because of the systematic manner in which Democratic Party authorities disseminated them.

The accuracy of the *Huntsville Southern Advocate*'s prediction that the yeomanry would back Clemens is difficult to gauge, because the voters never got a chance to judge Clemens at the ballot box. His alienation from party leaders and editors, especially southern-rights men, was too extreme for him to win a nomination in a party caucus. A return to the Senate was even less likely, since Senate elections were decided in the legislature.

The charge against Clemens, that he had achieved office through a backroom deal, resonated with genuine fears that behind-the-scenes managers controlled the political system and stymied democracy. One editor complained, "The people seem to be absolutely asleep as to what their representatives in Congress are doing. . . . Their lawmakers might enact laws to enslave them . . . and they would never know it, till they felt the chains around their own necks." Others worried that voters showed "criminal unconcern" about politics. The *Butler Standard* signaled the anxiety of independent men when it suggested they should monitor politics as "a subject they should as vigilantly watch over as they would the virtue of their own wives."[36] In using metaphors of enslaved white men and degraded women, the newspapers signaled that the concerns about politics held by many Alabamians raised fundamental anxieties about the future of the Republic.

In abandoning his opposition to the compromise when its popularity became clear, Clemens unwittingly highlighted ambiguity in Democratic doctrine. As a responsive Democratic representative, he embraced what he believed to be the will of the people. Yet the results for him were disastrous, because his hasty shift in position raised suspicions about his integrity and autonomy. While Alabama Democrats demanded that representatives fulfill their wishes, fawning acquiescence to public opinion could jeopardize the reputation for independence necessary for a man of honor. An editorial in the *Montgomery Advertiser* illuminated the dilemma that Clemens faced in deciding between charting a responsive course or maintaining chivalrous independence. The newspaper complained that "public men are no longer pillars of the state but weathercocks that veer and turn with every shifting breeze." The *Advertiser* suggested that if politicians always followed the popular will, they risked their honor, declaring that "the age of chivalry is gone indeed in the sense that nobody can be found in these degenerate times" to proffer independent political judgment.[37] Alabamians seemed ambivalent about what kind of democracy they wanted. They wanted politicians who represented the people's wishes, but pandering to the populace could seem dishonorable.

Frustrated with public life, Clemens retreated to his plantation. Except for a short stint as a newspaper editor in Memphis in 1859, he focused on writing novels from 1856 to 1860, during which he produced three works of historical fiction. *Bernard Lile* (1856), a tale of the Texas Revolution, told the story of a brave adventurer on the Texas frontier and was based on his own recollections of the conflict. Although the book received little critical attention, it gained a large enough audience to inspire a sequel on the Mexican War, *Mustang Gray*, in 1858. Clemens claimed that both books were based on actual events: "I knew that fiction must in a great measure give place to fact, and that imagination would be inconveniently restricted in its flight." *Bernard Lile* and *Mustang Gray* both harkened back to Clemens's youth and the frontier fighting that won him a reputation for valor. In 1860 he published *The Rivals*, a sympathetic treatment of Aaron Burr's early years. He combined "the main historical facts" with an imaginative account of Hamilton and Burr that he thought true of "what [he] believed each to be capable."[38]

Jeremiah Clemens's fiction does not measure up to that of his more famous cousin. While both writers examined the antebellum Southwest, Clemens's books clumsily imitate Sir Walter Scott. He produced exciting action scenes, but the characters in *Bernard Lile* and *Mustang Gray* serve as stick figures representing good or evil. The author's unrelenting racism makes his fiction disconcerting: he attributed the success of the United States in war against Mexican "greasers" to the "character of the races."[39] In all three of Clemens's pre–Civil War works of historical fiction, he substituted high-flown rhetoric for frontier vernacular, producing pretentious dialogue that bears no resemblance to the writing of Mark Twain. Clemens argued, "The South-West has a language of its own but . . . sometimes whole sentences are uttered not only in the purest English, but in the loftiest strain of eloquence." His attempt to preserve frontier language "exactly as it is" occasionally produced improbable and tedious dialogue that makes Scott's work seem understated. For example, Bernard Lile, a hero of Texas's war for independence, declares that he joined the struggle in Texas because of "the wild chivalry that gives it birth, the desperate odds, the iron men . . . all possess attractions." He later declares that Buena Vista "was a glorious field and will be embalmed forever in the hearts of the American people." Antebellum southern humorists such as Joseph Glover Baldwin and Johnson J. Hooper presented the voices of the antebellum South in a more plausible and engaging manner.[40]

As the work of a notable politician, Clemens's antebellum writing offers fascinating insights into Old South political culture. His novels, in which the protagonists embrace the cult of chivalry, illuminate Clemens's values by following a common theme, as the heroes are unjustly deemed unworthy by public opinion. Clemens presents these men as true heroes who overcome their inability to conform to community standards of honor. The central figure in *Mustang Gray* lives an outlaw life on the frontier and even participates in the illegal international slave trade. His Mexican War compatriots know of his valor in battle, but they are unaware of the chivalry he had shown as a young man, as he fled North Carolina authorities after fighting a duel to defend a woman's reputation. In placing heroic but despised young men on the same southwestern frontier where he had fought, Clemens symbolically rehabilitates his own damaged reputation.

Clemens's most exciting antebellum novel, *The Rivals*, attempts to repair the reputation of one of the most despised men in American political history—Aaron Burr. The novel focuses on the Revolutionary War career of Burr and the intrigue that culminated in his famous duel with Alexander Hamilton. In Clemens's account, Hamilton persecutes Burr, who has ample reason to challenge Hamilton. Despite Burr's extraordinary heroism in the Revolutionary War, Hamilton uses political influence to damage the reputation of his fellow officer, and Burr finds himself isolated from George Washington because of Hamilton's malicious rumors. But in Clemens's version it is not Hamilton's treachery against Burr that causes their duel. Instead, he portrays Hamilton as questioning the virtue of an innocent young woman who was a friend of Burr's. Displaying the respect for womanhood characteristic of a chivalrous man, Burr challenges Hamilton to a duel and kills him. The Jeffersonian disdain that Clemens harbored for Hamilton shaped the story, because since boyhood the author had "entertained strong prejudices against him." Clemens asserted that "slander was [Hamilton's] favorite weapon."[41] A political audience wrongly condemned Burr, not knowing that his only crime was defending the honor of a powerless young woman. Clemens clearly felt kinship with a man who had lost the respect of the public.

Like its predecessors, *The Rivals* showed that public opinion—the central element of the political culture of honor—could be unjust. But Clemens's antebellum work never rejected the system of honor. Rather, he merely suggested that society could be mistaken when judging men's honor. His heroes embodied many of the traits that Scott associated with chivalry: patriotism, love of personal freedom, generosity, gallantry, and an elevated concern for women. Yet they all lacked the one trait Scott believed was crucial to the "character of a perfect knight"—an unblemished reputation.[42] The evident parallel with Clemens himself illustrates the degree of importance he attached to honor and the extent to which he resented the decline in his standing.

The secession crisis of 1861 thrust Clemens back into politics when he joined the opposition to disunion. As in the debate over the Compromise of 1850, southern-rights activists characterized secession as a battle for honor. A month after the election of Lincoln, Alabama governor Andrew B. Moore remarked that the "honor of the state" was at stake in the secession debate. Similarly, secessionist leader Yancey declared in the secession convention that the men of the state had gone too far "to recede with dignity and self-respect."[43] Of course, Clemens's stand against secession promptly drew further attacks on his honor. Writing to the *Montgomery Advertiser* in late 1860, he declared, "I have been denounced throughout the state as a 'submissionist.'" Worse, he had for his devotion to the Union "encountered obloquy, reproach, and the alienation of friends in its defense."[44]

The attacks on Clemens's character illustrate the manner in which the secession crisis brought the intertwined issues of independent manhood, honor, and democracy to the forefront. Opponents of immediate secession found that "bitter epithets . . . were showered on the heads of the cooperationist men."[45] Alabamians elected a secession convention that met in January 1861 to decide the future of the state. Leading Democrats such as J. L. M. Curry feared that most citizens opposed secession. Some delegates at the secession convention spoke frankly of the need for representatives to act as independent men ready to "rise above the popular tumult and lead and control the popular multitudes." Those who advocated immediate secession stifled plans to submit the convention's results to the people for ratification. The danger, Lewis M. Stone explained, lay in the fact that "the public mind would again become agitated, new divisions would spring up among our people. . . . Our divisions would be exposed."[46] Proponents of secession, such as Yancey, declared that the convention had the power to act without consultation with the voters, and he made some none-too-subtle threats against the recalcitrant citizens of north Alabama.[47]

Clemens seemed irreconcilably opposed to disunion. He wrote to Senator John Crittenden of Kentucky that he believed Alabama could redress its grievances in the Union and that he refused to "admit the *right* of secession at all. I do not admit the right of a majority to drag me into treason." By denying the right of secession, Clemens differed from many of the cooperationist delegates to the secession convention who opposed immediate and independent secession by the state in favor of a convention of the slaveholding states that would unite them around a shared policy. Prior to secession, Clemens's position resembled the more radical stance of Tennessee's Senator Andrew Johnson, who also declared secession to be treason.[48]

Although his political pronouncements were Unionist before secession, Clemens would not, or could not, stand against his state after it left the Union. Although at the state convention in January 1861 he led the opposition and denounced secession in principle, he sided with Alabama when it left the Union. After the ordinance of secession passed, opposition to the state was unsafe, as Yancey warned when he declared, "There is a law of treason, defining treason against the State; and, those who shall dare oppose the actions of Alabama, when she assumes her independence of the Union will become traitors—rebels against her authority, and will be dealt with as such." After this explicit threat was issued, Clemens signed the ordinance of secession and offered his services to the state militia.[49]

It was during the secession crisis that Clemens first began to question the worth of honor as a code for regulating the conduct of southern men. Clemens also questioned the terms of debate, emphasizing practical politics rather than southern honor. In a letter to the *Huntsville Southern Advocate* he declared, "I will say nothing about honor for I put no punctilious notions of honor in the scales to weigh against national danger and disaster. It may be an excellent thing in its place, and I have heard dull men wax eloquent on it, but I shall abjure it in this letter." Union was more important than honor.[50] Clemens's evaluation of the political culture of southern honor had changed during the secession crisis. His novels had explored the lives of men who lived within a code of chivalry but had been unjustly denied the public recognition critical to honor. Now, he questioned the importance of honor and denigrated it in favor of a more pressing concern: Union.

The skepticism about honor in Clemens's public letter signaled extraordinary feelings of conflict and even despair over southern rights and the Union. When Alabama seceded from the Union, he maintained that the honorable course was to fight for the Confederacy: "A new era has dawned, and all that I can promise is that no effort will be spared on my part to prevent it from becoming an era of disgrace. . . . I shall drag my body to the nearest battlefield, and lay down a life that has lost its value." He went on explicitly to defend himself against the charge of submission and femininity, declaring, "I shall bear myself as becomes a man, and fall at last, if fall I must, with as much of honor as mere courage and manly bearing can win."[51] These sentiments show Clemens to be of two minds. He still avowed the value of honor in his own life, but he also questioned its worth in providing a political and moral compass in a time of crisis.

Clemens left the Alabama militia and crossed over to Union lines in 1862, at least in part because secessionist distrust had denied him a position in the Confederate army commensurate with his military experience. He quickly became a hated figure among secessionists in Alabama, known simply as the "arch-traitor." Although Clemens was the most prominent Alabamian in opposition to the Confederacy, he was not alone. Many in north Alabama shared his opinions, and the loyalty of north Alabama had been questioned by secessionist leaders such as Yancey, who in early 1861 threatened to hang "traitors and public enemies."[52] In fact, Confederate control of the citizens of north Alabama collapsed quickly in 1861 and 1862. Unionist citizens organized Peace Societies to push for reconstruction and draft evasion. These organizations represented half the male population left in the state and were particularly concentrated in north Alabama.[53] Between 1862 and 1865, former cooperationists, including Clemens, led the Peace Societies, although little concrete information exists on these secret bodies. Significant resistance to the Confederacy in north Alabama grew as more than two thousand white Alabamians enlisted in the First Alabama Calvary, U.S.A. Moreover, the 1863 Alabama elections reflected the depth of dissatisfaction with the war in the northern section of the state.[54]

Relative deprivation fueled up-country Unionism: one-third of the families in Clemens's home county of Madison were classified as indigent, and the widespread poverty spurred desertion. Men angered by economic disparities left the Confederate army to help provide for their families.[55] North Alabama reached near anarchy as competing Unionist and Confederate factions battled for control of up-country districts. One observer declared that "sheriffs and constables are as extinct as geological specimens." Both sides stopped taking prisoners.[56] The political culture of honor depended on community opinion. But the infighting brought by war meant that north Alabama lacked the shared values necessary to provide for community judgment of honor and reputation.

Confederate politicians' contempt extended to all Alabama Unionists, and before the end of his brief Confederate career Clemens himself joined in the derision. When his close friend George Lane accepted a federal judgeship in early 1861, Clemens remarked of the volunteers he commanded in Mobile, "Of the 500 men now here from North Alabama there are not five who would not rejoice at receiving an order to hang [Lane]." If the Confederate Congress did not declare Lane's action to be treason, Clemens declared, he knew "another remedy whose application is not a matter of doubt." Two years later, after Clemens had transferred his loyalty to the Union, Alabama's governor derided north Alabama Tories such as Clemens as men who chose "a life of cowardly shame."[57] Accusations leveled against the manhood of Alabama draft resisters, who were often nonslaveholders, boiled over into simple class prejudice. One Confederate officer suggested chasing deserters with dogs, as had been done with slaves.[58] In contrast, a more sympathetic observer noted that the Unionists were "mostly poor, though many of them are, or rather have been in reduced circumstances. . . . They are persecuted in every conceivable way."[59]

Partly because of his previous misdeeds, Clemens became a lightning rod for Confederate anger at north Alabama disloyalty. Initially he meant to stay in Alabama. Confederate leaders noted contemptuously that he could only do so by boarding federal officers in his house for protection. In the fall of 1862, the *Clarke County Democrat* approvingly wrote about a savage caning of Clemens by a Confederate officer, exclaiming that the "Yankeeizing southerner" was beaten "within inches of his life on the streets of Huntsville . . . disfiguring him horribly."[60] The newspaper may have exaggerated the physical damage done by the assailant. Nevertheless, the report must have humiliated Clemens, because duels were fought between social equals, and caning was reserved for an inferior. Clemens left no record of the beating and soon felt strong enough to travel from Alabama to the North. He hoped to negotiate a reconstruction of the Union with the help of Lincoln, but U.S. secretary of war Edwin M. Stanton brushed him off, telling Clemens and former Constitutional Union presidential candidate John Bell to "use their influence at home."[61] Between the contempt of his state and the indifference of federal authorities, Clemens suffered serious indignities.

He also continued to rework his thinking on southern honor. During the period between 1862 and 1865, he divided his time between the Union-occupied town of Huntsville and the North. In a remarkable letter, Clemens described the way that he believed the South's culture of honor had broken down during the war. Before the war, southern men had "independence," but the war had brought them "slavery" to Confederate despotism. Southern men had lost the autonomy central to honor. Clemens complained that Confederates still charged Union men with dishonor, writing that they had "disgraced themselves" by becoming "tools of the basest and most degraded

[Union] despotism." But he now felt emboldened to declare that Confederate fealty to Richmond and Jefferson Davis was worse than loyalty to the Yankees: "Good God! How blind must that infatuation be which bows the necks of an unquestionably brave and gallant people beneath a yoke so galling." Yeoman farmers, at the mercy of Confederate foraging parties, had to "submit, in powerless agony, to personal insult." Clemens virtually asserted that southern honor had disappeared, asking, "What has become of the boasted chivalry of the South? Where are the braggarts who could kill two yankees and run away two more before breakfast?" The Alabama Unionist, who first questioned the language of southern honor during the secession crisis, now went a step further by challenging the association between southern rights and chivalry.[62] He accused the Confederates of deliberately provoking the war to achieve their political objectives, describing one Alabama leader who in early 1861 implored Secretary of War Leroy P. Walker, "Unless you sprinkle blood in the face of the people of Alabama, they will be back to the old Union in less than ten days!"[63]

In 1863 and 1864, Clemens imaginatively worked through his difficult Civil War experience with a fictionalized account of guerrilla fighting in the north Alabama up-country, *Tobias Wilson*. The book is striking not only as a rare account of mountain partisan warfare but for presenting his changing vision of the ethical foundations for southern life. In *Tobias Wilson*, Clemens discarded the view of chivalry, so much like that of Sir Walter Scott, that pervaded his earlier books. While novels such as *The Rivals* tentatively questioned the culture of honor, *Tobias Wilson* rejected the relevance of honor in a warring society in which community standards had broken down. Although the novel continued the flowery language Twain derided in romantic fiction, it moved decisively away from a belief in the southern code of honor. Ultimately, the protagonist achieves manhood by internalizing a code of law and Christian ethics more suited to a world without the rule of chivalry.

Robert Johnson is the grandfather of the book's hero, Tobias Wilson, and a staunch Union man. He lives a humble life in the Alabama up-country but gives the impression that he is "an educated and cultivated man, and that he had been bred in a different society to that about him." Johnson presents a favorable contrast with his neighbors, none of whom is as "free, easy, independent, without a trace of that weak and unmanly spirit." Johnson exemplifies the values of independence and manhood honored within antebellum political culture. Johnson's grandson, Tobias Wilson, follows his mother's strict ideas "of the conduct which best became a Christian." The spiritual influence of Tobias's mother reflects that "in the South as in the North, piety figured among the attributes of the woman's role."[64] As Clemens describes it in the novel, the South had slid into war because of misguided notions of honor. Up-country Democrats were "led by their wily leaders from one act to another . . . to persuade them they cannot retrace their steps with honor." In contrast to Johnson's family, Confederates represent "the offscourings" of the South who would "rob" Unionist families and even, Clemens hinted, use rape as a tool of warfare.[65]

The novel represents the tensions encountered by southern Unionists who tried to defend themselves against Confederate depredations while remaining true to their Christian ethics. In the initial stages of the story, the protagonists attempt to protect their home. Clemens portrays Confederate rhetoric about protecting the household as hypocritical. Confederate leaders had promised to safeguard southern homes against the Union, but Johnson must secure his humble dwelling against Confederate raids. As he put it, "When the great secession orator, Mr. Yancey, traveled through this country, he told us that every cabin was a castle, from which we had a right to expel any intruding foot. It was about the only thing in his speech with which I agreed, and I am resolved to put it to the test. I shall harm no one except in my own just defense." The work presents Johnson's concept of self-defense of his household as a first step toward a personal moral compass in a society in which honor had failed to maintain order.[66]

Despite Johnson's resolution to defend himself, Confederate partisans murder him. After engaging in thorough detective work, Wilson deduces the identity of his grandfather's killers. But wartime chaos prevents Tobias from obtaining justice through the law: when his friend Thomas Rogers suggests taking the evidence to a court, he laughs at the possibility of bringing original secessionists to justice before a Confederate jury. Intent on punishing the murderers of his grandfather and aware that legal authority would not help, Tobias plans to assassinate the murderers. His Christian ethics are nearly broken when faced with despicable killers and a lawless society. Clemens's earlier heroes would have committed the murders without a second thought, but Tobias feels torn between his desire to avenge his grandfather and the demands of his conscience. He agonizes over his wish for revenge: "'Oh! mother,' he continued, striking his hand upon his breast, 'if you knew the hell that is burning here. . . . My thoughts were dark and bloody enough before. God grant they may not lead me to a retribution he will not pardon.'"[67]

Unlike Clemens's antebellum heroes, who always exacted rough justice,

Tobias abandons such action for the sake of a woman. In doing so, he moves beyond the vengeance demanded by southern honor. He loves a young neighbor, Sophy Rogers, an ethereal figure who stands "pure and sinless . . . upon a pinnacle so high above [him]." The beautiful and devout girl has "a rosy tinge of heavenly beauty spread over her cheeks . . . as pure as that of the star which shed its radiance o'er the cradle of the infant Redeemer." Sophy decides to turn Tobias from his course of vengeance because it would condemn him to hell. On hearing of Tobias's plot, she declares, "I will save him!" Sophy promises Tobias she will marry him if he will give up revenge "by any means but those which the law allows." He agonizes over his inability to punish his grandfather's killers but marries Sophy and joins the Union army.[68] The author portrays Tobias's moral triumph, because "alone and unaided, save by the prayers of one gentle and tender girl, he had won that mightiest of victories—a victory over himself." When Tobias abandons the temptation to commit revenge, he not only accepts Sophy's ethical guidance but remains faithful to the values he learned from his mother. Clemens presents a masculine hero embracing Christianity at a time when "there remained an eroding but still lively sentiment that male participation in church life was unmanly."[69]

Prior to the Civil War, northerners had developed an ideal of manhood that contrasted sharply with southern honor. The new image of manliness that took shape in the North dovetailed with the developing free labor ideology of the Republican Party. Northern men valued hard work and often explained financial success or failure in terms of self-discipline.[70] The free labor viewpoint emphasized industry and personal restraint in order to win success in a society based on a competitive market. After winning the war, however, northern men attacked southern "chivalry" as antithetical to their model of masculine self-control. Moreover, the irony that southern soldiers "who were supposed to epitomize the highest ideals of southern manhood" failed to defend their homes and families successfully was not lost on anyone, and many Confederates worried that their military defeat meant dishonor.[71]

The overthrow of slavery lay at the root of the enormous social and cultural change undergone by Alabamians. The radicalizing impact of war was evident in Clemens's pleas to Andrew Johnson, which asked that he appoint to office men ready to end slavery "with a firm and remorseless hand."[72] The social revolution brought by war forced white men to "transform" their conception of their own masculinity as the self-sufficient household gave way to an increasingly market-oriented economy. For many men, as for Tobias Wilson, social change produced a reexamination of religious convictions.

Enthusiasm for the symbols of chivalry declined after the collapse of the Confederacy. Medieval tournaments, a popular antebellum pastime that recalled Scott's *Ivanhoe*, faded into empty rituals drained of their former substance.[73] Research on gender and mental illness suggests Alabama men suffered psychologically from the exigencies of war and its accompanying changes in standards of masculinity. As Twain later noted, "the foundations of a social system had been broken up" by the war.[74] Among those foundations was the culture of honor.

Clemens could have ended his novel with Tobias transcending the code of honor for one of gentility, saving his soul and bravely fighting in the ranks for the Union. Yet Clemens could not quite reconcile his desire for Tobias to act as a Christian with his discomfort at leaving the three Confederate miscreants unpunished. Fortunately, Thomas Rogers vows to relieve Tobias of the responsibility for vengeance by taking on the project himself. While Tobias controls his desire for revenge, Clemens could not quite cheat his readers of the spectacle of retribution. As Rogers exacts vengeance from Confederate raiders, Clemens praises the Christian piety of Sophy and Tobias. Thomas declares that Tobias "is better, and braver, and more gifted than any of us. His proper place is in a higher walk than mine."[75] That Thomas speaks so admiringly of Tobias suggests that Clemens had come to value Christianity and law over chivalry. Yet Tobias's absence in the second half of the novel shows that Clemens was not quite comfortable with his new model of heroism. His ambivalence is evident even in the last paragraph of the novel. The author laments the fact that so many young men sought "glory at the risk of the grave." Yet he also notes that "higher aspirations and more noble impulses" moved men such as Tobias Wilson. Indeed, "the heroism they manifested may almost be claimed as the offspring of religion."[76] Here Clemens seems to make a decisive step away from southern honor, yet the language he uses indicates some uncertainty about his new archetype of heroism.

Tobias Wilson reflects the coexistence and competition in the South between honor and Christianity. As Christine Heyrman argues, evangelicals had made inroads among some men of honor during the antebellum years, but only by accommodating themselves to the total control over the domestic sphere demanded by independent masters.[77] Even as evangelicals made significant advances in the antebellum South, tension between their faith and slavery persisted. At least in principle, evangelicals rejected two fundamental tendencies of slave society: the grasping materialism of the master class and the dehumanization of the slave.[78] In *Tobias Wilson*, Clemens seems to have made Christianity central to his ideals while relegating southern honor to a secondary position. Tobias, with his self-control, was markedly different from the style of the reckless frontiersmen and duelists who populated Clemens's earlier novels. He represented a new prototype of masculinity.

If the "Sir Walter disease" consisted merely of pomposity and "adjective piling" in romantic fiction, then Jeremiah Clemens never cured it.[79] Moreover, Thomas's exacting revenge indicates that Clemens could never fully abandon his antebellum views as he straddled a historical divide between evangelical Christian ethics and the code of honor. Yet he underwent a remarkable transformation during the Civil War years. The rigid code of honor, appropriated by the Democratic leadership of Alabama to punish him for his Unionism and cooperation with Whigs, stalked his life. While Alabama's Democratic leadership had effectively used the language of honor against Clemens, he failed to sustain effectively a critique of chivalry in the antebellum years. Tortured by his exclusion from the political culture of honor espoused by the Democratic elite, he depicted chivalrous and vengeful fighting men in his novels. When the war came, Clemens the politician put the nation above notions of honor, shunning disunion and denouncing chivalry for serving the interests of foolhardy secessionist leaders.

As a Civil War novelist, he transcended southern honor by inventing a character who forswore the retribution taken by his earlier characters. Mark Twain left no record of having read the fiction of Jeremiah. He did, however, talk to a friend who told him "a good deal about Hon. Jere Clemens." He even proclaimed his relation to the politician in his autobiography.[80] Clemens's life does more than illuminate the way southern honor could limit the political autonomy of public men necessary to a popularly responsive democracy. It confirms the wisdom of Twain's condemnation of the chivalry embodied in Scott's fiction. Fittingly, *Tobias Wilson*, which marked such a departure from the political culture of honor in the Old South, was published just weeks after Appomattox, and Clemens, drained by his wartime ordeal, died on May 21, 1865.

7 Jefferson Davis and the Confederacy's Dysfunctional Democracy

Jefferson Davis, like most other Democrats in 1861, believed in a society of independent white men, a limited state and laissez-faire economy, strict construction of the Constitution, and slavery. The *Richmond Enquirer* testified to Davis's orthodoxy, citing his mainstream ideas as qualifications for the Confederate presidency. Davis represented a "logical choice" for president because he stood soundly on the issue of southern rights but was not an extremist fire-eater. The *Charleston Mercury* declared that "no man . . . could well dispute with him the highest place in Southern confidence." His experience as secretary of war during the Pierce administration and standing as a military hero in the Mexican War brought him to the attention of politicians gathered in the provisional Confederate capital in Montgomery in early 1861.[1] In terms of education, preparation in government service, and miliary expertise, Davis seemed to surpass his counterpart, Abraham Lincoln, in every respect. Although southern-rights activist Edmund Ruffin would have favored a president with more extreme secessionist views, he described Davis and his vice president, Alexander Stephens of Georgia, as men "who for intellectual ability and moral worth are superior to any President and Vice-President elected together . . . since Madison's administration."[2] Richard B. Jones, a clerk in the Confederate War Department in Richmond, testified to the Confederate president's public standing when he remarked, "So far, perhaps, no Executive has ever had such cordial and unanimous support of the people as President Davis."[3]

Yet by 1862 Davis had become profoundly unpopular, and he remained so until the war's end, as he seemed unable to unite Confederate citizens behind a long war effort. Complaints surfaced that Davis's public speeches failed to inspire mass enthusiasm: in 1862 the *Richmond Examiner* grumbled, "The public expected a much more important communication from the President."

His alleged shortcomings as president have led historians to argue that his failings as a popular leader played a crucial role in the defeat of Confederacy. In an essay on the Confederacy's demise, historian David Potter made the provocative argument that "if the Union and Confederacy had exchanged presidents with one another, the Confederacy might have won its independence." Among the flaws in Davis's leadership pointed out by Potter was his inability to raise morale: Davis "could scarcely even communicate with the people of the Confederacy. He seemed to think in abstractions and to speak in platitudes." Historian Paul Escott has argued that the Confederate president failed in "eliciting the enthusiasm and energies of the [Confederate] people." In this view, Davis's spectacular failure to articulate a clear political agenda and coherent philosophical justification for the sacrifice brought by war contributed to Confederate defeat.[4]

While virtually any Confederate newspaper provides evidence that the young nation witnessed extraordinary political squabbling, some historians dispute whether the new nation's factionalism had much effect in undermining its viability. Some contend that Davis did reasonably well as a political leader and that the real problems of the Confederacy lay in its relative economic and military weakness. In a classic essay, "God and the Strongest Battalions," historian Richard Current argued that the course of the war was dictated by the fact that the "Union went to war with an overwhelming preponderance in most sources of economic power." In this account, "objective conditions and events" made Confederate defeat all but inevitable. In a recent book, military historian Gary Gallagher has discounted explanations of Confederate defeat that focus on low morale, emphasizing the motivation of Lee's army and the political vitality of the Confederacy. In Gallagher's view, Lee's Army of Northern Virginia served as a symbol of national unity and remarkably strong national cohesion. In this view, military history best explains the outcome of the conflict.[5]

But the results of combat are never objectively determined by military factors in isolation from politics, particularly in a civil war, and at important junctures Lee factored morale and the political situation into his strategic calculations. Military strength, Carl Von Clausewitz wrote, is a function not just of the force available but also of the will to use it—that is, of "two inseparable factors, viz. the total means at his disposal and the strength of his will."[6] The judgment that Union victory flowed inexorably from a strong economy is based largely on hindsight and ignores the thoughtful calculation by many southerners that only poor morale could defeat the new nation. Confederates entered the war aware of the North's strengths, but they believed that they would have the advantages of popular revolutionaries defending their homeland, such as the Dutch in their war of independence and the American Revolutionary generation of 1776. The *Richmond Enquirer* explained that in 1861 Confederates staked their play "on the history of the genius and enterprise natural to all struggles originating revolutions." At the opening of the war, Confederates expected easy victory over "Yankee trash." Historian Allan Nevins wryly noted that making such brave statements before wars is commonplace in a variety of cultures, but the Confederates were unusual because they actually believed their boastful declarations. As Georgia Unionist Herschel Johnson put it, "Nothing else will conquer us. Our army can whip upon every field."[7]

Many historians have traced the relationship between politics and Confederate defeat, providing a wealth of material describing the political and ideological strains experienced by the new nation. This ample literature has focused on the political consequences of class divisions among whites.[8] Yet despite this emphasis on popular cohesion, little work has focused on the Constitution, which was central to Confederates' understanding of both their struggle for national independence and their concept of democracy. Confederates believed themselves to have inherited an American democratic tradition that dovetailed with constitutionalism, since the Constitution provided the rules under which democratic politics operated. Even lukewarm exponents of democracy, such as the editors of the *Charleston Mercury*, reminded readers about the Virginia and Kentucky Resolutions, written by Jefferson and Madison, which they believed proved that "Jefferson himself being the high authority, every State has a right to secede from the Union."[9]

To follow the Civil War travails of Jefferson Davis requires an appreciation of his constitutional thought and its relation to the Democratic political culture in which he came of age. Constitutional issues often provided the framework for the political wrangling that dominated public life in the Confederacy. The importance of constitutionalism was part of the political heritage of the antebellum South: nowhere was Tocqueville's remark that in antebellum society "the language of everyday party political controversy has to be borrowed from legal phraseology and conceptions" more true than in the South.[10] By 1860, proslavery southerners believed that only they correctly interpreted the true heritage of the Constitution—a view echoed in some recent scholarship.[11] The Confederate generation was particularly immersed in constitutional discourse because the debates that preceded the war gave them unprecedented popular expertise in constitutional theory.[12] Constitutional fervor grew as Americans fought over the issue of slavery in the territories during the 1850s. Despite Jacksonian rhetoric about limited government, politicians realized that "slavery, of all property in the world, most needs the protection of a friendly government."[13] The defense of slavery against abolitionists, free-soilers, and the slaves themselves required firm political power, especially in wartime.

Constitutionalism provided hope of reconciling the existence of power and liberty. Individuals and parties could be corrupt, but the Constitution was conceived as an impersonal device that would rein in the interests of politicians or spoils men. Because the Constitution seemed to provide an objective guide to government, many, including Jefferson Davis, called it a "machine" or a "mechanism."[14] Historian Perry Miller has argued that the Constitution's centrality to nineteenth-century American government indicated the dominance of values embodying the rational, scientific rule of the mind over that of the heart. Miller's sweeping generalization may not apply to the South as a whole, but it aptly describes the Confederate president. Davis, whose mind always ruled his heart, pointed out that the Constitution "distinguished our form of government from those confederacies or republics which preceded it."[15] Of course the Constitution was seen as a last bastion for the defense of southern rights in slave property: William Porcher Miles spoke of the "broad sword of the Constitution" that defended the South. But to many Democrats, states' rights blended seamlessly with individual liberties. Southern constitutionalism had a distinctly Jeffersonian tinge, and South Carolina's F. W. Pickens exemplified a tendency to speak of constitutional rights and individual rights interchangeably. So important was the "struggle to secure the personal rights of individuals" that Pickens declared it central to the history of the world. He designated individual rights as the moving spirit behind the American Constitution.[16]

After the war, popular historians constructed the notion of a gallant lost cause, epitomized by Robert E. Lee, ground down by the inexorable force of the Union.[17] But while the conflict continued, Davis believed that maintaining morale would be central to military success. Davis traveled within the Confederacy and delivered speeches meant to lift the spirits of the Confederate populace. Many critics of Davis have failed to realize that the president understood the importance of popular enthusiasm. Only a desire to lift political spirits explains Davis's long journey to Georgia in 1864. He made the journey on a poor railroad system despite the fact that Georgia was home to his critics Joseph Brown and Alexander Stephens. Davis admitted the devastating impact of sagging morale during a speech in Georgia, declaring that "two-thirds of our men are absent—some sick, some wounded, but most of them absent without leave." The president seemed sure "you can whip them, if all the men capable of bearing arms will do their duty by taking their places under the standard of their country." But by 1864 few heeded his call, and Davis seemed unable to understand why so many of the Confederacy's plain folk abandoned their arms. By 1865 he was certain that politics, not the irresistible might of the Union, had brought the Confederacy near defeat: "Faction has done much to cloud our prospects."[18]

Nevertheless, in the early months of the Confederacy Davis formed a coherent set of ideals based on building political unity through strict construction of the Constitution. Davis aimed at popular diffusion of democratic nationalist ideas through "print culture," a hallmark of democratic nationalism. He claimed that the United States Constitution provided the central principles of the Confederacy, arguing, "We have changed the constituent parts but not the system of government. The Constitution framed by our fathers is that of these Confederate States. In their expositions of it, and in the judicial construction it has received, we have a light that reveals its true meaning." Davis appealed to continuity with the American revolutionary heritage, insisting the Constitution's "mechanism was wonderful. . . . It has been the perversion of the Constitution; it has been the substitution of theories of morals for principles of government" that ended the Union.

Karl Marx contemptuously dismissed Davis's attempts to build a Confederate nation, declaring that "'the South' is neither a territory completely detached from the North geographically nor a moral unity. It is not a country at all, but a battle slogan."[19] But the Confederates were by no means unique: as historian Eric Hobsbawm has pointed out, political leaders in a variety of nations have found it necessary consciously to create a national identity.[20] Although the South shared a language and culture with the North, its most obvious distinguishing feature, slavery, seemed unlikely to unite the nation. But as much as anyone in the Confederacy, Jefferson Davis understood the necessity of appropriating American symbols such as the founding fathers and their Constitution. The Confederacy, Davis believed, would save the nation's democratic heritage. It represented the fulfillment, not the repudiation, of American freedom. Thus he insisted that the Confederate constitution differed "from that of our fathers only in so far as it is explanatory of their well-known intent." Leading southern legal theorist T. R. R. Cobb agreed with Davis, ably describing the new document as "really the old Constitution with . . . positive provisions against the inroads of latitudinal constructions."[21]

The attempt to build Confederate unity by appropriating the legacy of the founding fathers achieved extraordinary success in 1861. Confederate claims to defend the legacy of constitutional republicanism, combined with surprising successes on the battlefield, such as that at Bull Run, inspired southerners to fight for national independence. In widely publicized speeches such as his first inaugural address, Davis defended American democratic values. This stance produced the irony, noted by historian James McPherson, that troops both north and south marched to a "Battle Cry of Freedom." Davis scarcely made public mention of slavery in 1861, and in his 1881 memoir, *The Rise and Fall of the Confederacy*, he offered texts of his major speeches to argue that his chief concern had been constitutionalism.[22]

Davis's constitutionalism developed in antebellum Mississippi, a state dominated by Jacksonian politics. In 1828 Andrew Jackson carried every county in Mississippi. He appealed especially to the frontiersmen, proclaiming, "I have saved your women and children from the tomahawk and scalping knife. . . . and annexed to your State, an extensive domain." The spirit of Jacksonian democracy moved the state to approve one of the country's most democratic constitutions in 1832. As a recent study has argued, Mississippi Democrats "offered themselves as defenders of an egalitarian world, a world they believed imperiled by the influence of self serving aristocrats. They wanted to provide all white Mississippians an equal chance at securing their economic and political liberty." Party lines hardened as politicians struggled over issues such as banking and internal improvements in the state, and party alignments influenced the controversy over secession, which found the Democrats in the vanguard of disunion.[23]

Davis grew up in a prominent planter family, but his privileged background proved no handicap in Democratic politics: in his home county, public officials consistently came from the wealthiest 20 percent of the community.[24] Davis's political career prospered as he adopted Jacksonian stances, such as opposition to national spending for internal improvements. The young politician argued that all Mississippians shared an interest in limited government, and he presented his laissez-faire economic beliefs as beneficial to the humblest citizens. In an early speech he argued that the tariff created "much higher duties . . . on articles that entered largely into the consumption of the common and lower classes, and how low duties were on luxurious articles consumed and used by the rich." In stumping the state for his party, he had proved adept in a new style of popular politics, and as a young man he seemed "full of the genuine fire of democracy."[25] Later in his career, he boasted, "My devotion to the party is life long. . . . I derived [principles] from a revolutionary father—one of the earliest friends of Mr. Jefferson, who, after the Revolution . . . bore his full part in the second revolution, which emancipated us from usurpation and consolidation." As class resentments simmered in Mississippi over issues such as banking and debt repudiation, Davis denied charges that he represented the planter interest of the state's wealthy river counties. He proclaimed his devotion to white men's democracy and remarked, "It is mortifying to me to feel that any section of the state should assume the attitude of opposition to me under the idea that one part of Mississippi is less dear to me than another."[26]

After Jackson's death in 1845, Vicksburg Democrats called on Davis to give a eulogy for the former president. The aspiring politician presented the conventional narrative of Jackson's heroic Revolutionary boyhood and his exploits in fighting the British and Native Americans. Like other Democrats, he pointed to the character of Old Hickory, describing him as a "son of . . . poverty." But in this speech, Davis avoided partisan issues framed by Jackson, such as the war with the Bank of the United States. Instead he declared that Jackson's foremost political virtue lay in his strict construction of the Constitution. Davis had not "spoken fully of President Jackson's course in office" because he wanted to highlight the principles of a man who "gallantly bore, to the close of his life, the ark of our covenant, the Constitution of the U. States." For Davis, Jackson's life epitomized respect for the Constitution, and he defended Jackson's position on nullification. Jackson's stand during the nullification crisis in South Carolina represented dedication to constitutionalism, as he realized that "resistance to the laws it was his duty to suppress by all the means at his command, and when loud and deep were heard threats of disunion . . . he resolved, cost what it might, to save it."[27]

Although Davis endorsed Jackson's political philosophy in 1845, it is by no means clear that he fully understood the constitutional implications of Jackson's stand against South Carolina. At the time of the nullification crisis in South Carolina, Jackson declared that "the power to annul a law of the United States, assumed by one State, [is] incompatible with the existence of the Union, contradicted expressly by the letter of the Constitution, unauthorized by its spirit, inconsistent with every principle on which it was founded, and destructive of the great object for which it was formed." In words that brooked no opposition, the president argued that South Carolinians who felt the tariff was unconstitutional should seek a remedy through "recourse to the judiciary." Jackson believed that a government that could not enforce its laws was an absurdity, and he based his constitutional doctrines on an "ultranationalist" interpretation of the Constitution's origin.[28]

Davis and Jackson shared an emotional attachment to the Constitution with other Democrats. Jackson's emphasis on the Constitution meshed with antebellum states' rights Democratic beliefs. Democrats lauded the Constitution for defending the individual rights and personal independence viewed as central to a healthy polity. Since the time of Jefferson, Democrats believed the protection of individual rights was the crucial function of the document.[29] The attitude of North Carolina Democrat Miles, that he had "been trained in a school that looks upon constitutions as sacred things," was not unusual. Virginia governor Henry Wise did not exaggerate when he said southerners regarded the document with "a reverence approaching religious devotion." The Constitution was central to many southerners' political identity, as Louis T. Wigfall demonstrated in declaring, "I am a Democrat. By that I mean that I believe in a strict construction of the Constitution." Tocqueville recognized the importance of the law in political culture, noting "there is hardly a political question in the United States which does not sooner or later turn into a judicial one."[30] Davis apparently understood that the importance of constitutional issues in sectional wrangling created a generation with extraordinary interest in constitutional theory.

Despite emphasizing liberty, Davis could not completely escape the issue of slavery. In a March 1861 speech, Vice President Stephens declared, "Our new government is founded. . . . Its cornerstone rests, upon the great truth that the negro is not equal to the white man; that slavery, subordination to the superior race, is his natural and normal condition." Davis, concerned with winning the loyalty of the plain folk of the South and diplomatic recognition from European powers, could not have been pleased. Yet in starkly defining the war as one over slavery, Stephens's speech was an exception to the pose of moderation on slavery presented by most leading Confederates in the tense months before the war.

Although slavery was the Confederacy's reason for being, Davis's argument that he defended the Constitution was undoubtedly sincere. States' rights constitutionalism was both central to Davis's worldview and a politically sound means to mobilize a new nation. Constitutionalism embodied both American and southern identity: in 1858 Davis explained that "we became a nation by the Constitution, whatever is national springs from the Constitution; and national and constitutional are convertible terms."[31] For tactical reasons, Davis's emphasis on constitutional rights grew in the early days of the Confederacy: by stressing constitutional doctrine he could sidestep the issue of slavery. An overly frank defense of the peculiar institution would likely hurt the Confederacy in the border states such as Tennessee and Kentucky, where slaveholders were relatively few. As pioneering historian James Ford Rhodes wrote, Davis focused on constitutional rights because he wished to "obscure" the issue of slavery, which was "the true reason for the conflict."[32] Having worried about the support of nonslaveholders for slavery earlier in his career, he hoped to maintain their loyalty to the southern cause.[33]

Davis's appeal to constitutional purity was appropriate for a Democrat who valued a strict, almost fundamentalist, construction of the nation's founding document. Yet faith in Confederate constitutionalism virtually collapsed by 1863. In 1861, as Davis drew on popular aversion to centralized government to unite southerners against the Lincoln administration, he seemed to have a winning formula for energizing the people of the Confederacy. Confederate morale quickly eroded, however, and a firestorm of criticism against Davis broke out by the spring of 1862. John Daniel, a Richmond newspaperman and critic of Davis, diagnosed the problem when he wrote that the Confederacy staked its survival on "the history of the genius and enterprise natural to all struggles originating revolutions." Unfortunately, Daniel concluded, the hope for an outpouring of self-sacrifice and popular enthusiasm was "sadly contradicted by our experience in this war." Davis ally Senator James Phelan pointed to sagging morale in 1863, informing the president that "the enthusiasm of the masses of the people is dead!" Davis responded to the Richmond Bread Riot of 1863 in the manner of a "paternalist" dealing with poor whites, throwing money on the ground to stop citizens from storming shops. He learned of declining spirits in the army when he endured the humiliation of addressing a crowd of demoralized soldiers who interrupted him with cries of "furlough!"[34]

After the Mexican War, American politicians became increasingly concerned with slavery, and congressional votes began to break down over sectional rather than party lines.[35] Inevitably, as southern Democrats lost hope in the northern wing of the party, they were drawn to the states' rights ideas of John Calhoun. In the midst of the political crisis of 1850, Davis abandoned the Jacksonian nationalism he espoused in 1845. Davis emerged as a states' rights Democrat, as he pursued an extraordinarily confrontational stance on sectional issues out of fear for the future of slavery.[36] His increasingly militant position represented a marked departure from his political past: "What had she [South Carolina] done ... was she faithless to the Constitution? Never—always its defender!" His increasingly positive view of South Carolina and states' rights led him to denounce those "in certain quarters even in the South" for whom the state evoked "a peculiar sentiment of dread." Davis shared Calhoun's self-righteous insistence that those who disagreed with southern-rights politics ignored the Constitution's "plain meaning, its true intent." In 1860 Davis demanded a strict southern-rights construction of the Constitution, which he insisted was "the spirit in which it was made."[37]

For the rest of his life, Davis viewed Calhoun as the ultimate authority on the Constitution. In 1861 he called the South Carolinian "the wisest man I ever knew." He declared his intellectual debt during a Civil War visit to Charleston and proclaimed that Calhoun looked upon "our present struggle, and in our trial watches over us with all a guardian angel's care." Political scientist Marshall DeRosa has noted that the Confederacy's leaders, especially Davis, emulated Calhoun's approach to constitutional questions.[38] Like the Jacksonian Democrats, Calhoun spoke of a fixed original intent in the Constitution, but his "original meaning" differed from that of other Democrats. Calhoun, who dominated political life in the most militantly proslavery state in the antebellum South, viewed constitutionalism primarily as a means of protecting community prerogatives rather than individual rights. Further, while Jacksonians embraced the theory of majority rule, followers of Calhoun denounced the "almighty power of numbers" in the political arena associated with Jacksonian democracy.[39] After the sectional crisis of 1850 heightened Davis's interest in Calhoun, he maintained a lifelong respect for his political philosophy, which overrode his early infatuation with Jacksonian principles.

Calhoun's states' rights particularism, which so influenced Davis, clashed with the majoritarian principles espoused by many Confederates. Calhoun's thought changed dramatically during his long political career, but he did logical back flips as he sought to affirm his consistency to principle. A campaign biography written with Calhoun's input referred to his "matchless constancy" in pursuing public goals, but even a friendly writer in the *Southern Quarterly Review* noted, "If [Calhoun] has a prominent weakness it is his earnest desire to be classed among those who have never changed the opinions they have once expressed."[40] In his lengthy *Discourse on the Constitution*, Calhoun ignored the abundance of evidence that the Constitution was an ambiguous document, with meanings contested by the framers even before ratification. Madison, who lived to witness Calhoun's constitutional theorizing in the 1830s, disputed Calhoun's attempt to provide the sole true reading of the Constitution, but Calhoun cavalierly dismissed the founder's views as "strange." During his lifetime, Calhoun's views represented an idiosyncratic attempt to develop a political philosophy workable for both the United States and South Carolina, which was distinguished for its social and political eccentricity.[41]

Calhoun advocated a materialist political theory based on the belief that the self-interest of competing factions would inevitably overwhelm constitutional restraints. In *A Disquisition on Government*, he argued that because communities, like individuals, acted out of self-interest, in a polity representing diverse interests, democracy inevitably brought the oppression of minority communities. In his view, "the more extensive and populous the country, the more diversified the condition and pursuits of its population, and the richer, more luxurious and dissimilar the people, the more difficult it is to equalize the action of the government." Written constitutions would prove unavailing, as "there is no means by which [minorities] could compel the major party to observe the restrictions."[42] He stated his belief that majority oppression would overwhelm minorities in an 1847 Senate speech: "We shall be at the entire mercy of the nonslaveholding states. . . . Ought we to trust our safety and prosperity to their sense of mercy and justice?" Calhoun explicitly rejected Jackson's version of constitutionalism based on majority rule: "Of what possible avail is the strict construction of the major [faction], when [it] would have all the powers of government?" Calhoun insisted that a majority faction would follow its class interests: he was, in historian Richard Hofstadter's famous phrase, the "Marx of the Master Class."[43]

While in his abstract theorizing Calhoun concerned himself with the problem of protecting minorities, his critics suspected that his real interest lay in protecting communities led by slaveholders. Calhoun's constitutionalism seemed inextricably bound up with proslavery ideology that declared only slavery, and slaveholders, could sustain republican government. Historian Louis Hartz may have exaggerated when he called Calhoun "a profoundly disintegrated political theorist," but the South Carolinian did seem unable to define clearly the vision of community that he derived from proslavery thought.[44] Whatever the merits of his political philosophy, Calhoun's thought contradicted much of the heritage of men raised in the party of Jackson, such as Davis. Calhoun's ideas contradicted the "bristly independence" espoused by many Jacksonians. Suspicion grew among many Democrats as South Carolina theorists challenged Jacksonian orthodoxy regarding majority rule, denying the prevailing opinion that regarded "the numerical [majority] as the only majority."[45]

Historians, most notably William Freehling, have shown that the South Carolina nullification crisis concerned the institution of slavery as much as its ostensible object, tariffs. Nullification came when slaveholders were jolted by the Denmark Vesey conspiracy and Nat Turner rebellion, a divisive debate over constitutional reform and emancipation in Virginia, and the publication of William Lloyd Garrison's abolitionist newspaper, the *Liberator*. With slavery under siege, 1831 was a "turning point" for its defense. The emergence of Thomas Dew's argument for slavery as a positive good marked an increasingly intolerant climate in which slavery could not be questioned.[46] The nullification crisis was exposing increasing sectional tensions, but it also revealed geographic and class divisions within the South's political community of white men. In arguing for the right of South Carolina to nullify national laws, Calhoun pitted himself against a fellow slaveholder, Andrew Jackson. South Carolinians could complain about Yankee tariffs, but they were stood down by a president portrayed as a champion of the southern yeomanry. In 1828, Jackson had won all but 9 of the South's 114 electoral votes and two-thirds of its popular votes. Ultimately, the failure of slave states, even those in the Deep South, to back Calhoun killed nullification. South Carolina remained isolated politically because of its unique social structure, which included a greater proportion of slaves than in any other state.[47]

The doctrines of both Jackson and Calhoun coexisted among Democrats in the antebellum South. In the secession crisis, southern Democrats found themselves torn between the competing legacies of Jackson and Calhoun, and most, like Davis, embraced the doctrines of the latter. Tennessee's Senator Andrew Johnson, the only southerner to remain in the Senate after secession, recalled Jackson's Unionist legacy as he condemned secessionists who claimed to represent Democratic principles. "I believed that the position taken then [1833] by General Jackson, and those who came to his support, were the true doctrines of the Constitution." Johnson invoked Jackson's authority in order to denounce both secession and nullification. He effectively linked Calhoun's states' rights constitutional doctrine with South Carolina's aristocratic reputation, arguing that the state's leaders "have an early prejudice against this thing called democracy—a government of the people." Perceptively, Johnson placed his finger on the flaw in the theory of proslavery constitutionalism, its assumption of a unified southern interest. The

Tennessean argued that secessionist doctrine had antidemocratic implications, because "if you cannot trust a free State in the confederacy, can you trust a non-slaveholder in a slaveholding State to control the question of slavery?"[48]

States' rights Democrats also tried, although without much success, to claim the mantle of Jackson. Davis made an unconvincing attempt to invoke Jackson's memory. In an 1861 Senate speech, Davis declared his allegiance to the principles of "Jackson, glorious old soldier, who, in his minority, upon the sacred soil of South Carolina, bled for the cause of revolution and the overthrow of a Government which he believed to be oppressive." Davis also referred to Jackson's famous episodes of insubordination as a general and argued that Old Hickory had "the same cast of character . . . which would today be called rebellion and treason." Those who made such wildly implausible appeals about Jackson as a would-be secessionist simply failed to grapple with his nationalism. Southerners such as the Alabamian who signed an antisecession editorial with the pseudonym "Andrew Jackson" appropriated the former president's legacy with more success.[49] Yet Davis could not repudiate the heritage of Old Hickory, a political figure still revered by southerners.

In 1860, Davis remained more cautious than any of his counterparts in the Mississippi Democratic Party, and his views on disunion prior to the breakup of the Democratic convention at Charleston are exceedingly difficult to discern.[50] But he had already begun to propound a coherent constitutional doctrine. His theory of southern constitutionalism was rooted in materialism resembling that of Calhoun. Davis noted that "he is a poor statesman who does not understand that communities at last must yield to the dictates of their interests." Instead of relying on constitutional machinery to balance competing factions, Davis staked his hopes on "a new association composed of States homogenous in interest, in policy, and feeling." Davis's inaugural address constituted a genuine departure from Jacksonian democracy: the president declared that the Confederacy and its constitution must be based on social unity rather than individual rights. Only a homogeneous social basis would prevent a "despotism of numbers." Without such a firm grounding, he wrote to Robert Barnwell Rhett Jr., disaster would follow: "Interest controls the policy of states, and finally all the planting communities must reach the same conclusion."[51]

Davis's namesake, Thomas Jefferson, had idealized the yeoman farmer, but Davis's use of the term "planting communities" signified his expectation that slaveholders would play a leading role in the Confederacy, just as they had in the antebellum South. Davis opposed the idea of asking northwestern free states, whose economies were based largely on agriculture, to join the Confederacy. After all, yeoman farmers in the Northwest overwhelmingly supported the Republican Party.[52] He staked his hopes for the Confederate constitution on the organic unity of a slaveholding community, because he believed that these communities were more stable, and for whites, more equitable, than those based on free labor. This echoed the central contention of proslavery writers; because slavery promoted the general diffusion of wealth throughout the white population of the southern states, it strengthened social cohesion and a community based on organic unity.[53] Davis believed this unity of slaveholding communities would produce a nation of "brethren . . . of one flesh, one bone, one purpose, and of identity of domestic institutions."[54]

Yet the dream of a homogeneous slaveholding republic foundered on the reality that only a minority of white southerners, about one family in three, owned slaves. In Davis's Mississippi, the most consistent dissent against secession came from nonslaveholders.[55] Some southerners warned in 1861 that political harmony would prove elusive, since after secession "new divisions would spring up among our people."[56] The struggles between Whigs and Jacksonians that characterized the second party system never threatened slavery, but they contradicted Davis's belief in the organic unity of the slave states, as southern leaders had long regarded the loyalty of the yeomanry as "somewhat problematic." As Unionist James W. Sheffrey declared in the Virginia Secession Convention, a "diversity of interests" existed within the South. If Davis's theory "applied to our state, to the interests of the East and the West, [it] would be calculated above all things to stir up strife."[57]

Calhoun shared little of the concern for the primacy of individual rights central to antebellum Democratic political discourse. Calhoun's doctrine of state sovereignty, later adopted by Davis, promoted state power. Slaveholding politicians used the doctrine of state sovereignty in "overriding local law and local custom and negating the idea of local self-government" in regard to the conflict over fugitive slaves and the fight over slavery in the territories. Broad construction meant that the idea of state sovereignty "was a nationalistic doctrine, not a localistic one." Nowhere was the tendency of proslavery doctrine toward a consolidation of national power more evident than in the Dred Scott case, which appeared to limit the power of territories to regulate slavery and fueled Republican fears of a "Slave Power Conspiracy" to control the national government. The potential for centralism was highlighted by the fact that in the Confederate constitution the right to secede is implied by the phraseology of the preamble but never explicitly stated.[58]

In fact, increased national power to control slaves, not individual rights, provided one key rationale for the Confederacy. Georgia's *Augusta Daily Constitutionalist* warned that "the question is, secession from the Union, and a self-defending, homogenous southern Republic, or submission to the Union, and the fate of Jamaica and St. Domingo." With the election of Lincoln, a southern "crisis of fear" regarding slave rebellion emerged in South Carolina and the Mississippi Valley, as "rampant insurrection anxiety" was a key factor driving secession.[59] Davis declared that "our servants" would never rise in rebellion, but he added an important qualification as he argued that slaves might rebel if incited by "bad men" with abolitionist views. The diary of South Carolina's Mary Chesnut reveals a fear of slave rebellion that many slaveholders shared. Southern fears of slave insurrection in 1860 and 1861 may have been exaggerated, but many believed a "self-defending" republic would require strong measures to contain potential rebellion.[60]

The Confederate constitution ensured that a strong president could deal with the twin threats of war and slave revolt. However, the Confederate framers failed to provide a basis for nullification and, remarkably, did not explicitly recognize the right of secession. As historian Donald Fehrenbacher has noted, the Confederate constitution was shaped by "men committed to the principles of states' rights but addicted, in many instances, to the exercise of national power."[61] The constitution granted increased power to the executive branch, such as a line-item veto that allowed the president to cancel spending he viewed as unwise. The requirement for a two-thirds vote in both houses for appropriations not requested by the president further strengthened the executive branch. In their most bold constitutional innovation, the Confederate framers vested power in an executive limited to a single six-year term, hoping that a president ineligible to succeed himself would rise above popular politics: Alexander Stephens called this measure "a decidedly conservative change." The *Richmond Whig* overstated matters when it called Davis an "elective king," but he did have remarkably strengthened powers compared with the old United States Constitution. Some Confederates wished for more, perhaps even a military strongman: Richmond newspaper editor John M. Daniel, no friend of Davis's, declared, "To the dogs with Constitutional questions, what we want is an effectual resistance."[62]

Despite Davis's extraordinary power, he seemed an unlikely despot in 1861 as he appealed to citizens on the basis of defending constitutional rights. In the state conventions that met to ratify the Confederate constitution, virtually no protest emerged regarding increased executive power.[63] Early in the war,

Davis proudly compared his record on civil liberties to the Union. There, he said, Lincoln was "making war without the assent of Congress," suspending the writ of habeas corpus, and trampling "justice and law ... under the heel of military authority." Such northern actions, the Confederate president believed, signaled a "radical incompatibility" between Americans north and south. Many Confederates echoed Davis's arguments, since by condemning northern tyranny he tapped into long-standing southern fears of centralized authority. One Confederate broadside proclaimed,

> They talk of Union and the Flag
> Old blessed guards of liberty
> and all that's good from both they drag
> Debase them both by tyranny!
> Hear, O hear, the battle's call
> Gallant Southrons one and all:
> Sons of freedom now awake
> And the chains of tyrants break!

Davis did not create the argument for southern independence, but his constitutional arguments meshed with ideals of freedom that brought Confederate soldiers into the ranks.[64]

By 1862, Davis's appeals to liberty left him open to charges of hypocrisy as the Confederacy began a national program of conscription. One historian of the yeomanry has described conscription, which many perceived to be unfair and illegal, as one of "the greatest mistakes of the Confederate government." The Confederate president hardly relished the power to draft soldiers, but that task was forced on him by the sheer numbers of Union troops arrayed against the South. Davis argued that he had no choice but to institute a draft and that he continued to "deeply ... regret the character of the contest" that made conscription unavoidable. He wrote sincerely that "arbitrary measures are not more congenial to my nature than to the spirit of our institutions."[65]

Even as the president bent his prewar constitutional principles, he took pains to present his course as consistent with southern constitutionalism. Congress, Davis noted, had the constitutional power to raise armies, and it had judged conscription "a necessary and proper" means of executing that power. He argued that to deny Congress the ability to draft citizens would be to deny its authority to raise an army, and he pointed out the Confederate constitution's nearly unqualified assignment of the war power to the national government. Although each state could successfully administer its domestic government, Davis argued, they were "yet too feeble successfully to resist powerful nations" and so sought "safety with other states in like condition."[66] Although the famous thesis that the Confederacy "died of states' rights" is overstated, Davis's centralized war effort and its nationalistic justification did shock many Confederates who were committed to states' rights. The president's insistence on the constitutionality of conscription and the necessity of military centralization no doubt worsened the state of affairs, as he seemed impatient with critics. He believed that because he led a nation in which all citizens had a mutual interest in preserving slavery, his critics were "weak" men too concerned "with local and personal interests."[67]

Davis's broad construction of the "necessary and proper" clause of the constitution angered many Confederates who disliked centralized power. Since Davis had been a strict constructionist under the Union, it seemed that his reading of the Confederate constitution, which contained language strictly limiting central authority, was disingenuous. Because he was a symbol of the civilian Confederacy, Davis incurred the displeasure of a people fearful of strengthened national power as the Confederate administration transformed the central government into a powerful national state. Davis could, and did, argue that military necessity made conscription and impressment of supplies essential. While he never made the argument that the urgency of the situation justified unconstitutional measures, some of his supporters did. Mississippi's Albert Gallatin Brown remarked, "It would be bad to have it said, after we were in our graves, that our liberty had been lost [to the North] whilst we were struggling over petty constitutional questions." Louis Wigfall, also of Mississippi, completely rejected antebellum constitutionalism, arguing, "It was no time now to talk of the rights of man, while war was being made on us like beasts."[68]

Yet Davis never reformulated his theory of constitutionalism, and he fell into unconvincing rationalizations for policies that, however necessary from a military standpoint, contradicted his earlier principles. Davis contended that the war justified aid to railroads, even though the Confederate constitution expressly prohibited such spending.[69] He referred to England as a precedent for suspending the writ of habeas corpus, claiming that its history proved that "a country whose reverence for the great bill of rights is at least as strong as our own" had done so and yet maintained free institutions. For many southerners, looking to an abolitionist center with an unwritten constitution must have seemed obnoxious. Complaints that Davis abused his constitutional authority multiplied, eroding his popularity. Davis's few close political allies fretted, "Your labors are heavy, and your trials are vexatious." To friends of the president, growing discontent meant that "many who ought to hold up your hands are pushing them down."[70]

Some southerners accused Davis of violating the very constitution he had sworn to uphold. Richmond newspaperman Edward Pollard, a Davis critic, declared after the war that conscription "necessarily established a consolidated government, founded on military principles." Confederates who maintained a Jacksonian disdain for central power were appalled by "a departure from all the constitutional precedents known in the country, a direct assault on State Rights." The president made some accommodations to outraged public opinion, giving ground on habeas corpus and altering conscription laws to end special exemptions that angered many southerners. But while criticism grew, Davis defended the constitutionality of conscription. Yet even Davis came close to conceding the arguments of critics such as Joseph Brown, as he admitted to the Georgia governor that the right of each state to judge its reserved powers in relation to "the general government is too familiar and well-settled a principle to admit of discussion." Here, Davis practically admitted the existence of a gap between principle and practice. Centralization and conscription made Davis's wish "to avoid collisions" with state authorities impossible.[71]

As the president's popularity collapsed in the final three years of the war, opposition to him reflected not just the class resentment and war weariness noted by historians such as Paul Escott but also anger at his abandonment of principles of strict construction. Alienated from the administration, Stephens, who left Richmond in 1862, retired to his plantation and wrote dozens of acerbic letters criticizing Davis's newfound constitutional flexibility: "I am surprised at some things in the President's letter coming from a strict constructionist. Such as that Congress is the judge of its powers. . . . What think you of this coming from a man who held the United States Bank was unconstitutional under the old Government?"[72] The exasperated lament of a Confederate senator from Tennessee who noted that "hardly a subject would come up in the Senate that gentleman did not say that the identical thing had dissolved the Union" signaled the depth of dissatisfaction. Even some of Davis's defenders believed that the exigencies of war had forced him "to sacrifice on the altar of his country the principles of a lifetime."[73]

To take the place of principles, he encouraged fear. In mobilizing support, Davis repeatedly warned of the threat of "subjugation." The word suggested not just military defeat but social humiliation, the possibility of rape, and a peeling away of the privileges that masters of households shared. Indeed, manhood permeated the rhetoric of the war, as Davis constantly complained of attacks on women and children: they resulted because the Union was "invading our home." Confederate men must therefore defend the heritage as free men "purchased by the blood of [their] revolutionary sires." For men across the country, fighting in the Civil War became a test of their masculinity.[74] The rhetoric had little effect. After his early success in rallying the populace for states' rights constitutionalism, Davis seemed to have reneged on his beliefs. Worse still, he offered no new philosophy of government that could shore up the spirits of ordinary citizens and soldiers.

Angry Jacksonians such as newspaper editor William Woods Holden, who denounced Davis and the war in the columns of North Carolina's largest Democratic newspaper, the *Raleigh Weekly Standard*, focused on the decline of constitutional liberty in the Confederacy. Holden had been a leading figure in the antebellum North Carolina Democratic Party who had reluctantly supported secession, while warning that the Confederacy must abide by "strict construction" and "the reserved rights of the states." Holden declared that "this war will have been accomplished in vain . . . if the people of North Carolina continue to sit still and allow the enemies of 'self-government' to rob them piece by piece of those same liberties and privileges" that the North had conspired to take.[75] Davis pressured North Carolina authorities to suppress Holden's paper, claiming that Holden was "engaged in the treasonable purpose of exciting the people of North Carolina to resistance against their government and cooperation with the enemy." Confederate secretary of war James A. Seddon advised North Carolina governor Zebulon B. Vance to curb "our tolerance and compassion to the few bad men who are busy feeding disaffection." But Holden continued his denunciations of Davis even as the *Raleigh State Journal* complained, "North Carolina troops . . . are leaving nightly in large numbers. . . . The troops are advised to desert by relatives, who say that Holden will defend them." North Carolina politicians realized that Holden's scathing indictments of Davis were effective because the prominent Jacksonian had "extraordinary influence . . . on the common people."[76] Yet they felt powerless to act in the wake of Holden's widespread support.

The Confederacy presented the singular spectacle of a nation in the midst of revolution squabbling over the construction of legal documents. Davis never abandoned his claim that he acted in "compliance with the whole letter and spirit of the Constitution," and he became increasingly intolerant of opposition on that score. Personal arrogance hampered Davis's ability to respond to criticism: he confided to Robert E. Lee, "There has been nothing which I have found to require a greater effort of patience than to bear the criticisms of the ignorant."[77] Politicians who complained, he warned in a speech meant to silence opposition, exhibited "treasonous design . . . masked by a pretense of devotion to State Sovereignty." By 1864, Davis shifted from a defense of his constitutional bona fides to an attack on "traitors" and "conspirators" who exploited "technicalities of the law."[78] In describing violations of the Constitution as "technicalities," Davis had truly abandoned his role as a defender of strict construction.

Beginning in late 1862, Davis had gradually deemphasized constitutionalism as a factor in his appeals for public support and shifted to warnings of racial apocalypse in the event of Confederate defeat. Freed slaves threatened southern families: in 1863, the *Huntsville Confederate* published a message from Davis asking deserters to return to the army, as he warned that the Union's "malignant rage aims at nothing less than the extermination of yourselves, your wives, and children. . . . They design to incite servile insurrection." Speaking to the Army of Tennessee, Davis advised the troops that "gentle women, feeble age and helpless infancy have been subjected to outrages without parallel." The work of historian Martha Hodes indicates that a wartime increase in sexual assaults on white women is unlikely, and Reid Mitchell argues that assaults against white women by Union soldiers were rare. Still, Davis could argue that generals such as Benjamin Butler encouraged Union soldiers to "insult and outrage the wives, the mothers and the sisters of our citizens."[79] Having lost his reputation as a strict constructionist, Davis propagated his fantasies about sex and conquest as a substitute for a coherent political ideology. He also shifted his emphasis to another staple of Jacksonian rhetoric: independent manhood. The president invoked the memory of the Revolution and praised soldiers for meeting the standard set by fathers who "fought against a manly foe." The young soldiers of Jackson's generation "grew to manhood among its struggles," and so too would the soldiers of the Confederacy.[80]

While the Confederate president continued to defend the war effort in 1863 and 1864, increasingly he abandoned constitutional arguments in favor of calls for self-denial. The trials of war required southerners to show that they deserved to be a nation. In calling for days of fasting, prayer, and humiliation on nine separate occasions, he conveyed the necessity for collective unity as the key to Confederate nationalism. By testing themselves in the "severe crucible" of war, southerners were tried "in order to cement us together" in social unity. Davis asked for collective sacrifice, pointing out that a society based solely on self-interest could not survive the necessities of total war. Constitutional issues receded as many Confederates came to view the war as a moral test. Alabama governor John Gill Shorter argued, "Our people must make sacrifices—and endure privations—until we achieve our independence. If we are not prepared to do this we do not deserve to be free." In his view, liberties would be earned "in proportion to the sacrifice they cost." Davis invoked the will of God as he asked troops to achieve "that self-denial which rejects every consideration at variance with the public service as unworthy to the holy cause."[81]

In calling for sacrifice and economic regulation, Davis became further entangled with the region's Jacksonian heritage. Democrats had long insisted on a rigid separation of church and state. Jackson had alienated some evangelical voters with his harsh Indian removal policy and insistence on delivering the mail on Sunday and by resisting Henry Clay's call for a day of fasting during an 1832 cholera epidemic.[82] Early in the war, the *Richmond Examiner* complained that the fast days violated the principle that "religion is the sentiment of individuals" and "are regarded by the people as cant." Eventually, Davis's politically motivated days of prayer became an object of sarcastic jibes, as the *Charleston Mercury* composed a prayer declaring "the Confederate Government is most bountiful—most considerate—most wise."[83]

Many accounts have portrayed the Confederacy as relatively successful in maintaining internal freedom, as historians have long concluded that the contrast between Lincoln and Davis on civil liberties "is all in favor of the southern leader." Yet the impositions of the Confederate government went far beyond conscription. A recent study indicates that arrests of civilians in the South were roughly proportional to those in the North. In many ways, the Confederate citizen was less free than his northern counterpart, since a domestic passport system inhibited freedom of movement.[84] Because impressment of agricultural goods seemed like the arbitrary act of a "kingly government," it bred resentment.[85] Southern newspapers, which had been subjected to legislation enacted to stifle criticism of slavery since the 1830s, engaged in self-censorship because of fears of the authorities.[86] These measures meant that the rhetoric of constitutional liberty that had given legitimacy to the war effort in 1861 sounded increasingly hollow as the war progressed.

Increasingly discredited as a defender of liberty, the president failed to increase his public approval through panicked appeals to racial fear. As many as 50 percent of the men in the demoralized armies deserted, and Davis could find no means of stopping "the disposition to avoid military service" that Herschel Johnson described as widespread and "humiliating." Davis's popularity fell so low that in late 1864 his friend Clement Claiborne Clay warned his wife, Virginia, not to visit or even contact him, advising her that Davis "has less and less power to intimidate his enemies, and they grow more numerous every day."[87] Thomas Bocock, former Speaker of the Confederate House of Representatives, stated that a vote showing the country lacked confidence in the cabinet would gain the approval of three-fourths of the members of Congress.[88] Ruffin, who applauded Davis's selection to head the Confederacy, now referred to him as "our tender conscienced and imbecile President." Ultimately, the deluge of criticism took a toll on Davis's health as his migraines and his neuralgia worsened.[89]

In the immediate aftermath of the war, Davis suffered considerable personal humiliation. While fleeing from Richmond, the head of the collapsing government had serious difficulty in finding citizens in Greensboro, North Carolina, willing to lodge him for the night. His capture provoked great merriment in the North because when his carriage was stopped by Union soldiers, he had slipped on his wife's shawl. Davis claimed that he simply wished protection from the rain, but northern journalists claimed that Davis dressed as a woman in order to sneak away from Union authorities. Northern cartoons of Davis in petticoats, running away as a "feminized and feckless fugitive," drove home the message that the dissipated southern men lacked the discipline and self-restraint required for genuine manhood, and implied that northern men were more masculine than their southern counterparts.[90] At Fort Monroe, Davis spent almost two years in conditions he considered abysmal; for the first five days he faced the indignity of wearing leg irons.[91] Hated by Confederate enemies, jailed for nearly two years, humiliated by a victor that he believed was bent on vengeance, and fearful for his property in Mississippi, Davis hit bottom in both his public and personal life. During Reconstruction his fortunes revived, however, and doubts about his presidential performance had faded. Confederate nostalgia had grown in the New South. By the 1870s, Davis became a popular public speaker and enjoyed a new measure of respect from his fellow southerners. At his death in 1889, seventy thousand people visited his body, and his enormous funeral in New Orleans honored both Davis and the lost cause he represented. The *New Orleans Picayune* declared that for the South Davis represented "the cause for which a million of her most chivalrous sons drew their swords."[92]

While the Confederate president was remembered by some as chivalrous, his constitutionalism, derived from Calhoun, proved wanting when put into practice. The organic unity of a white community based on slavery proved to be a fiction, and the notion that a proslavery government could protect individual freedom collapsed. Calhoun's assumption, based on proslavery ideas, that a slaveholding community would prove extraordinarily united was disproved during the war. The appeals to constitutional liberty in 1861, which initially were effective, foundered as the war progressed. In raising the specter of racial subjugation in 1864 and 1865, Davis implicitly conceded that the war was, after all, about slavery.

Jefferson Davis's adoption of Calhoun's constitutional theory estranged him and the Confederacy from the common farmers and soldiers on whose support the new government depended. The Confederate experiment in government proved a failure, if judged by the values of independence and democracy, which were touchstones of the antebellum Democratic Party. Yet Davis was unrepentant: more than twenty years after the war, he wrote, "If a young man should ask me where he could, in a condensed form, get the best understanding of our institutions and the duties of an American patriot, I would answer, 'In Calhoun's speech in the Senate on what is known as the "Force Bill."'"[93] Undaunted by defeat, Davis held to the principles of the man whom he saw as the greatest political theorist of the antebellum South. In doing so, he rejected the individualistic heritage of Jefferson and Jackson for an ideal of an organic slaveholding community.

Conclusion

After the war, Alexander Stephens wrote that Lincoln's Unionism "rose to the sublimity of a religious mysticism." It would have been more accurate to say that, as a successful attorney, Lincoln cared deeply about orderly government and believed that it was bestowed by the Constitution and the Declaration of Independence. He shared his attachment to these values during a lecture in Springfield in 1838, in which the young Lincoln denounced vigilantism and asked his fellow citizens to "never . . . violate in the least particular, the laws of the country, and never to tolerate their violation by others." Americans should make a "political religion" of upholding the law, especially the supreme law as expressed in the Constitution and the Declaration of Independence.[1] The Lincoln-Douglas debates of 1858, occasioned by competition for selection as senator from Illinois, reveal that Lincoln was absorbed by the constitutional implications of sectional tensions. As he declared, "There is no reason in the world why the negro is not entitled to all the natural rights enumerated in the Declaration of Independence, the right to life, liberty, and the pursuit of happiness."[2] This practice of reading the Constitution in light of the Declaration's promise of equality would continue. Lincoln's democratic vision, combined with his attachment to the Union, would guide his actions as the conflict intensified.

Lincoln enacted conscription, suspended the writ of habeas corpus, and drew the fire of opponents for violating the Constitution, just as Jefferson Davis had. In border states, where guerrilla fighting was rampant, civil liberties were strictly constrained. But Union infringements on individual rights were not limited to combat zones. Lincoln assented to a decision by General Ambrose Burnside to arrest Ohio Democrat Clement Vallandigham, a Copperhead opponent of the war, and expel him from the country. In arresting Vallandigham, a civilian expressing antigovernment sentiments in an area where there was no imminent Confederate military threat, the administration overstepped its bounds.³ Indeed, for a generation after the Civil War, Democrats would assail Lincoln's record on civil liberties, and many would argue that the entire war effort was unconstitutional. Under the pressure of events, many argued, Lincoln played fast and loose with the Constitution.⁴ But unlike Davis, who repeated stale, inflexible constitutional arguments for his position, Lincoln found new ways to justify the war effort.

In a supreme irony, northern politicians such as Lincoln, allied with antislavery radicals who stubbornly pushed slavery to the forefront of political debate in the Civil War, would rejuvenate Jeffersonian democracy and ensure the survival of the dream that all men are created equal. The process was set in motion before Lincoln was born. During the late eighteenth century's "Age of Revolution," abolitionists emphasized the connection between democratic liberalism and opposition to slavery. Northern states abolished slavery in the wake of the American Revolution. Rebellious slaves such as those in Haiti fought to win democratic principles of "liberty and equality" influenced by the French radicalism that so moved Jefferson. Even Nat Turner, the messianic Virginia slave rebel, spoke "in the accents of the Declaration of Independence."⁵ Yet during the thirty years of reaction in the South that followed the Turner revolt, African Americans realized the horrible contradiction between the American democratic creed and their personal experience of democracy in the United States. In an 1854 Fourth of July address, Frederick Douglass emphasized the exclusion of blacks from American democracy: "The rich inheritance of justice, liberty, prosperity, and independence, bequeathed by your fathers, is shared by you, not by me. . . . This Fourth of July is yours, not mine." Douglass angrily denounced the racism inherent in the heritage represented by the Fourth of July, as it was "a day that reveals to [the slave], more than all other days in the year, the gross injustice and cruelty to which he is the constant victim." To the slave, "your shouts of liberty and equality [are] hollow mockery."⁶ Yet Douglass never questioned the ideals of liberty and equality the holiday was meant to represent. He simply noted the failure of white Americans to live up to their principles.

Like Douglass, many abolitionists realized the efficacy of a political strategy that drew on constitutional democracy as a means of making freedom universal. In 1851, a slave owner and federal marshals entered Christiana, a Pennsylvania hamlet near the Maryland border, seeking a fugitive slave. Shots were exchanged, and the master was killed. Two African

Americans who had engaged in the fight against the slave catchers were tried for treason and acquitted. The good news brought one black newspaper to declare, "We are glad that . . . a few voices are raised in defense of the eternal truths for which Jefferson wrote, and [Crispus] Attucks . . . bled."[7] After abolitionist John Brown made his 1859 raid on the federal arsenal at Harpers Ferry, where his vain attempt to incite slave rebellion was crushed, many attempted to depict the old man as a lunatic. Yet the leading advocate of nonviolence in the abolitionist movement, William Lloyd Garrison, linked Brown to Jeffersonian democracy. Perhaps, Garrison argued, Jefferson was a co-conspirator because his ideas had helped to inspire Brown's raid: "It must have been Thomas Jefferson—another Virginian—who said of the bondage of the Virginia slaves, that 'one hour of it is fraught with more misery than ages of that which our fathers rose in rebellion to oppose.'" Garrison argued that Brown had learned from Jefferson "the SELF-EVIDENT TRUTH, that all men are created equal, and endowed by their Creator with AN INALIENABLE RIGHT TO LIBERTY."[8]

Despite his antislavery convictions, Lincoln disavowed any intention to interfere with slavery in the existing slave states after his election to the presidency. This position, unpalatable to abolitionists in his party, flowed from his constitutionalism. He declared, "I have no purpose, directly or indirectly, to interfere with the institution of slavery in the states where it already exists. I believe I have no lawful right to do so, and I have no inclination to do so." Lincoln believed that the Constitution provided adequate safeguards to protect the South's slaveholders, and, sensitive to the constitutional issues at stake, he assured the slave states that "all the vital rights of minorities, and of individuals, are so plainly assured to them, by . . . the Constitution, that controversies never arise concerning them." He went further to state that he had no objection to a constitutional amendment expressly guaranteeing the "irrevocable" authority of states to regulate their own "domestic institutions."[9] Lincoln adamantly insisted that he would rule the country, including the South, according to the Constitution. Even after the shelling of Fort Sumter, he was willing to support a resolution sponsored by Kentucky's John Crittenden that the Union fought solely "to defend and maintain the supremacy of the Constitution."[10]

When southern states seceded from the Union in the winter of 1861, Lincoln feared for the future of constitutional democracy. He had good reason: never before had the results of a presidential election brought defiance from a large part of the populace. In focusing on the maintenance of constitutionalism, he chose the icon of southern democracy, Thomas Jefferson, to illustrate that the Confederates had abandoned traditions of freedom. "Our adversaries have adopted some Declarations of Independence; in which, unlike the good old one, penned by Jefferson, they omit the words 'all men are created equal.'" Similarly, he noted, the Confederate constitution eliminated the words "we the people." Lincoln characterized this as a "deliberate pressing out of view, the rights of men, and the authority of the people."[11] He held that government based on "a majority, held in restraint by constitutional checks, and limitations . . . is the only true sovereign of a free people." If minorities were to reject the principle of majority rule and secede rather than submit to this rule, the logical outcome would be chaos. Disunion would destroy America's constitutional heritage because "the central idea of secession is the essence of anarchy."[12] In defining his essential war aim as defense of the Constitution, Lincoln found an issue that could unite both northern War Democrats, such as Stephen Douglas, and southern Unionists in the border states behind the war effort. The political leaders of both sections, each for their own reasons, ignored in their early pronouncements on the war the four million African Americans held in bondage.

In fact, Lincoln knew that the root of the war lay in slavery. As he wrote his former congressional ally Stephens in 1860, "You think slavery is right and ought not to be extended; while we think it is wrong and ought to be restricted. That I suppose is the rub."[13] Lincoln understood that a war about slavery inevitably brought the issue of liberty to the forefront as the contested nature of freedom became evident. For Unionists, Lincoln declared, freedom meant each man could enjoy "the product of his labor." Like antebellum Republicans, the president placed economic autonomy and rough social equality, buttressed by social mobility, at the center of his understanding of freedom. On the other hand, Lincoln noted, for the Confederates, freedom implied mastery—the right to do "as they please with other men, and the product of other men's labor." By the fall of 1862, he understood that the war would determine which definition of freedom would prevail.[14]

Nevertheless, after more than a year of war, Lincoln was unwilling to stand boldly on the side of freedom. Especially concerned with maintaining the loyalty of border states such as Kentucky, he approached the question of emancipation with great deliberation. Lincoln pushed plans for voluntary emancipation in the border states, but they fell through because of a lack of support by slaveholders. This passivity regarding slavery drew criticism in the North. As the Union war effort stalled in 1862 during George McClellan's failed Peninsula campaign in Virginia, abolitionists and radical Republicans pushed Lincoln to turn the Civil War into a battle against slavery. Newspaper editor Horace Greeley asked him to free the slaves and stop handling traitors with "kid gloves."[15] While Lincoln maintained his personal opposition to slavery, he reiterated his commitment to conservative constitutionalism in a letter responding to Greeley's call for emancipation. He wrote that his determination to view the conflict as a crisis of Union meant he "would save the Union": "I would save it the shortest way under the Constitution. . . . My paramount object in this struggle is to save the Union, and is not either to save or destroy slavery."[16] Yet at the time he wrote these words minimizing the importance of slavery, Lincoln was planning to issue an emancipation proclamation. The expansion in the scope of the war moved Lincoln to reconsider his position on emancipation, and it became one of several measures meant to increase pressure on the South as the conflict moved toward an uncompromising "hard war."[17]

After the Battle of Antietam in September 1862, Lincoln announced a preliminary emancipation proclamation, which he framed only as a war measure, with no reference to freedom or indictment of slavery. Although this approach to emancipation flowed logically from his reading of the Constitution, historian Richard Hofstadter has derided Lincoln's pronouncement for "having all the moral grandeur of a bill of lading."[18] Nevertheless, the proclamation proved remarkably effective. As word of freedom spread, slaves fled their masters, and the institution entered a terminal decline, brought down by federal armies and fugitive slaves. In the North, the short-term political response to emancipation was unfavorable. But the proclamation made the war a battle between not just armies but competing societies, because northern victory would bring revolution to the South. In such a battle there could be no compromise.[19]

Jefferson Davis, who had virtually abandoned his Jeffersonian principles as the war ground on, could never find a higher cause in which to justify the Confederate struggle for national existence. When Davis found himself under attack for violating the letter and the spirit of the Confederate constitution, he virtually abandoned discussion of constitutional issues and shifted to apocalyptic rhetoric of racial subjugation, spinning out scenarios of black social and political domination. In the Confederacy's rights-oriented political culture, Davis became increasingly unpopular, and he could provide no clear rationale for the horrible sacrifices made by the Confederate people. Davis, who served a six-year term and therefore did not have to face the voters, almost certainly would not have been reelected.[20] He understood the need to lift popular morale; he traveled extensively and issued numerous proclamations. He failed because while he knew the importance of communication, compared with Lincoln, he simply had little to say. Lincoln's popularity fluctuated throughout the war, but his dogged persistence in defending Union and emancipation won him reelection.[21]

While slaveholding Democrats appropriated the ideology of Jefferson for increasingly conservative purposes in the antebellum period, there was nothing intrinsically reactionary about those ideas. African Americans, who had drawn on democratic ideals even before the Civil War, have proved most persistent in claiming their rights in the language of American democracy. For example, in the first year of Radical Reconstruction, South Carolina's Reconstruction convention declared to the state's white residents, "We adopt the language of the Declaration of Independence that 'all men are created equal' and that 'life, liberty, and the pursuit of happiness' are the right of all."[22] Demands for "forty acres and a mule" echoed Jefferson's wish to base democracy on a propertied citizenry. Union Leagues, which supported the Republican Party, organized across racial lines and invoked the Declaration at meetings.[23] Opponents of Radical Reconstruction, on the other hand, found themselves adopting racist arguments that tended toward repudiation of the Declaration. For example, one Baltimore writer declared that white southerners refused to be taken in by the "tinsel tattle of Radical orators, by appeals to the Declaration of Independence, and all that muck-mammocky rot about liberty and equality and 'the philosophy of first principles'; in which the Senators indulged."[24]

When the United States retreated from Reconstruction, it condemned African Americans to a shadow of freedom and narrowed the scope of American liberty. John R. Lynch, an African American Republican who had served as Speaker of the Mississippi House during Congressional Reconstruction, later summed up his experiences in a memoir, *The Facts of Reconstruction*. In a South that witnessed segregation and disenfranchisement, Lynch declared, "Jeffersonian democracy, therefore, seems now to be nothing more than a meaningless form of expression."[25] Writing during the Gilded Age, a period of economic boom that witnessed deteriorating conditions for former freedmen, Lynch had reason for despairing of the future of the Jim Crow South. He argued that the leaders of the United States, in abandoning southern blacks, had also abandoned the egalitarian vision of Jefferson and Lincoln. It could hardly be coincidental that 1877, the year that witnessed the nation's withdrawal of support for southern black laborers, also witnessed unprecedented violence against workers in the North.[26]

Nevertheless, African American resistance to Jim Crow never disappeared, and historians are still recovering evidence of the remarkable persistence of black struggles against oppression.[27] On rare occasions workers and farmers organized across racial lines despite massive opposition.[28] But southern workers, including whites, were vulnerable to racial divisions that thwarted union organizing and stunted wage growth. For too long, the persistence of southern poverty has seemed to confirm Marx's dictum that "labor in white skin cannot emancipate itself where the black skin is branded."[29]

Marx's insight into the relationship between black and white labor, reached during the Civil War, has much to offer historians of the slave South. The peculiar institution was not just a business arrangement but a way of life. Slavery built a social hierarchy based on violence and terror. Because it was a way of life, it necessarily left its mark on virtually every aspect of society, including political institutions such as the Democratic Party. The peculiar institution produced a peculiar democracy, distorted by a culture of mastery and social inequality. When Civil War came, democracy crumbled, and Democratic Party leaders proved unable to contain the divisions in white society.

Notes

ABBREVIATIONS

ADAH	Alabama Department of Archives and History
CRG	Allen D. Candler, ed., *Confederate Records of the State of Georgia* (New York, 1972)
DUL	Duke University Library
LC	Library of Congress
MDAH	Mississippi Department of Archives and History
OR	*The War of the Rebellion: A Compilation of the Official Records of the Union and Confederate Armies* (Washington, 1894)
SCDAH	South Carolina Department of Archives and History
SCL	South Caroliniana Library, University of South Carolina
SHC	Southern Historical Collection, University of North Carolina
UC	University of Chicago
UGA	University of Georgia
VHS	Virginia Historical Society

INTRODUCTION

1. *New York Times*, June 1, 1865; *Douglass' Monthly*, April 1863, in Douglass, *Life and Writings of Frederick Douglass*, 3:63. For Douglass and the nonslaveholders, see Douglass, *Narrative of the Life of Frederick Douglass*, 35, 45–47, 70–71, 87–104; Douglass, *Life and Times of Frederick Douglass*, 65–70, 115–27, 176–87.

2. *Richmond Enquirer*, 1856, quoted in Oakes, *Slavery and Freedom*, 80; *Montgomery Advertiser*, May 6, 1857.

3. Catherine Anne Devereux Edmonston, December 30, 1864, in Crabtree and Patton, *"Journal of a Secesh Lady,"* 651; J. D. B. De Bow, *Interest in Slavery of the Southern Nonslaveholder*.

4. Ashworth, *"Agrarians" and "Aristocrats,"* v; Geertz, "Ideology as Cultural System," 47–50.

5. On "herrenvolk democracy," see Fredrickson, *Black Image in the White Mind*, 61–68. In a more recent essay, Fredrickson argues that neither "an aristocratic ethos" nor "popular democracy" fully describes the contradictory reality of the Old South. See *Arrogance of Race*, 137. See also J. Mills Thornton III, *Politics and Power in a Slave Society*, xviii, 457. Ford, *Origins of Southern Radicalism*, 112–13; Shade, *Democratizing the Old Dominion*, 16; Carey, *Parties, Slavery, and the Union in Antebellum Georgia*, xv; Watson, *Jacksonian Politics and Community Conflict*, 198–246; Atkins, *Parties, Politics, and the Sectional Conflict in Tennessee*, 11; Kruman, *Parties and Politics in North Carolina*, 107; Inscoe, *Mountain Masters*, 9, 181. William Cooper's *The South and the Politics of Slavery* emphasizes national politics and party consensus on slavery. For a survey of the literature on politics and class, see Watson, "Conflict and Collaboration," 273–98. For a discussion of the issues on a national scale, see Wiebe, *Self-Rule*, 8–9.

6. Eugene Genovese, "Yeoman Farmers in a Slaveholder's Democracy," 10; Genovese, *Roll, Jordan, Roll*, 25–49; Greenberg, *Masters and Statesmen*; Wyatt-Brown, *Southern Honor*, 62–80; Wyatt-Brown, "Andrew Jackson's Honor," 1–36; Johnson, *Toward a Patriarchal Republic*; McCurry, *Masters of Small Worlds*, 242; Cecil-Fronsman, *Common Whites*, 1–8, 82–96; Bolton, *Poor Whites*, 113–38. J. William Harris, in *Plain Folk and Gentry in a Slave Society*, 5, draws from both major streams of interpretation of the slave South. Altschuler and Blumin, "Limits of Engagement in Antebellum America," 855–85; Ashworth, "Agrarians" and "Aristocrats," 24.

7. Kruman, *Parties and Politics in North Carolina*, xi. Social historians have had some notable successes in viewing the Civil War era as a whole, including Escott, *Many Excellent People*; Hahn, *Roots of Southern Populism*; Fields, *Slavery and Freedom on the Middle Ground*; Ayers, *Vengeance and Justice*; Whites, *Civil War as a Crisis in Gender*; Burton, *In My Father's House*.

8. *Speech of the Hon. L. Q. C. Lamar of Mississippi*, 27.

9. Escott, *After Secession*; Donald, "Died of Democracy," 77–91; Current, *Lincoln's Loyalists*; Rable, *Confederate Republic*, esp. 174–94; Beringer et al., *Why the South Lost the Civil War*, 430; Durill, *War of Another Kind*, 41–67; Freehling, "Divided South," 220–54. Gallagher's *The Confederate War* emphasizes Confederate unity and Union might, as does Current, "God and the Strongest Battalions," 15, 30. See also McPherson, "Why Did the Confederacy Lose?," 113–36.

10. Thornton, *Politics and Power in a Slave Society*, 4. Habermas, *Structural Transformation of the Public Sphere*, 175–222; Fraser, "Rethinking the Public Sphere," 109–42.

11. Chambers, *Reasonable Democracy*, 206.

12. Oakes, *Slavery and Freedom*, 93.

13. Ward, *Andrew Jackson*, 3–12; Schlesinger, *Age of Jackson*, x; Watson, *Jacksonian Politics and Community Conflict*, 198–246; Ashworth, "Agrarians" and

"Aristocrats," 47–52, 87–111; Hofstadter, *American Political Tradition and the Men Who Made It*, 59–86; Sellers, *Market Revolution*, 273–82; Watson, *Liberty and Power*, 132–71; Meyers, *Jacksonian Persuasion*, 2–15; Kohl, *Politics of Individualism*, 22–28.

14. William S. Powell to Cordelia Powell Mansfield, July 28, 1853, in John Lipscomb Johnson Papers, SHC; Sharp, *Jacksonians versus the Banks*, 326.

15. Baldwin, *Party Leaders*, 282.

16. Davis, *Jefferson Davis*, 11–12.

17. Ellis, *American Sphinx*, 295.

18. Jefferson in Petersen, *Portable Thomas Jefferson*, 214.

19. Holt, *Rise and Fall of the American Whig Party*, 213–15; Wilson, *Honor's Voice*, 296.

20. "Address at Sanitary Fair, Baltimore, Maryland," in Fehrenbacher, *Speeches and Writings*, 589; "Annual Message to Congress, December 1, 1862," in Fehrenbacher, *Speeches and Writings*, 414–15.

21. Wills, *Lincoln at Gettysburg*, 145.

22. Paludan, *Presidency of Abraham Lincoln*, 228; Neely, *Fate of Liberty*, 218–20; "Response to Serenade," July 7, 1863, in Basler, *Collected Works of Abraham Lincoln*, 319–20.

23. Lincoln, "Gettysburg Address," in Fehrenbacher, *Speeches and Writings*, 536.

24. Foner, *Reconstruction*, 7; Du Bois, *Black Reconstruction in America*, 125–26.

1. JEFFERSON, JACKSON, AND DEMOCRATIC POLITICS

1. Parton, *Andrew Jackson*, 3:282.

2. Brown, *Manhood and Politics*, 179–188. McCurry has discussed the relationship between gender and inequality among white men in the Old South in *Masters of Small Worlds*, 92–129.

3. Brown, "Missouri Crisis, Slavery, and the Politics of Jacksonianism"; Ashworth, *Slavery, Capitalism, and Politics*, 323–50.

4. Petersen, *Jeffersonian Image in the American Mind*.

5. Foner, *Tom Paine and Revolutionary America*, 96; Miller, *Jefferson and Nature*, 27.

6. Thomas Jefferson to John Adams, in Cappon, *Adams-Jefferson Letters*, 2:335. McCoy, *Elusive Republic*, 244–45, and Marx, *Machine in the Garden*, 142–50, discuss Jeffersonian ambivalence about manufactures.

7. Thomas Jefferson, *Notes on the State of Virginia*, in Petersen, *Portable Thomas Jefferson*, 214–15.

8. McCoy, *Elusive Republic*, 240–42; Miller, *Wolf by the Ears*, 38–46; Jordan, *White over Black*, 273, 430–35.

9. Jefferson, *Notes on the State of Virginia*, in Petersen, *Portable Thomas Jefferson*, 216–17.

10. Ellis, *American Sphinx*, 89; Thomas Jefferson to E. Pendleton, August 13, 1776, in Boyd, *Papers of Thomas Jefferson*, 1:442.

11. Thomas Jefferson to Mr. Lithson, January 4, 1805, in Ford, *Writings of Thomas Jefferson*, 11:55.

12. Wilson, *Jefferson's Literary Commonplace Book*, 172–73; Thomas Jefferson to Robert Skipwith, August 3, 1771, in Petersen, *Portable Thomas Jefferson*, 341.

13. Hofstadter, *American Political Tradition*, 48. For an overview of the voluminous literature on republican political thought, see Robert E. Shallhope, "Toward a Republican Synthesis," 49–80; Shallhope, "Republicanism and Early American Historiography," 334–56; Rodgers, "Republicanism," 11–38. McCoy, *Elusive Republic*, 10, describes republicanism as "an ideology in transition." James Oakes explores the historic transformation in "From Republicanism to Liberalism," 551–71. On Jefferson and liberalism, see also Appleby, *Capitalism as a New Social Order*, 50.

14. Randolph, *Domestic Life of Thomas Jefferson*, 229. On the pastoral, see Williams, *Country and the City*, 17; Gray, *Writing the South*, 18–29; Miller, *Jefferson and Nature*, 108–9; Grammer, *Pastoral and Politics in the Old South*, 10–43; Simpson, *Dispossessed Garden*, 32. On the relationship between manhood and debt, see Norton, *Founding Mothers and Fathers*, 210. For a more sympathetic picture of Jefferson's thought, see Mathews, *Radical Politics of Thomas Jefferson*, 43.

15. McCoy, *Elusive Republic*, 227–33; Thomas Jefferson to Benjamin Austin, February 19, 1816, and January 9, 1816, in Ford, *Writings of Thomas Jefferson*, 10:7–11.

16. MacPherson, "Preface to Fingal," 36.

17. Wilson, *Jefferson's Literary Commonplace Book*, 150–51.

18. "Thomas Jefferson's Notes of Proceedings," in Boyd, *Papers of Thomas Jefferson*, 1:315–19.

19. Simpson, *Dispossessed Garden*, 32; Thomas Jefferson to D. Curie, 1787, in Boyd, *Papers of Thomas Jefferson*, 2:683.

20. Thomas Jefferson to John Adams, October 28, 1813, in Cappon, *Adams-Jefferson Letters*, 389; Thomas Jefferson, "Report of the Commissioners for the University of Virginia, August 4, 1818," in Petersen, *Portable Thomas Jefferson*, 334–44.

21. Morgan, *Inventing the People*, 163–74.

22. Sutton, "Nostalgia, Pessimism, and Malaise," 41–42.

23. Burstein, *Sentimental Democracy*, xvii.

24. Tucker, *Valley of the Shenandoah*, 45; Lewis, *Pursuit of Happiness*, 164–68.

25. Breen, *Tobacco Culture*, 9.

26. Thomas Jefferson to Thomas Mann Randolph, February 13, 1792, in Betts, *Farm Book*, 12–13; Thomas Jefferson to John W. Eppes, June 30, 1820, in Betts, *Farm Book*, 45–46.

27. Thomas Jefferson to Philip Mazzei, April 24, 1796, in Ford, *Writings of Thomas Jefferson*, 8:239.

28. Ellis, *American Sphinx*, 89. On Jefferson's managerial efficiency, see Sobel, *World They Made Together*, 58–59; Smith, *Mastered by the Clock*, 240.

29. McLaughlin, *Jefferson and Monticello*, 110–11; Ellis, *American Sphinx*, 140–41; Sutton, "Nostalgia, Pessimism, and Malaise," 41–42; Appleby, "Commercial Farming and the 'Agrarian Myth,'" 844–49; Lewis, *Pursuit of Happiness*, 106–68.

30. Taylor, *Arator*, 316; Taylor, *Inquiry into the Principles and Policy*, 279–304; Shallhope, *John Taylor of Caroline*, 185–89.

31. Benton, *Thirty Years' View*, 1:45.

32. James Madison to James Monroe, September 15, 1793, in Hunt, *Writings of James Madison*, 6:197–98.

33. Smith, *Wealth of Nations*, 439–41.

34. Taylor, *Inquiry into the Principles and Policy*, 157–58; Lenner, "John Taylor and the Origins of American Federalism."

35. Sellers, *Market Revolution*, 164–67; Greene, *Constitutional Development in the South Atlantic States*, 942; Greene, "Democracy in the Old South."

36. Morgan, *Inventing the People*, 148; Cash, *Mind of the South*, 21–22.

37. Upshur, "Mr. Jefferson"; Petersen, *Jeffersonian Image in the American Mind*, 68–76.

38. Adams, *John Randolph*, 43.

39. Thomas Jefferson to John Adams, October 28, 1813, in Cappon, *Adams-Jefferson Letters*, 2:389; Cash, *Mind of the South*, 61–66, 70–81.

40. The shift between Jeffersonian and Jacksonian politics is effectively described in Wiebe, *Opening of American Society*, 143–67.

41. On honor, leadership, and masculinity, see Wyatt-Brown, *Southern Honor*, 62–80.

42. Abernethy, *From Frontier to Plantation in Tennessee*, 123; Wyatt-Brown, "Andrew Jackson's Honor," 1.

43. Kann, *Republic of Men*, 150.

44. Oakes, *Ruling Race*, 57–65; Sellers, *Market Revolution*, 47; Tocqueville, *Democracy in America*, 263. On the development of market relations in the West, see Dunaway, *First American Frontier*.

45. Tocqueville, *Democracy in America*, 273–78.

46. Ward, *Andrew Jackson*, 3–10; *Richmond Enquirer*, March 1, 1815; George Troup in *National Intelligencer*, February 16, 1815.

47. Andrew Jackson in *National Intelligencer*, March 17, 1815; Andrew Jackson to Secretary of War James Monroe, January 9, 1815, Bassett, *Correspondence of Andrew Jackson*, 2:137; *National Intelligencer*, February 6, 1815.

48. "Address from the City Battalion of Uniform Companies to Major

General Jackson," Camp Jackson, March 16, 1815, in *National Intelligencer*, April 24, 1815.

49. General John Coffee in *Richmond Enquirer*, January 28, 1815.

50. Andrew Jackson in Bassett, *Correspondence of Andrew Jackson*, 2:195; Thomas Jefferson quoted in Remini, *Andrew Jackson and the Course of American Empire*, 109.

51. McHenry, *Jackson Wreath*; John Henry Eaton to Rachel Jackson, February 8, 1824, in Moser, Hoth, and Hoesmann, *Papers of Andrew Jackson*, 5:353; Eaton, *Letters of Wyoming*, 103; Andrew Jackson to Andrew Jackson Donelson, November 21, 1819, in Bassett, *Correspondence of Andrew Jackson*, 2:441.

52. Reid and Eaton, *Life of Andrew Jackson*, 12.

53. Fliegelman, *Prodigals and Pilgrims*. Several historians have explored the psychological roots of Jackson's will to power. See Sellers, *Market Revolution*, 176; Killen, *Manhood in America*, 35; and Rogin, *Fathers and Children*, 46–74.

54. *Memoirs of General Andrew Jackson*, 20; Goodwin, *Biography of Andrew Jackson*, 4; McHenry, *Jackson Wreath*, 11; *A History of the Life and Public Services of Major General Andrew Jackson*, 2–3; "McCallister's Eulogy," in Dusenbery, *Monument to the Memory of Andrew Jackson*, 121; *Political Mirror or Review of Jacksonism*, 47.

55. Reid and Eaton, *Life of Andrew Jackson*, 142–43.

56. *Political Mirror*, 69; Reid and Eaton, *Life of Andrew Jackson*, 143.

57. On paternalism see Genovese, *Roll, Jordan, Roll*, 3–7.

58. Hugh A. Garland, Petersburg, Virginia, July 12, 1845, in Dusenbery, *Monument to the Memory of Andrew Jackson*, 147.

59. Remini, *Andrew Jackson and the Course of American Empire*, 364.

60. *Speech of Hon. Henry Clay in the House of Representatives*, 27–30; Martineau, *Society in America*, 1:8; Joseph Story to S. P. Fay, February 18, 1834, cited in Schlesinger, *Age of Jackson*, 11.

61. Garland, in Dusenbery, *Monument to the Memory of Andrew Jackson*, 188–89.

62. Andrew Jackson, "First Inaugural Address," in Richardson, *Messages and Papers of the Presidents*, 1001; Remini, *Andrew Jackson and the Course of American Empire*, 311; Reid and Eaton, *Life of Andrew Jackson*, 381.

63. Adams, *Memoirs of John Quincy Adams*, 7:274.

64. Andrew Jackson to Samuel Swarthout, March 4, 1824, in Bassett, *Correspondence of Andrew Jackson*, 3:233–34; Prentice, *Biography of Henry Clay*, 216.

65. Remini, *Andrew Jackson and the Course of American Empire*, 7.

66. Goldsmith, *Vicar of Wakefield*, 3, 12.

67. Ibid., 12, 14; Dykstal, "Story of O," 330.

68. Nelson, *National Manhood*, 76.

69. Andrew Jackson to Andrew Jackson Donelson, February 24, 1817, in Bassett, *Correspondence of Andrew Jackson*, 2:274; Andrew Jackson to Ezra Stiles, March 23, 1829, in Parton, *Andrew Jackson*, 3:188–89.

70. "History of the Life and Public Services of Major General Andrew Jackson" (1828), in McHenry, *Jackson Wreath*, 13.

71. Ashworth, *Slavery, Capitalism, and Politics*, 220–40.

72. Remini, *Andrew Jackson and the Course of American Freedom*, 203–5; Petersen, *Great Triumvirate*, 183; Basch, "Marriage, Morals, and Politics," 890–918.

73. Marszalek, *Petticoat Affair*; Wood, "'One Woman So Dangerous To Public Morals,'" 237–75.

74. Andrew Jackson to John Calhoun, May 30, 1830, in Wilson, *Papers of John C. Calhoun*, 11:192–93; *Washington Globe*, February 19, 1831.

75. John Calhoun to Andrew Jackson, May 29, 1830, in Wilson, *Papers of John C. Calhoun*, 11:173–76.

76. Andrew Jackson to John Calhoun, July 19, 1830, in Bassett, *Correspondence of Andrew Jackson*, 4:162–63.

77. Eaton, *Autobiography of Peggy Eaton*, 87–88.

78. C. G. Memminger, quoted in Jenkins, *Pro-Slavery Thought in the Old South*, 210; Fox-Genovese, *Within the Plantation Household*, 38; Taylor, *Cavalier and Yankee*, 145–51; Wyatt-Brown, *Southern Honor*, 199–225.

79. Freehling, *Prelude to Civil War*, 128; John Calhoun, "Reply to John Eaton's Address, October 19, 1831," in Wilson, *Papers of John C. Calhoun*, 11:474–75.

80. On politics and sociability, see Isaac, *Transformation of Virginia*; Marszelak, *Petticoat Affair*, 114; Gienapp, "'Politics Seems to Enter into Everything,'" 15–69.

81. Goldsmith, *Vicar of Wakefield*, 28; Andrew Jackson to John C. McLemore, April 5, 1829, Bassett, *Correspondence of Andrew Jackson*, 4:20–21.

82. Remini, *Andrew Jackson and the Course of American Freedom*, 209.

83. A. J. Donelson to Andrew Jackson, June 10, 1830, Bassett, *Correspondence of Andrew Jackson*, 4:145; "Memorandum, September 1831," Bassett, *Correspondence of Andrew Jackson*, 4:343; J. G. Harris, "Eulogy Delivered at Charlotte, Tennessee, July 17, 1845," in Dusenbery, *Monument to the Memory of Andrew Jackson*, 329; Wiebe, *Self-Rule*, 73.

84. Parton, *Andrew Jackson*, 3:287.

85. *Washington Globe*, March 16, 1831.

86. Eaton, *Autobiography of Peggy Eaton*, 147, 44–45.

87. Andrew Jackson to Joel R. Poinsett, January 24, 1833, Bassett, *Correspondence of Andrew Jackson*, 5:11.

88. Greenberg, "Representation and the Isolation of South Carolina," 723–43; McCurry, *Masters of Small Worlds*, 248–49; Freehling, *Road to Disunion*, 268–368.

89. Andrew Jackson, Second Inaugural Address, March 1, 1833, in Bassett,

Correspondence of Andrew Jackson, 5:27; Andrew Jackson to Brigadier General John Coffee, March 16, 1833, in Bassett, *Correspondence of Andrew Jackson*, 5:30.

90. Andrew Jackson to Reverend Andrew J. Crawford, May 1, 1833, in Bassett, *Correspondence of Andrew Jackson*, 5:71.

91. *United States Telegraph*, December 11, 1830; James K. Polk, "To a Philadelphia Committee," April 10, 1834, in Weaver, *Correspondence of James K. Polk*, 2:381.

92. Remini, *Andrew Jackson and the Bank War*, 177.

93. Roger B. Taney to Andrew Jackson, March 1833, in Bassett, *Correspondence of Andrew Jackson*, 5:37; Amos Kendall to Jackson, March 20, 1833, in Bassett, *Correspondence of Andrew Jackson*, 5:43–44.

94. McCurry, *Masters of Small Worlds*, 85–91; Watson, *Jacksonian Politics and Community Conflict*, 14–15.

95. Baldwin, *Flush Times*, 72; Martin Van Buren in Rogin, *Fathers and Children*, 290–91; Thomas Hart Benton, "Speech in the United States Senate, July 13, 1832," in Benton, *Thirty Years' View*, 1:262.

96. Jenkins, *Life and Public Services of Gen. Andrew Jackson*, 179; Archibald Yell to James K. Polk, January 16, 1833, Weaver, *Correspondence of James K. Polk*, 2:27; "Resolutions Adopted at a Public Meeting, July 16, 1832," *Niles' Weekly Register*, July 21, 1832.

97. Gordon, *War on the Bank of the United States*, 13; P. P. Barbour in Goodwin, *Biography of Andrew Jackson*, 358.

98. Andrew Jackson to Rev. Hardy M. Cryer, April 7, 1833, in Bassett, *Correspondence of Andrew Jackson*, 5:53.

99. Fredrickson, *Black Image in the White Mind*, 26–27; Ashworth, "Agrarians" and "Aristocrats," 223; Dew, *Review of the Debate*, reprinted in *The Pro-Slavery Argument* (Charleston, 1851), 287–490.

100. *Washington Globe*, June 12, 1831; *Washington Globe*, July 23, 1831.

101. Wyatt-Brown, "Andrew Jackson's Honor," 36.

102. Henry Clay to Daniel Webster, April 29, 1830, in Wiltse, *Papers of Daniel Webster*, 3:63; Nicholas Biddle to Henry Clay, August 1, 1832, in McGrane, *Correspondence of Nicholas Biddle*, 196.

103. Frost, *Pictorial Life of Andrew Jackson*, 537–38; Daniel Webster in Wiltse, *Papers of Daniel Webster*, 1:528.

104. Andrew Jackson, "Farewell Address," Richardson, *Messages and Papers of the Presidents*, 1515.

105. Andrew Jackson to Francis P. Blair, April 19, 1841, in Bassett, *Correspondence of Andrew Jackson*, 6:105.

106. Andrew Jackson to Andrew Jackson Jr., December 31, 1839; Andrew Jackson to Mrs. Sarah Jackson, January 4, 1840; Andrew Jackson to Francis P. Blair, February 29, 1844, in Bassett, *Correspondence of Andrew Jackson*, 6:46–47, 267.

107. Varron, "Tippecanoe and the Ladies, Too," 492–521.

108. Andrew Jackson to Francis P. Blair, April 9, 1840, in Bassett, *Correspondence of Andrew Jackson*, 6:57.

2. THE APPROACHING STORM

1. Woodward, *Mary Chesnut's Civil War*, 204–5. The complexity of this account is highlighted by sharply divergent readings of it provided by two leading historians of antebellum South Carolina. See Ford, *Origins of Southern Radicalism*, 372–73; McCurry, *Masters of Small Words*, 128–29.

2. Olmsted, *Journey to the Seaboard Slave States*, 84; Wilson, *Patriotic Gore*, 219–30; Olmsted, *Cotton Kingdom*, 86.

3. Oakes, *Slavery and Freedom*, 120.

4. Baldwin, *Party Leaders*, 278.

5. Meyers, *Jacksonian Persuasion*, 121–41; Hofstadter, *American Political Tradition*, 57–87; Hartz, *Liberal Tradition in America*, 89–96.

6. Watson, *Jacksonian Politics and Community Conflict*, 321; Thornton, *Politics and Power in a Slave Society*, 267–99; Ford, *Origins of Southern Radicalism*, 310–70; Kruman, *Parties and Politics in North Carolina*, 55.

7. Tocqueville, *Democracy in America*, 636.

8. McCurry, "Two Faces of Republicanism," 1245–64.

9. Daniel Martin to Clement Claiborne Clay, January 1857, in Clay Family Papers, UGA.

10. Watson, *Jacksonian Politics and Community Conflict*, 14; Wright, *Political Economy of the Cotton South*, 62–74.

11. Speech of John Wilson Cunningham of North Carolina, June 11, 1856, in John Wilson Cunningham Papers, SHC.

12. Sellers, "Who Were the Southern Whigs?," 335–46; Watson, "Conflict and Collaboration," 293.

13. Jefferson Buford in *Montgomery Advertiser*, January 2, 1856.

14. Ephraim Foster, speech at Courtland, Alabama, December 24, 1860, in *Huntsville Southern Advocate*, January 16, 1861.

15. Hon. J. D. Ashmore of South Carolina, March 1, 1860, in *Charleston Mercury*, March 7, 1860.

16. Patterson, *Slavery and Social Death*, 34.

17. William Lowndes Yancey, MS (n.p., n.d.) Yancey file, ADAH, 6, 3; *Address of William C. Harris before the Mississippi Senate*, 35.

18. Foner, *Free Soil*, 17; Genovese, *Political Economy of Slavery*, 247–64; Morrison, *Slavery and the American West*, 276.

19. Hon. John J. McRae, quoted in *Jackson Weekly Mississippian*, July 4, 1859.

20. Thornton, *Politics and Power in a Slave Society*, xx; Genovese, *Slaveholders'*

Dilemma, 10–45. For the attempts of a proslavery southerner to reconcile slavery and progress, see Ambrose, *Henry Hughes and Proslavery Thought*, 5.

21. On the prewar "modernization crisis," see William L. Barney, "Towards the Civil War: The Dynamics of Change in a Civil War County," in Burton and McMath, *Class, Conflict, and Consensus*, 148.

22. *Mobile Daily Register*, March 22, 1859.

23. *North Carolina Standard*, January 11, 1854.

24. *Montgomery Advertiser*, August 6, 1858; *Mobile Daily Register*, March 31, 1859; J. L. M. Curry, February 24, 1859, Appendix to *Congressional Globe*, 35th Cong., 2d sess., 270.

25. Thomas L. Clingman, "Speech in the House, April 4, 1854," in *North Carolina Standard*, April 26, 1854.

26. *Mobile Daily Register*, March 1, 1859; William Greene to Alabama Governor John Winston, March 22, 1857, Winston Correspondence, ADAH; *North Carolina Standard*, January 18, 1854.

27. *Mobile Daily Register*, March 1, 1859; William Greene to Alabama governor John Winston, March 22, 1857, Winston Correspondence, ADAH; J. L. M. Curry to Clement Claiborne Clay, July 18, 1854, Clay Family Papers, UGA.

28. Alabama governor John Winston to William Greene, March 22, 1857, Winston Correspondence, ADAH; *Montgomery Advertiser*, February 20, 1856; Hon. William Porcher Miles, quoted in *Charleston Mercury*, February 25, 1860.

29. Col. John B. Walker, Democratic Convention President, *Milledgeville Southern Recorder*, June 21, 1859.

30. Kruman, *Parties and Politics in North Carolina*, 55, 140; Thornton, *Politics and Power in a Slave Society*, xxix, 268; Ford, *Origins of Southern Radicalism*, 308–37; Genovese, *Slaveholders' Dilemma*, 13. Fogel, *Without Consent or Contract*, 94–101.

31. Hahn, *Roots of Southern Populism*, 36; Alexander Stephens, February 12, 1859, in Cleveland, *Alexander Stephens in Public and Private*, 118; Howe, *Political Culture of the American Whigs*, 248–49.

32. "Address of Thomas J. Hudson at the Agricultural Fair," reprinted in *Journal of the Mississippi Senate* (Jackson, 1858), 57.

33. Governor John W. Ellis, November 20, 1860, in *Raleigh Weekly State Journal*, November 28, 1860.

34. Hofstadter, *Idea of a Party System*, 248.

35. *Tuskegee True Union* in *Montgomery Advertiser*, May 6, 1857; P. H. Bingham to Senator Clement Claiborne Clay, June 1, 1857, Clay Family Papers, UGA; S. Baughton to Howell Cobb, October 30, 1855, Howell Cobb Papers, UGA; *Mobile Daily Register*, April 28, 1855.

36. Oakes, *Ruling Race*, 69–95; Genovese, *Political Economy of Slavery*, 251–74; Barney, *Secessionist Impulse*, 61–76.

37. Potter, *Impending Crisis*, esp. 328; W. B. Davis to Governor John J. Pettus, November 23, 1859, Pettus Papers, MDAH; John Forsythe to Stephen A. Douglas, December 28, 1860; Stephen Douglas Papers, UC.

38. *De Bow's Review* 24:573, in Wender, *Southern Commercial Conventions*, 207; McCardell, *Idea of a Southern Nation*, 91–140.

39. *Sumter Democrat* in *Mobile Daily Register*, August 30, 1855; *Huntsville Southern Advocate*, December 28, 1860.

40. John Hays to Clement Claiborne Clay, June 1, 1857, in Clay Family Papers, UGA.

41. R. M. Hatton to Clement Claiborne Clay, June 5, 1857, in Clay Family Papers, UGA.

42. On Winston, see Thornton, *Politics and Power in a Slave Society*, 322–40. See also Parks, *Joseph E. Brown of Georgia*, 83; Harris, *William Woods Holden*; McKitrick, *Andrew Johnson and Reconstruction*, 87.

43. *Montgomery Advertiser*, May 6, 1857; *Montgomery Advertiser*, August 26, 1857.

44. Thornton, *Politics and Power in a Slave Society*, 327–41; Hahn, *Roots of Southern Populism*, 36–37; Kruman, *Parties and Politics in North Carolina*, 140.

45. A. E. Psabre, Asst. Superintendent New Orleans and Ohio Telegraph Company, to John Winston, March 9, 1855, in Gov. John Winston Papers, ADAH. On the telegraph, see Rodriquez, "Wired to the World," 137–55.

46. A. B. Moore, "Second Inaugural Address, November 4, 1859," in *Montgomery Advertiser*, November 15, 1859; "Progress, with Safety," *Montgomery Advertiser*, January 30, 1856.

47. De Bow, *Interest in Slavery*, 6, 9.

48. *Address of the Hon. William C. Harris before the Mississippi Senate*, 533; "James Barbour in Virginia House of Delegates, February 16, 1860," *Richmond Enquirer*, February 28, 1860.

49. Butts, "'Irrepressible Conflict,'" 44–61; Jeffrey, *State Parties and National Politics*, 268–70; Escott, *Many Excellent People*, 67–71.

50. Jefferson Davis, "Speech at Jackson, November 4, 1857," in Crist, *Papers of Jefferson Davis*, 6:282.

51. *Edgefield Advertiser*, January 18, 1860; *Address of the Hon. William C. Harris before the Mississippi Senate*, 531.

52. McMichael, "Slavery in Capitalism," 334; Shore, *Southern Capitalists*, 55, 77; Harrold, *Abolitionists and the South*, 152.

53. Jeremiah Morton of Orange in Virginia State Convention, February 28, 1861, in *Richmond Enquirer*, March 21, 1861; Governor Henry Wise in *Richmond Enquirer*, January 8, 1861; "C. G. Memminger before the Assembled Authorities of the State of Virginia, January 16, 1860," *Charleston Mercury*, February 6, 1860; Johnson, *Toward a Patriarchal Republic*, 83–101; Curry, *Perils and Duties of the South*. On nonslaveholders and Republican patronage, see Bolton, *Poor Whites*, 140.

54. T. R. R. Cobb, "Thomas R. R. Cobb's Secessionist Speech, Monday Evening, November 12," in Freehling and Simpson, *Secession Debated*, 30; De Bow, *Industrial Resources*, 2:196; Watson, "Conflict and Collaboration," 274.

55. James W. Gillock, in Dyer and Moore, *Tennessee Civil War Veterans Questionnaires*, 1:42; William Landon Baab and John Wilson Barnett, in Dyer and Moore, *Tennessee Civil War Veterans Questionnaires*, 1:8, 1:10; Bailey, "Class and Tennessee's Confederate Generation," 31–60.

56. On slave ownership, prices, and stratification, see Wright, *Political Economy of the Cotton South*, 34–37, 42; Hahn, *Roots of Southern Radicalism*, 36, 40, 46–47.

57. Leonidas Spratt, *Resolutions on the Slave Trade* (n.p., 1858), 12, Curry Pamphlet Collection, ADAH; Takaki, *A Pro-Slavery Crusade*, 66; J. D. B. De Bow in Cole, *Irrepressible Conflict*, 74–75; J. D. B. De Bow to William L. Yancey, in *Weekly Mississippian*, July 27, 1859; "Jefferson Davis in U.S. Senate, March 25, 1859," in Rowland, *Jefferson Davis, Constitutionalist*, 4:49.

58. Clay, *Life of Cassius Marcellus Clay*, 192; "Cassius Clay, Speech at Lexington, 1855," Parsons, *Inside View of Slavery*, 293; Clay, *Life of Cassius Marcellus Clay*, 507.

59. Hinton Rowan Helper, *The Impending Crisis of the South*, in Wish, *Antebellum*, 201; Horace Greeley quoted in Foner, *Free Soil*, 42.

60. Bailey, *Hinton Rowan Helper*, 80–81; Crenshaw, "Speakership Contest of 1859–60," 323–38.

61. Genovese, *Southern Front*, 31–41; Genovese, *World the Slaveholders Made*, 118–244; Faust, *Ideology of Slavery*, 1–20; Ambrose, *Henry Hughes and Proslavery Thought*, 183.

62. Genovese, *World the Slaveholders Made*, 128–29; William Lowndes Yancey in Wender, *Southern Commercial Conventions*, 218.

63. William Lowndes Yancey in *Huntsville Southern Advertiser*, January 30, 1861.

64. J. L. M. Curry to Howell Cobb, October 18, 1860, Cobb Papers, UGA; Scarborough, *Diary of Edmund Ruffin*, 1:576.

65. T. R. R. Cobb, in Freehling and Simpson, *Secession Debated*, 30.

66. L. W. Spratt, *The Philosophy of Secession, a Southern View*, broadside in Boston Atheneum Pamphlet Collection; Dennis Hart Mahan to James D. Davidson in Greenawalt, "Unionists in Rockbridge County," 83; A. P. Aldrich to James Henry Hammond, November 25, 1860, in James Henry Hammond Papers, LC, copy at SCL.

67. "Resolutions of Public Meeting of January 9, 1861," *Huntsville Southern Advocate*, January 16, 1861; "Andrew Jackson," in *Huntsville Southern Advertiser*, January 30, 1861; *Public Meeting of Mechanics and Workingmen in Winchester, Virginia, January 9, 1861*, broadside, n.p. in Douglas Papers, UC.

68. James M. Jones, Corinth, Mississippi, to Andrew Johnson, December 29, 1860, Graf and Haskins, *Papers of Andrew Johnson*, 4:99.

69. Mr. Willey in Virginia State Convention, February 21, 1861, *Richmond*

Enquirer, February 22, 1861; "The Ballot Box," *Raleigh Weekly Standard*, August 15, 1860.

70. Fields, *Slavery and Freedom*, 90–91; Klein, *Days of Defiance*, 213–30. For an account emphasizing the strength of upper South Unionism, see Crofts, *Reluctant Confederates*.

71. Gov. William H. Gist to Gov. John J. Pettus, November 6, 1860, MDAH.

72. Gienapp, "Political System," 121; Potter, *Impending Crisis*, 498–501; Shugg, *Origins of Class Struggle in Louisiana*, 157–70; Freehling, "Divided South," 167; Wooster, *Secession Conventions of the South*, 265; McCurry, *Masters of Small Worlds*, 294–97; Eaton, "Mob Violence in the Old South," 351–70; Nevins, *Ordeal of the Union*, 328.

3. THE "SELF-ANALYSIS" OF JOHN C. RUTHERFOORD

1. "Resolutions offered at Goochland Court House, August 20, 1866 upon the death of J. C. Rutherfoord," Rutherfoord Papers, VHS.

2. Report of Col. Charles L. Fitzhugh, Sixth New York Cavalry, March 19, 1865; OR, ser. 1, vol. 46, 496–98.

3. "Resolutions offered at Goochland," Rutherfoord Papers, VHS.

4. John C. Rutherfoord Diary, October 17, 1858, Rutherfoord Papers, VHS.

5. McCurry, *Masters of Small Worlds*, 47, 235–38; Faust, *James Henry Hammond*, 188.

6. Fredrickson, *Black Image in the White Mind*, 61–68; Shade, *Democratizing the Old Dominion*; Thornton, *Politics and Power in a Slave Society*, xviii.

7. John C. Rutherfoord Diary, October 17, 1858, Rutherfoord Papers, VHS.

8. Slaveholders controlled 63 percent of the seats in the House of Delegates in 1860, while they made up roughly 20 percent of the population. Wallenstein, "Incendiaries All," 154.

9. Larkin Smith to Littleton Waller Tazewell, August 17, 1804, Tazewell Papers, in Lewis, *Pursuit of Happiness*, 121.

10. Taylor, *Arator*, 68; Sutton, "Nostalgia, Pessimism, and Malaise," 41–42; Smith, *Inside the Great House*, 50–54. On planter consumption and increasing debt in eighteenth-century Virginia, see Breen, *Tobacco Culture*, xi–xiv.

11. Sellers, *Market Revolution*, 237; Appleby, "Commercial Farming and the 'Agrarian Myth.'"

12. Lewis, *Pursuit of Happiness*, 164; Oakes, *Slavery and Freedom*, 40–80; William T. Sutherlin in Siegal, *Roots of Southern Distinctiveness*, 144.

13. Edmund Ruffin in Olmsted, *Cotton Kingdom*, 536.

14. McCurry, *Masters of Small Worlds*, 59–61; Taylor, *Arator*, 316, 122.

15. William L. Yancey, misc. material found by John DuBose, n.d., ADAH; Ephraim

Foster, speech at Courtland, Alabama, December 24, 1860, in *Huntsville Southern Advocate*, January 16, 1861; Hodgson, *Science the Handmaid of Republicanism*; Curry Pamphlets, ADAH; Habermas, *Structural Transformation of the Public Sphere*, 3. On the relationship between yeoman independence and planter power, see McCurry, *Masters of Small Worlds*, 92–129.

16. Rutherfoord, *Autobiography of Thomas Rutherfoord*, i–iii.

17. Ibid., 10–11, 20, 32, 38, 48–51, 52–61, 63.

18. Ibid., 60–63.

19. Lewis, *Pursuit of Happiness*, 155; Taylor, *Arator*; Burstein, *Inner Jefferson*, 280; Oakes, *Ruling Race*, 57; McCoy, *Elusive Republic*, 259.

20. Thomas Jefferson to John Adams, October 28, 1813, in Cappon, *Adams-Jefferson Letters*, 388.

21. John C. Rutherfoord Diary, 1861–63, n.p., Rutherfoord Papers, VHS; Page, *Social Life in Old Virginia*, 80, 45.

22. Jefferson to J. C. Cabell, January 24, 1816, in Cabell, *Early History of the University of Virginia*, 48; Thomas Jefferson to William Wirt, August 15, 1815, quoted in Gray, *Writing the South*, 19.

23. Thomas Jefferson, *Notes on the State of Virginia*, in Petersen, *Portable Thomas Jefferson*, 215; Thomas Jefferson, "Report of the Commissioners for the University of Virginia, August 4, 1818," in Petersen, *Portable Thomas Jefferson*, 332.

24. Matthew Singleton to Richard Singleton, September 11, 1836, in Wyatt-Brown, *Southern Honor*, 279.

25. John C. Rutherfoord, Commonplace Book, 1844–46, p. 56 (n.d.), Rutherfoord Papers, VHS; John C. Rutherfoord Diary, October 17, 1858; John C. Rutherfoord Commonplace Book, 1852–56, July 10, 1852; Rutherfoord Papers, VHS.

26. Rutherfoord, *Oration Delivered before the Jefferson Society*, 8, 6.

27. John C. Rutherfoord speech, c. 1846, Rutherfoord Papers, VHS; Ashworth, *Slavery, Capitalism, and Politics*, 1:205–10.

28. John C. Rutherfoord Diary, January 1, 1847; John C. Rutherfoord Commonplace Book, 1848, Rutherfoord Papers, VHS.

29. "Speech Against the Revolutionary Movement of the Anti-Slavery Party, Delivered in the Senate of the United States," January 16, 1860, in *Speeches and Writings of the Hon. Thomas L. Clingman*, 458; *Address of the Southern Rights Association*.

30. Hundley, *Social Relations in Our Southern States*, 43, 30, 49.

31. *Richmond Enquirer*, February 17, 1860; Genovese, *Slaveholders' Dilemma*, 1–10.

32. Hundley, *Social Relations in Our Southern States*, 49.

33. Thomas Rutherfoord to J. R. Callender, May 1, 1851, Rutherfoord Papers, VHS.

34. "Rock-Castle," typescript, 1922, Nannie Rutherfoord Johnson, Rutherfoord Papers, VHS.
35. John C. Rutherfoord, October 17, 1858; Rutherfoord Papers, VHS.
36. John C. Rutherfoord Diary, April 23, 1861, Rutherfoord Papers, VHS.
37. Ibid., January 1, 1862.
38. John S. Wise, R. L. Dabney, quoted in Genovese, *Roll, Jordan, Roll*, 75, 80.
39. John Rutherfoord, "miscellany," no date, Rutherfoord Papers, VHS; John C. Rutherfoord, October 17, 1858, Rutherfoord Papers, VHS.
40. John C. Rutherfoord, Commonplace Book, 1852–60, n.d., p. 7, Rutherfoord Papers, VHS.
41. John C. Rutherfoord, "Miscellany," n.d.; John C. Rutherfoord Commonplace Book, 1852–56, n.d., p. 5; John C. Rutherfoord Diary, October 17, 1856, Rutherfoord Papers, VHS.
42. John C. Rutherfoord Diary, October 17, 1858, Rutherfoord Papers, VHS.
43. Greenberg, *Masters and Statesmen*, viii–ix; Kojeve, "Introduction to the Reading of Hegel," 111.
44. John Keane, quoted in Eley, "Nations, Publics, and Political Cultures," and Ryan, "Gender and Public Access," 310; Stevenson, *Life in Black and White*, 84.
45. *Speech of John C. Rutherfoord*, 3, 7; Rutherfoord, *Speech on the Banking Policy*, 15, 33.
46. Rutherfoord, *John C. Rutherfoord of Goochland in the House of Delegates*, 11.
47. Rutherfoord, *Speech on the Banking Policy*, 16.
48. Oakes, *Slavery and Freedom*, 80.
49. Ashworth, *"Agrarians" and "Aristocrats,"* v.
50. John C. Rutherfoord Commonplace Book, 1856, p. 9, Rutherfoord Papers, VHS.
51. Thornton, *Politics and Power in a Slave Society*, 291–301.
52. Genovese, *Slaveholders' Dilemma*, 13.
53. Anne C. Rutherfoord to Aunt Sarah Alexander Bruce, June 11, 1856; John C. Rutherfoord, undated entry, Commonplace Book, November 7, 1859–May 28, 1861, Rutherfoord Papers, VHS.
54. Rutherfoord, *Speech on the Banking Policy*, 1.
55. Buckle, *History of Civilization in England*, 1:602, 668–69.
56. John C. Rutherfoord to Thomas H. Ellis, June 20, 1855, Rutherfoord Papers, VHS; William Cook to John Rutherfoord, August 7, 1855, Rutherfoord Family Papers, Perkin Collection, DUL.
57. Henry Wise, May 26, 1854, in Wise Papers, SHC; William Cook to John Rutherfoord, August 7, 1855, Rutherfoord Family Papers, Perkin Collection, DUL; John C. Rutherfoord to John Rutherfoord, May 18, 1855, Rutherfoord Family Papers, Perkin Collection, DUL.

58. John C. Rutherfoord, Commonplace Book, 1848; John Rutherfoord to Thomas H. Ellis, June 20, 1855, Rutherfoord Papers, VHS.

59. John C. Rutherfoord Diary, 1854–58, n.p.; John C. Rutherfoord Diary, October 17, 1858, VHS.

60. Brown, *Manhood and Politics*, 71–126.

61. John C. Rutherfoord Diary, January 9, 1858, Rutherfoord Papers, VHS.

62. Dodd, *Statesmen of the Old South*.

63. John C. Rutherfoord quoted in Wallenstein, "Incendiaries All," 154. On sectional tensions on slavery within the Democratic Party, see Link, "Jordan Hatcher Case," 636.

64. *John C. Rutherfoord of Goochland in the House of Delegates*, 16.

65. John C. Rutherfoord Diary, November 19, 1860, Rutherfoord Papers, VHS; *John C. Rutherfoord of Goochland in the House of Delegates*, 24; Rutherfoord Diary, November 19, 1860, Rutherfoord Papers, VHS. On key leaders during secession, see Shanks, *Secessionist Movement in Virginia*, 142; Simpson, *Good Southerner*, 219–51; Boney, *John Letcher of Virginia*, 91–113.

66. John C. Rutherfoord Diary, November 19, 1860, Rutherfoord Papers, VHS.

67. Shanks, "Conservative Constitutional Tendencies," 200–202.

68. John C. Rutherfoord Diary, April 15, 1861, Rutherfoord Papers, VHS.

69. *Charleston Mercury*, April 1, 1861.

70. John C. Rutherfoord Diary, April 15, 1861; June 11, 1861, Rutherfoord Papers, VHS.

71. Mr. Fisher in Virginia State Convention, November 30, 1861, in *Richmond Enquirer*, December 3, 1861; Mr. Gannett in Virginia State Convention, December 4, 1861, in *Richmond Enquirer*, February 25, 1862.

72. John C. Rutherfoord Diary, April 15, 1861, Rutherfoord Papers, VHS; Shanks, "Conservative Constitutional Tendencies," 28–48.

73. Reese, *Proceedings of the Virginia State Convention*, 2:66, 15, 137, 358.

74. John C. Rutherfoord Diary, February 22, 1862, Rutherfoord Papers, VHS.

75. Jefferson Davis, "Farewell Address to U.S. Senate," in Crist, *Papers of Jefferson Davis*, 20; Jefferson Davis, "Inaugural Address," in Rowland, *Jefferson Davis, Constitutionalist*, 6:200–202.

76. Dodd, *Statesmen of the Old South*, 262.

77. Jefferson Davis to Confederate Congress, November 18, 1861, in Rowland, *Jefferson Davis, Constitutionalist*, 5:170; Jefferson Davis to Army of Tennessee, October 14, 1863, in Rowland, *Jefferson Davis, Constitutionalist*, 61.

78. Mitchell, *Vacant Chair*, 3–19; Mitchell, "Soldiering, Manhood, and Coming of Age," 43–45.

79. John C. Rutherfoord Diary, April 23, 27, 25, 1861, Rutherfoord Papers, VHS.

80. Ibid., April 27, July 25, 1861.

81. Ibid., January 30, 1862, February 22, 1862.

82. John C. Rutherfoord, "miscellany," n.d.; John C. Rutherfoord, letter c. 1862; John C. Rutherfoord Diary, November 26, 1865, 68, Rutherfoord Papers, VHS.

83. Edmund Ruffin, June 17, 1865, Scarborough, *Diary of Edmund Ruffin*, 3:723.

84. John C. Rutherfoord Diary, June 9, 1866, Rutherfoord Papers, VHS.

85. William Hauchins to John C. Rutherfoord, c. 1855, Rutherfoord Papers, VHS.

86. Thornton, *Politics and Power in a Slave Society*, xviii; Shade, *Democratizing the Old Dominion*, 281–91; Shanks, "Conservative Constitutional Tendencies," 128–48. My formulation draws on Eugene Genovese's discussion of James Henry Hammond in *Slaveholders' Dilemma*, 99.

4. AN AMBIGUOUS DEMOCRAT

1. J. Henley Smith to Alexander Stephens, June 21, 1862, in Alexander Stephens Papers, LC, copy at UGA. For a harsh indictment of Brown as "vacillating," see Davis, "Government of Our Own," 54–71, 131.

2. Phillips, *Georgia and States' Rights*, 182; Joseph Brown to Dr. Lewis, December 9, 1857, Hargrett Collection, UGA.

3. Parks, *Joseph E. Brown of Georgia*, 4–9.

4. Howe, *Political Culture of the American Whigs*, 248.

5. Robert Toombs to John J. Crittenden, April 4, 1856, quoted in Cooper, *South and the Politics of Slavery*, 279.

6. John B. Lamar to Howell Cobb, February 7, 1860, in Howell Cobb Papers, UGA.

7. A. E. Cochran to Howell Cobb, June 3, 1855, in Cobb Papers, UGA.

8. John C. Rutherfoord to John Rutherfoord, May 18, 1855, in Rutherfoord Family Papers, Perkin Collection, DUL. On the Know-Nothings and antislavery, see Anbinder, *Nativism and Slavery*.

9. Robert Toombs to Thomas W. Thomas, July 31, 1856, in Clay Family Papers, UGA; Herschel V. Johnson to John T. Smith et al. June 8, 1855, in Herschel V. Johnson Papers, Perkin Collection, DUL; Robert Toombs to T. Lomax, June 6, 1855, in Phillips, *Correspondence*, 352.

10. Herschel V. Johnson to John T. Smith et al., June 8, 1855, in Johnson Papers, Perkin Collection, DUL; S. Barclay to Howell Cobb, August 3, 1855, in Cobb Papers, UGA; Robert Toombs to Alexander Stephens, August 4, 1857, in Phillips, *Correspondence*, 409.

11. Avery, *History of the State of Georgia*, 5.

12. Thomas W. Thomas to Alexander Stephens, June 15, 1857, Phillips, *Correspondence*, 2:400. On the Buchanan administration and the Lecompton controversy, see Stampp, *America in 1857*, 174–77.

13. Parks, *Joseph E. Brown of Georgia*, 83.

14. Linton Stephens to Alexander Stephens, July 4, 1857, in Stephens Papers, Manhattanville College, copy at UGA.

15. T. Allan to Howell Cobb, October 4, 1855, Cobb Papers, UGA; Avery, *History of the State of Georgia*, 5.

16. Alexander Stephens to Thomas W. Thomas, December 29, 1856, in Phillips, *Correspondence*, 386; Thomas W. Thomas to Alexander Stephens, January 12, 1857, in Phillips, *Correspondence*, 389–91; Howell Cobb to Alexander Stephens, July 23, 1857, in Phillips, *Correspondence*, 408.

17. Joseph Brown to Alexander Stephens, February 9, 1857, in Phillips, *Correspondence*, 432.

18. Hahn, *Roots of Southern Radicalism*, 37; Gov. Joseph Brown, Democratic Convention, June 15, 1859, in *Milledgeville Southern Recorder*, June 21, 1859.

19. Joseph Brown to Alexander Stephens, June 21, 1859, in Phillips, *Correspondence*, 446.

20. Flippin, "From the Autobiography of Herschel Johnson," 324; Freehling and Simpson, *Secession Debated*.

21. Avery, *History of the State of Georgia*, 5; Phillips, *Georgia and States' Rights*; Bryan, "Secession of Georgia," 89–111; Coulter, *Georgia*, 319. Johnson, *Toward a Patriarchal Republic*. A new history of antebellum Georgia politics argues, contrary to Johnson, that secession represented a cross-class "white men's revolution." The author recognizes the ambiguity of Joseph Brown's politics, however, describing him as a "bank-bashing Baptist yeoman who doubled as an astute manager of the lucrative Western & Atlantic Railroad." See Carey, *Parties, Slavery, and the Union*, 216. See also a view contrary to mine, Collins, "Governor Joseph Brown," 225.

22. T. Allan to Howell Cobb, December 19, 1860, in Cobb Papers, UGA.

23. Joseph Brown before Georgia House and Senate, November 6, 1861, in CRG, 2:12; Joseph Brown before Georgia House and Senate, November 6, 1861, in CRG 2:125, 122.

24. Hill, *Joseph Brown and the Confederacy*, 50, 36; John Anderson to Howell Cobb, February 11, 1861, in Cobb Papers, UGA; Jefferson McCoy to Howell Cobb, February 11, 1861, in Cobb Papers, UGA; Freehling and Simpson, in *Secession Debated*, xxix–xx, discuss the "inertia" of Georgia Unionists and Brown's key role in winning secession. On nonslaveholder opposition to secession, see Johnson, *Toward a Patriarchal Republic*, 66–67.

25. Potter, *Impending Crisis*, 386–89.

26. *Governor Brown on the Present Crisis* (n.p., n.d.), Hargrett Collection, UGA; Collins, "Governor Joseph Brown," 222; Robert Toombs to Alexander Stephens, February 10, 1860, in Phillips, *Correspondence*, 462.

27. Flippin, *Herschel Johnson*, 201.

28. Doyon and Hodler, "Secessionist Sentiment and Slavery," 323–48.

29. On "ambiguous democracy," see Sellers, *Market Revolution*, 332–54, Du Bois, *Black Reconstruction in America*, 241.

30. Karl Marx to Johann Baptist Schweitzer, January 24, 1865, quoted in Draper, *Karl Marx's Theory of Revolution*, 294; Engels, *Revolution and Counterrevolution in Germany*, in Marx and Engels, *Selected Works*, 1:304.

31. Rable, *Confederate Republic*, 256–62.

32. Joseph Brown, in *Milledgeville Federal Union*, May 17, 1861; McCurry, "Politics of Yeoman Households," 22–42; Joseph Brown in *North Carolina State Journal*, February 27, 1861; Joseph Brown to Georgia Senate and House of Representatives, November 5, 1863, CRG, 2:484; Whites, *Civil War as a Crisis in Gender*, 17.

33. Alexander Stephens to Herschel V. Johnson, June 22, 1864, Johnson Papers, Perkin Collection, DUL.

34. Joseph E. Brown to Dr. O. R. Boyles, January 23, 1863, Hargrett Collection, UGA. Thomas, *Confederacy as a Revolutionary Experience*, explores the connection between social transformation and popular discontent.

35. Joseph Brown to Major J. H. Howard, May 20, 1861, Hargrett Collection, UGA.

36. Joseph Brown to Editor, *Brunswick Advocate*, May 11, 1861, Hargrett Collection, UGA.

37. Joseph Brown to Charles C. Jones Jr., May 18, 1861, Hargrett Collection, UGA.

38. James W. Ailes to Joseph Brown, February 15, 1861, Telamon Cuyler Collection, UGA; Joseph Brown to A. H. Stephens, January 1, 1862, Hargrett Collection, UGA; Joseph Brown in the *Confederacy*, November 16, 1862.

39. Joseph Brown to Jefferson Davis, September 17, 1861, in National Archives File 437, copy held at Jefferson Davis Association, Rice University; Owsley, *States' Rights in the Confederacy*, 272–81.

40. Joseph Brown to Senate and House, November 6, 1862, CRG, 2:305; Joseph Brown to Major J. H. Howard, June 7, 1861, Hargrett Collection, UGA; Joseph Brown to Jefferson Davis, June 21, 1862, Jefferson Davis Papers, Perkin Collection, DUL; William Lowndes Yancey in DuBose, *Life and Times of William Lowndes Yancey*, 671.

41. Joseph Brown, to Senate and House, November 6, 1861, CRG, 285–86; Joseph Brown, to Senate and House, March 5, 1864, CRG, 2:609–16.

42. Alexander Stephens to Linton Stephens, June 20, 1862, Manhattanville College Collection, copy at UGA.

43. *Richmond Enquirer*, March 25, 1862; *Charleston Mercury*, January 8, 1863.

44. Joseph Brown to Senate and House, November 6, 1862, CRG, 2:287; Joseph Brown to Senate and House, November 12, 1862, CRG, 2:337.

45. *OR*, ser. 4, vol. 2, 10–13.

46. Joseph Brown to Jefferson Davis, June 21, 1862, Davis Papers, Perkin Collection, DUL; Joseph Brown to House of Representatives, November 26, 1861, CRG, 2:155; Hill, *Joseph E. Brown and the Confederacy*, 91.

47. Joseph Brown to Linton Stephens, February 25, 1862, Hargrett Collection, UGA; Joseph Brown to Alexander Stephens, March 28, 1862, Stephens Papers, LC, copy at UGA.

48. V. N. Jackson to Howell Cobb, December 2, 1860, Cobb Papers, UGA.

49. Joseph Brown to House and Senate of Georgia, November 5, 1863, CRG, 2:505; Joseph Brown to Senate and House of Representatives, March 25, 1863, CRG, 2:369; Joseph Brown to Robert E. Lee, February 21, 1862, CRG, 3:164.

50. Howell Cobb, Robert Toombs, and M. J. Crawford in *Richmond Enquirer*, January 20, 1862; *Milledgeville Southern Recorder*, September 8, 1863; P. W. Threatt to Alexander Stephens, March 10, 1862, Stephens Papers, CRG, copy at UGA; Howell Cobb and T. R. R. Cobb, "Appeal to Planters," *Richmond Enquirer*, June 13, 1861.

51. Joseph Brown to Major J. F. Cummings, February 6, 1864, CRG, 3:475; Joseph Brown to the Senate and House of Representatives, November 6, 1862, CRG, 2:273–74; Joseph Brown to Senate and House of Representatives, November 6, 1861, CRG, 2:103.

52. Proclamation of Joseph Brown, February 11, 1862, CRG, 2:192. Joseph Brown, "To the People of Georgia," CRG, 2:469; Joseph Brown to the General Assembly, June 22, 1863, CRG, 2:458; Joseph Brown, Inaugural Address, November 8, 1861, CRG, 1:130.

53. Joseph Brown to Herschel V. Johnson, April 21, 1862, Johnson Papers, UGA.

54. Jefferson Davis to Joseph Brown, January 9, 1864, Perkin Collection, DUL.

55. Howell Cobb, January 9, 1863, Cobb Papers, UGA.

56. "Governor's Letter Books, 1861–65," 451, Georgia Department of Archives and History, Atlanta.

57. *Substance of the Remarks of General Howell Cobb*.

58. Current, *Lincoln's Loyalists*, 213–16.

59. "To the Mechanics of Georgia," Governor Joseph Brown, February 20, 1862, CRG, 2:194; Joseph Brown to General Assembly, December 12, 1862, CRG, 2:347.

60. Herschel Johnson to A. E. Cochran, October 25, 1862, Johnson Papers, Perkin Collection, DUL; Joseph E. Brown to Alexander Stephens, March 28, 1862, Stephens Papers, LC, copy at UGA.

61. Davis, *Long Surrender*, 63–83.

62. Mitchell, "Perseverance of the Soldiers," 124–25; Fredrickson, *"Blue over Gray,"* 79. For an overview of military strategy, see Gallagher, *Confederate War*, 113–55.

63. Secretary of War Leroy P. Walker to Joseph Brown, CRG, 3:114; Joseph Brown to Jefferson Davis, "Governor's Letterbooks, 1861–65," 45, Georgia Department of Archives and History, Atlanta.

64. Joseph Brown to Georgia Senate and House of Representatives, November 5, 1863, CRG, 2:483.

65. *Milledgeville Southern Recorder*, February 28, 1865.

66. Mohr, *On the Threshold of Freedom*, 215.

67. Alexander Stephens to Herschel V. Johnson, June 22, 1864, Stephens Papers, Perkin Collection, DUL; Benjamin Henry Hill to Jefferson Davis, March 25, 1865, in War Department, Collection of Confederate Records in National Archives, Roll No. 67, at Jefferson Davis Association, Rice University; Herschel V. Johnson to Alexander Stephens, April 1, 1864, Perkin Collection, DUL.

68. Joseph Brown to House of Representatives and Senate of Georgia, November 6, 1862, CRG, 2:302; Joseph Brown to House of Representatives and Senate of Georgia, November 3, 1864, CRG, 2:739. Thornton, *Politics and Power in a Slave Society*, 25–26, discusses the yeomanry's fear of being reduced to slavery. Joseph Brown to Jefferson Davis, October 18, 1862, CRG, 3:300.

69. Flippin, "From the Autobiography of Herschel V. Johnson," 332.

70. Joseph Brown to James Seddon, December 29, 1864, in CRG, 3:462; Jefferson Davis, "Speech to the Army of Tennessee, October 14, 1863," in Rowland, *Jefferson Davis, Constitutionalist*, 186.

71. Powell and Wayne, "Self-Interest and the Decline of Confederate Nationalism," 30; Faust, *Mothers of Invention*, 236; Faust, *Creation of Confederate Nationalism*, 22–41.

72. Joseph E. Brown to House of Representatives and Senate of Georgia, November 3, 1864, CRG, 2:749.

73. Joseph Brown in *Augusta Weekly Chronicle and Sentinel*, April 19, 1865; Joseph Brown to Hiram Warner, January 18, 1865, Hargrett Collection, UGA.

74. Alexander Stephens to Herschel V. Johnson, October 2, 1864, Stephens Papers, Perkin Collection, DUL.

75. William T. Sherman to H. W. Halleck, September 7, 1863, OR, ser. 1, 30, pt. 3, 695–96; Sherman, *Memoirs of General William T. Sherman*, 2:138–39, 188–91.

5. THE PRICE OF MODERATION

1. Rable, *Confederate Republic*, 61; Freehling, "Spoilsmen and Interests," 25–42; Ford, "Inventing the Concurrent Majority," 19–58.

2. *Edgefield Advertiser*, September 24, 1862.

3. Cauthen, *South Carolina Goes to War*, 139–52; White, "Fate of Calhoun's Sovereign Convention," 757–71; Edmunds, *Francis W. Pickens*, 167; Ware, "South Carolina Executive Councils," 32.

4. Banner, "Problem of South Carolina," 36–60; Ford, *Origins of Southern Radicalism*, 50, 113; Greenberg, "Representation and the Isolation of South Carolina," 723–43. See also Weir, "South Carolinian as Extremist," 86–103.

5. This judgement has been reflected in historiography. See Cauthen, *South Carolina Goes to War*, 140–41; White, "Fate of Calhoun's Sovereign Convention," 758.

6. Edmunds, *Francis W. Pickens*, 65.

7. White, "Calhoun's Sovereign Convention," 762-3.

8. *Message No. 1 of His Excellency F. W. Pickens to the Legislature*, 18.

9. For a far different analysis of party dynamics, see Banner, "Problem of South Carolina," 89–93.

10. Schultz, *Nationalism and Sectionalism*, 134–231; White, "National Democrats in South Carolina," 570–87; Leemhuis, *James L. Orr*, 29–69; Kibler, *Benjamin Perry*, 302.

11. Kibler, "Unionist Sentiment in South Carolina," 346–66.

12. John C. Calhoun, "Remarks on the Executive Patronage Report in Exchange with Thomas H. Benton," February 13, 1835, in Wilson, *Papers of John C. Calhoun*, 12:473–75.

13. White, *Robert Barnwell Rhett*, 163–91; Channing, *Crisis of Fear*, 195–295; McCurry, *Masters of Small Worlds*, 277–304.

14. Boucher, *Sectionalism, Representation*, 6–7, 11.

15. Schaper, "Sectionalism and Representation," 437.

16. Kibler, *Benjamin Perry*, 304–13.

17. W. W. Churchwell to Francis W. Pickens, February 12, 1860, Pickens Family Papers, Perkin Collection, DUL.

18. Wilson, *Papers of John C. Calhoun*, 11:xiii–xxxix.

19. Greenberg, "Representation," 723–43.

20. Benjamin Perry, quoted in Takaki, *Pro-Slavery Crusade*, 187; Benjamin Perry in *Greeneville Mountaineer*, February 7, 1856; James Henry Hammond letter, "To the Public," November 8, 1860, SCL.

21. Ford, "Origins of the Edgefield Tradition," 337–39, 345.

22. Klein, *Unification of a Slave State*; Freehling, *Road to Disunion*, 213–28.

23. W. C. Moragne in *Edgefield Advertiser*, February 20, 1856.

24. Schultz, *Nationalism and Sectionalism*, 436–37.

25. "The Electoral Question," Francis W. Pickens, *Edgefield Advertiser*, October 5, 1854.

26. *Edgefield Advertiser*, March 12, 1856.

27. Alfred Huger to William Porcher Miles, September 30, 1858, William Porcher Miles Papers, SHC.

28. McCurry, *Masters of Small Worlds*, 247–49.

29. Schultz, *Nationalism and Sectionalism*, 54–55.

30. James L. Orr to C. W. Dudley, *Edgefield Advertiser*, December 19, 1855.

31. S. G. Bailey to William Porcher Miles, October 13, 1856, Miles Papers, SHC; Hiram Powers and H. Gourdin to William Porcher Miles, October 23, 1856, Miles Papers, SHC.

32. "Upper Country," in *Edgefield Advertiser*, June 4, 1856; Lawrence Keitt to Susanna Sparks Keitt, January 20, 1855, Lawrence Keitt Papers, Perkin Collection, DUL.

33. Robert B. Rhett Jr. to William Porcher Miles, April 7, 1858, Miles Papers, SHC.

34. Edward McCrady, *Charleston Courier*, September 29, 1860; Freehling, "Spoilsmen and Interests," 25–42.

35. Francis W. Pickens to Gov. Manning, May 12, 1857, Williams-Chesnut-Manning Papers, SCL.

36. Francis W. Pickens to Benjamin F. Perry, June 22, 1857; June 27, 1857, Benjamin Perry Papers, SHC.

37. Francis W. Pickens to Benjamin F. Perry, January 13, 1854, Perry Papers, ADAH; Francis W. Pickens to Andrew Pickens, c. early 1857, Pickens Family Papers, Perkin Collection, DUL.

38. Francis W. Pickens to G. N. Sanders, May 16, 1857, Pickens Family Papers, Perkin Collection, DUL; Francis W. Pickens to Benjamin F. Perry, April 24, 1859, Perry Papers, ADAH.

39. Francis W. Pickens to Beaufort T. Watts, October 24, 1857, Beaufort Watts Papers, SCL.

40. Isaac Hayne to James Henry Hammond, June 3, 1860, James Henry Hammond Papers, LC, copy at SCL; William Henry Trescot to William Porcher Miles, March 10, 1860, Miles Papers, SHC; Robert B. Rhett Jr. to William Porcher Miles, March 28, 1860, Miles Papers, SHC.

41. Robert Barnwell Rhett Jr. to William Porcher Miles, May 12, 1860, Miles Papers, SHC; William Henry Trescot to James Henry Hammond, April 28, 1860, Hammond Papers, LC, copy at SCL.

42. Benjamin F. Perry, "Democratic Convention Address," in Meets, *Writings of Benjamin F. Perry*, 115–17.

43. White, "National Democrats in South Carolina," 382.

44. Francis W. Pickens to J. Glancy Ivins, September 2, 1859, Francis Pickens Papers, SCL.

45. Francis W. Pickens to Benjamin F. Perry, November 21, 1859, Perry Papers, SHC.

46. Francis W. Pickens to G. N. Sanders, May 16, 1857, Pickens Family Papers, Perkin Collection, DUL; Francis W. Pickens to Benjamin F. Perry, April 24, 1859, Perry Papers, ADAH.

47. Francis W. Pickens to Benjamin F. Perry, June 22, 1857, Perry Papers, SHC; W. W. Churchwell to Francis W. Pickens, October 8, December 30, 1859, Pickens Family Papers, Perkin Collection, DUL.

48. Francis W. Pickens, May 25, 1860, Pickens Papers, SCL; Edmunds, *Francis Pickens*, 151–52.

49. White, *Robert Barnwell Rhett*, 185; W. A. Porter to James Henry Hammond, November 11, 1861, Hammond Papers, LC, copy at SCL; Cauthen, *South Carolina Goes to War*, 80–81.

50. Cauthen, *South Carolina Goes to War*, 92–118.

51. Robert Barnwell Rhett to James Orr, February 9, 1861, Orr-Patterson Collection, SHC; Robert Barnwell Rhett to Robert Barnwell Rhett Jr., February 11, 1861, SCL.

52. Major Robert Anderson to Col. S. Cooper, Fort Sumter, OR, ser. 1, vol. 1, 183.

53. J. L. Pugh to William Porcher Miles, January 24, 1861, Miles Papers, SHC.

54. William Gilmore Simms to William Porcher Miles, February 22, 1861, Miles Papers, SHC; Robert Barnwell to James Orr, February 9, 1861, Orr-Patterson Collection, SHC.

55. A. P. Aldrich to James Henry Hammond, December 6, 1860, SCL.

56. I. W. Hayne to Francis W. Pickens, January 16, 1861, Pickens-Bonham Collection, LC, copy at SCDAH; "Letter of Hon. I. W. Hayne," in *Correspondence and Other Papers*.

57. Francis W. Pickens to Jefferson Davis, January 23, 1861, Pickens Papers, SCL; Francis W. Pickens to General Evans, February 3, 1861; March 2, 1861, Pickens Papers, SCL.

58. Lawrence Keitt to James Henry Hammond, February 13, 1861, Hammond Papers, LC, copy at SCL.

59. Francis W. Pickens to Jefferson Davis, January 23, 1861, Pickens Papers, SCL.

60. William Porcher Miles to Milledge L. Bonham, December 23, 1860, Orr-Patterson Collection, SHC.

61. Capt. J. G. Foster to Gen. Joseph G. Totten, January 12, 1861, OR, ser. 1, vol. 1, 138.

62. Francis W. Pickens to Adjt. General Evans, March 2, 1861, Pickens Papers, SCL; Minutes of South Carolina Executive Council, February 6, 12, 1861, SCDAH.

63. *Charleston Mercury*, August 7, 1861.

64. William Henry Trescot to William Porcher Miles, November 25, 1861, Miles Papers, SHC.

65. Langdon Cheves to William Porcher Miles, August 1861, Miles Papers, SHC.

66. Saville, *Work of Reconstruction*, 36.

67. *Edgefield Advertiser*, November 13, 1861, quoted in Harris, *Plain Folk and Gentry*, 146.

68. Francis W. Pickens to William Porcher Miles, May 9, 1861, Miles Papers, SHC.

69. Gov. Francis W. Pickens to Hon. A. G. Magrath, December 1861, Pickens Papers, SCL.

70. *Columbia Guardian*, January 9, 1862, in *Edgefield Advertiser*, January 15, 1862; James Henry Hammond to William Gilmore Simms, November 10, 1861, Hammond Papers, LC, copy at SCL.

71. "A Back Country Man," in *Edgefield Advertiser*, April 30, 1862; James Hammond to J. D. Ashmore, April 1861, Hammond Papers, LC, copy at SCL.

72. *Edgefield Advertiser* in *Charleston Courier*, January 23, 1862; I. W. Hayne to Francis W. Pickens, March 5, 1862, Pickens Family Papers, Perkin Collection, DUL; Henry Buist to Francis W. Pickens, April 2, 1862, Pickens Family Papers, Perkin Collection, DUL.

73. *Charleston Mercury*, December 1, 1862.

74. Francis W. Pickens to H. G. Magrath, December 1861, Pickens Papers, SCL.

75. *Charleston Mercury*, December 1, 1862; Executive Council Minutes, August 5, 1862, SCDAH; Executive Council Minutes, August 29, 1862, SCDAH.

76. *Charleston Courier*, January 12, 1862; *Edgefield Advertiser*, October 1, 1862; William Gilmore Simms to James Henry Hammond, December 11, 1862, Hammond Papers, LC, copy at SCL.

77. *Charleston Courier*, July 9, 1862, August 20, 1862.

78. *Tri-Weekly Southern Guardian*, July 7, 1862; *Journal of the Convention of the People of South Carolina*, 649–58; James Henry Hammond to William Gilmore Simms, August 29, 1862, Hammond Papers, LC, copy at SCL.

79. *Edgefield Advertiser*, September 24, 1862; Pickens, November 25, 1862, *Journal of the Senate of South Carolina*, 33, 12.

80. *Message No. 1 of His Excellency F. W. Pickens to the Legislature*, 14.

81. Ibid.

82. William Gilmore Simms to James Henry Hammond, December 4, 11, 1862, Hammond Papers, LC, copy at SCL.

83. James B. Campbell to Benjamin F. Perry, November 6, 1862, Perry Papers, ADAH.

84. "Speech of Mr. B. F. Perry on Mr. Whaley's Resolution in the House of Representatives, November 7, 1862," in Perry Scrapbook, SCL.

6. CURING THE "SIR WALTER DISEASE"

1. Twain, *Life on the Mississippi*, 272; Twain, "The Private History of a Campaign That Failed," *Tales, Speeches, Essays, and Sketches* (New York, 1994), 164.

2. Osterweis, *Romanticism and Nationalism*, 51; Landrum, "Sir Walter Scott," 256–76; Orians, "Walter Scott, Mark Twain, and the Civil War," 342–59.

3. See Hoole, "Jeremiah Clemens, Novelist," 1–37; Martin, "Senatorial Career of Jeremiah Clemens," 186–235. Two less recent but still useful treatments of Clemens are Bedsole, "Life of Jeremiah Clemens," and Drummond, "Biography of Jeremiah Clemens." For an overview of the literary scene, see Williams, *Literary History of Alabama*, 58–68.

4. Thornton, *Politics and Power in a Slave Society*, 143.

5. Wyatt-Brown, *Southern Honor*, 14, 22–23.

6. Greenberg, *Masters and Statesmen*, 6; Ayers, *Vengeance and Justice*, 9–34.

7. Wyatt-Brown, "God and Honor in the Old South," 283–96; Heyrman, *Southern Cross*, 207–52, contains a useful discussion of the tangled relationship between evangelical Christianity and the southern culture of mastery and honor.

8. Greenberg, *Honor and Slavery*, 20–22; Wyatt-Brown, "Andrew Jackson's Honor," 1–37.

9. On independence in Alabama political culture, see Thornton, *Politics and Power in a Slave Society*, 443–47; W. E. Clarke to Gov. John Winston, May 12, 1855, Gov. John Winston Papers, ADAH.

10. Fox-Genovese, *Within the Plantation Household*, 32, 38–39; McCurry, *Masters of Small Worlds*, 37–91.

11. Daniel Martin to Clement Claiborne Clay, January 1857, Clay Family Papers, UGA.

12. On the evolution of the northern middle-class family, see Ryan, *Cradle of the Middle Class*, 102–4; Cott, *Bonds of Womanhood*, 92–100; Welter, "Cult of True Womanhood," 151–74.

13. Patterson, *Slavery and Social Death*; McCurry, "Two Faces of Republicanism," 1245–64.

14. Baldwin, *Party Leaders*, 292–95. On the continuing appeal of Jacksonian themes in antebellum Alabama, see Thornton, *Politics and Power in a Slave Society*, xxi.

15. Thornton, *Politics and Power in a Slave Society*, 45–49, 281–285; McCurry, *Masters of Small Worlds*, 85–91; Watson, *Jacksonian Politics and Community Conflict*, 14–15.

16. Baldwin, *Flush Times*, 61; P. P. Barbour, quoted in Goodwin, *Biography of Andrew Jackson*, 358.

17. Clay-Clopton, *Belle of the Fifties*, 13–14.

18. Bedsole, "Life of Jeremiah Clemens," provides the most complete biographical information on Clemens.

19. Greenberg, *Masters and Statesmen*, 142–43.

20. Jeremiah Clemens et al. to H. W. Collier, December 14, 1849, Collier Papers, ADAH; H. W. Collier, to Clemens et al., December 22, 1849, Gov. H. W. Collier Papers, ADAH.

21. *Columbus (S.C.) Telegraph* in *Huntsville Southern Advocate*, March 20, 1850; Jeremiah Clemens in *Congressional Globe*, 31st Cong., 1st sess., December 20, 1849, 51.

22. Jeremiah Clemens in *Congressional Globe*, 31st Cong., 1st sess., May 20, 1850, 587.

23. *Montgomery Advertiser* in *Huntsville Democrat*, March 20, 1851; John Morysett to H. W. Collier, October 29, 1850, Collier Papers, ADAH; *Huntsville Democrat*, October 14, 1851.

24. *Florence Gazette* in *Huntsville Southern Advocate*, September 10, 1851.

25. Robert Barnwell Rhett, *Congressional Globe*, 32d Cong., 1st sess., February 27, 1852, 644–56.

26. Robert Barnwell Rhett, *Congressional Globe*, 32d Cong., 1st sess., February 27, 1852, 648; Thornton, *Politics and Power in a Slave Society*, 203.

27. *Huntsville Democrat*, October 23, 1851.

28. For its continued support of Clemens after the compromise, see the *Huntsville Southern Advocate*, October 1851. On the power of party leaders to break politicians' careers, see Thornton, *Politics and Power in a Slave Society*, 128.

29. William Gilmore Simms, quoted in Greenberg, *Honor and Slavery*, 14; Wyatt-Brown, "Andrew Jackson's Honor," 10–11.

30. "To the Public," from the *Spirit of the South* in the *Democrat*, July 31, 1851, copied in Drummond, "Biography of Jeremiah Clemens," 394.

31. Jeremiah Clemens in *Congressional Globe*, 32d Cong., 1st sess., February 27, 1852, 660.

32. Jeremiah Clemens in *Huntsville Democrat*, October 23, 1851; *Huntsville Democrat*, October 23, 1851; F. Sanford to John Winston, February 1, 1856, Winston Papers, ADAH.

33. Clemens quoted in Bedsole, "Life of Jeremiah Clemens," 81; Clement Comer Clay to Clement Claiborne Clay, January 23, 1855, Clay Family Papers, UGA.

34. *Huntsville Southern Advocate*, September 11, 1856, quoted in Dorman, *Party Politics in Alabama*, 132.

35. P. H. Bingham to Clement Claiborne Clay, June 1857, Clay Family Papers, UGA; Daniel B. Dallas to Clement Claiborne Clay, May 14, 1857, Clay Family Papers, UGA.

36. *Alabama State Sentinel* in *Mobile Daily Register*, March 18, 1853; *Butler Standard*, February 17, 1851.

37. *The South* in the *Montgomery Advertiser*, May 6, 1857. The *Advertiser* stated the article "deserves the thanks and hearty support of the people in every section."

38. Clemens, *Mustang Gray*, v; Clemens, *Rivals*, viii.

39. Clemens, *Mustang*, 185; Clemens, *Bernard Lile*, 258.

40. Clemens, *Bernard Lile*, x, 236, 21; Baldwin, *Flush Times*; Hooper, *Adventures of Captain Simon Suggs*. See also Gray, *Writing the South*, 62–74.

41. Clemens, *Rivals*, viii.

42. Scott, "Essay on Chivalry," 6:10, 28.

43. "Proclamation of A. B. Moore to the People," December 17, 1860, A. B. Moore Papers, ADAH; William Yancey in Alabama State Convention, January 11, 1861, reprinted in *Huntsville Democrat*, February 6, 1861.

44. Jeremiah Clemens in *Montgomery Advertiser*, December 17, 1860; Jeremiah Clemens in *Montgomery Advertiser*, December 5, 1860.

45. *Huntsville Southern Advocate*, January 9, 1861.

46. J. L. M. Curry to Howell Cobb, October 18, 1860, Howell Cobb Papers, UGA; W. R. Smith in Smith, *History and Debates*, 438; Lewis M. Stone in Smith, *History and Debates*, 332.

47. Bailey, "Disaffection in the Alabama Hill Country," 182–94; Bailey, "Disloyalty in Early Confederate Alabama," 522–28.

48. Jeremiah Clemens to John J. Crittenden, November 24, 1860, Crittenden Collection, LC, in McMillan, *Alabama Confederate Reader*, 14; McPherson, *Battle Cry of Freedom*, 304.

49. Clemens's course at the convention can be followed in Smith, *History and Debates*. For Yancey's threats against Unionists, see 147–48. For a judicious examination of Clemens's stand regarding the Union and cooperationism, see Barney, *Secessionist Impulse*, 199–201. Denman, in *Secession Movement in Alabama*, 129, describes Clemens's stand as typical of his "vacillations."

50. Jeremiah Clemens, *Huntsville Southern Advocate*, December 5, 1860.

51. Jeremiah Clemens to George W. Neal, January 11, 1861, *Huntsville Southern Advocate*, January 16, 1861.

52. OR, ser. 1, vol. 32, pt. 3, p. 750; Fleming, *Civil War and Reconstruction*, 53.

53. Fleming, *Civil War and Reconstruction*, 138. For a survey of conflict in contested areas of the South, see Ash, *When the Yankees Came*, and Horton, "Submitting to the 'Shadow of Slavery,'" 111–36. Thompson, *Free State of Winston*, discusses the relationship between Clemens and Winston County Unionists. Johnston, *Sword of "Bushwacker" Johnston*, offers a Confederate perspective on the fighting.

54. Hoole, *Alabama Tories*; Wiggins, *Scalawag in Alabama Politics*, 7.

55. Martin, *Desertion of Alabama Troops*, 121–27; Lt. A. H. Burch to Gov. Thomas H. Watts, February 20, 1865, Watts Papers, ADAH.

56. Edward Betts to Governor Thomas H. Watts, February 8, 1864, Watts Papers, ADAH; Fleming, *Civil War and Reconstruction*, 65.

57. Jeremiah Clemens to Secretary of War, April 4, 1861, OR ser. 1, vol. 2, pt. 2, 35; Annual Cyclopedia (1863) in Fleming, *Civil War and Reconstruction*, 135.

58. Lt. Col. W. L. Maxwell to Captain T. B. Sykes, April 29, 1864, OR ser. 1, vol. 32, pt. 3, 853.

59. Col. A. D. Streight to Captain William A. Schlater, July 16, 1862, in Moore, *Rebellion Record*, 5:281–84.

60. *Chattanooga Rebel*, reprinted in *Charleston Mercury*, September 20, 1862; *Clarke County Democrat*, October 30, 1862.

61. Maj. Gen. O. M. Mitchel to Sec. of War E. M. Stanton, May 6, 8, 1862, Asst. Sec. of War P. H. Watson to O. M. Mitchel, May 8, 1862, OR ser. 1, vol. 10, pt. 2, pp. 167, 174–75.

62. Jeremiah Clemens to an unidentified addressee, October 1864, as quoted in Drummond, "Biography of Jeremiah Clemens," 210–18. For an excellent survey of the home front during the Civil War, see Atkins et al., *Alabama*, 204–23.

63. Jeremiah Clemens, speech in Huntsville, Alabama, March 13, 1864, reported in *New York Tribune*, March 24, 1861, quoted in Nevins, *Ordeal of the Union*, 3:68.
64. Clemens, *Tobias Wilson*, 13–14, 17–18, 33; Fox-Genovese, *Within the Plantation Household*, 232.
65. Clemens, *Tobias Wilson*, 16, 25, vii.
66. Ibid., iv, 40.
67. Ibid., 64, 48–49.
68. Ibid., 96–107.
69. Ibid., 122; Wyatt-Brown, "God and Honor," 290; Ryan, *Cradle of the Middle Class*, 103, 231–32.
70. Foner, *Free Soil*, 11–18, 24–29; Rotundo, *American Manhood*, 167–85.
71. *William L. Yancey at the National Democratic Convention, April 26, 1860* (pamphlet, n.p., in Yancey file, ADAH); Nina Silber, "Intemperate Men, Spiteful Women, and Jefferson Davis," in Clinton and Silber, *Divided Houses*, 289; Rable, *Civil Wars*, 154, 277.
72. Jeremiah Clemens to Andrew Johnson, November 19, 1864, Andrew Johnson Papers, LC.
73. Whites, *Civil War as a Crisis in Gender*, 115, 130, 140; Roark, *Masters without Slaves*, 203–4.
74. Silber, "Intemperate Men," 283–305; Hughes, "Madness of Separate Spheres," 56; Clemens, *Tobias Wilson*, 168.
75. Clemens, *Tobias Wilson*, 121, 327.
76. Ibid., 328.
77. Heyrman, *Southern Cross*, 248–49.
78. Oakes, *Ruling Race*, 108–10.
79. Twain, *Life on the Mississippi*, 272.
80. Samuel Clemens to Jane Lampton Clemens, June 21, 1866, in Robert Hirst, ed., *Mark Twain's Letters*, vol. 1, *1853–1866* (Berkeley, 1987), 343; Twain, *Mark Twain's Autobiography*, 1:86. In *Politics and Power in a Slave Society*, 3, J. Mills Thornton III argues that Twain "could hardly have been ignorant of the notoriety" of Clemens.

7. DAVIS AND THE DYSFUNCTIONAL DEMOCRACY

1. *Richmond Enquirer*, February 15, 1861; *Charleston Mercury*, February 23, 1861; William C. Davis, "Government of Our Own," 157; Thomas, *Confederate Nation*, 59.
2. McPherson, *Abraham Lincoln*, 94; Scarborough, *Diary of Edmund Ruffin*, 1:551.
3. John B. Jones, *Rebel War Clerk's Diary*, June 17, 1861, 27.
4. *Richmond Examiner*, February 24, 1862, in Daniel, *Richmond Examiner during the War*; Potter, "Jefferson Davis and the Political Factors in Confederate Defeat," 276, 284; Escott, *After Secession*, 269.

5. Current, "God and the Strongest Battalions," 15, 30; Gallagher, *Confederate War*, 63–111.

6. Clausewitz, *On War*, 77.

7. *Richmond Examiner*, February 26, 1862, in Daniel, *Richmond Enquirer during the War*, 43; Nevins, *Ordeal of the Union*, 3:95; Herschel Johnson to Alexander Stephens, April 4, 1863, Herschel V. Johnson Papers, Perkin Collection, DUL.

8. Faust, *Creation of Confederate Nationalism*, 60, 84; Beringer et al., *Why the South Lost the Civil War*, 434–38; Hahn, *Roots of Southern Populism*, 132–33; Durill, *War of Another Kind*, 37, 241; Faust, *Mothers of Invention*, 238, 247; Bailey, *Class and Tennessee's Confederate Generation*, 104; Wiley, *Road to Appomattox*, 120–21; Sellers, "Travail of Slavery," 71; Rable, *Civil Wars*, 211–13; Escott, *After Secession*, xi; Ramsdell, *Behind the Lines*; Donald, "Died of Democracy," 77–91.

9. *Charleston Mercury*, February 11, 1861.

10. Tocqueville, *Democracy in America*, 263.

11. Bradford, *Remembering Who We Are*, 145; Genovese, "Slaveholders' Contribution to the American Constitution," 116.

12. *Correspondence between Henry A. Wise and Hon. Fernando Wood*, Richmond, 1860; Hyman, *More Perfect Union*, 5.

13. Wharton, *Journal of the State Convention*, 142.

14. Kammen, *Machine That Would Go of Itself*, 115; Jefferson Davis, "Remarks on the Special Message on Affairs in South Carolina, January 10, 1861," in Rowland, *Jefferson Davis, Constitutionalist*, 5:21; *Address of William Lowndes Yancey to the Alabama State Democratic Convention*, 30.

15. Miller, *Life of the Mind in America*, 156–182; Jefferson Davis, "The Resolution Concerning the Relations of the States," May 8, 1860, in Rowland, *Jefferson Davis, Constitutionalist*, 4:252.

16. "Communication from Governor F. W. Pickens, March 28, 1861," *Journal of the Convention of the People of South Carolina*.

17. Connelly, *Marble Man*, 93.

18. Speech of Jefferson Davis in Macon, Georgia, September 29, 1864, in Rowland, *Jefferson Davis, Constitutionalist*, 6:342; Speech of President Davis in Columbia, October 6, 1864, in Rowland, *Jefferson Davis, Constitutionalist*, 6:351; Jefferson Davis to Mrs. Howell Cobb, March 30, 1865, in Rowland, *Jefferson Davis, Constitutionalist*, 6:525.

19. Karl Marx, "The Civil War in the United States," November 7, 1861, in *Karl Marx on America and the Civil War*, ed. Saul K. Padover (New York, 1972), 87.

20. Hobsbawm, *Nations and Nationalism since 1780*, 10; Anderson, *Imagined Communities*, 39–47; Faust, *Creation of Confederate Nationalism*, 5.

21. Davis, *Rise and Fall*, 1:234; Jefferson Davis, "Remarks of Jefferson Davis on the Special Message on Affairs in South Carolina, January 10, 1861," in Rowland,

Jefferson Davis, Constitutionalist, 5:25; Davis, "Inaugural Address of the President of the Provisional Government, February 18, 1861," in Rowland, *Jefferson Davis, Constitutionalist,* 5:52; T. R. R. Cobb, *Southern Banner,* April 10, 1861.

22. McPherson, *Battle Cry of Freedom,* vi; Davis, *Rise and Fall,* 6.

23. Andrew Jackson, *Port Gibson Correspondent,* November 3, 1827; Miles, *Jacksonian Democracy in Mississippi,* 169; Bond, *Political Culture in the Nineteenth-Century South,* 88; Rainwater, *Mississippi,* 11.

24. Morris, *Becoming Southern,* 149.

25. "Notice of a Political Meeting—Speeches by Jefferson Davis, Peter B. Starke, and Henry S. Foote," in *Macon (Miss.) Jeffersonian,* August 8, 1844, in Crist, *Papers of Jefferson Davis,* 2:196–97; "Notice of a Political Meeting—Speech by Jefferson Davis," *Vicksburg Sentinel and Expositor,* September 10, 1844, in Crist, *Papers of Jefferson Davis,* 2:209.

26. Jefferson Davis to William R. Cannon, January 8, 1850, in Crist, *Papers of Jefferson Davis,* 4:55.

27. Jefferson Davis, "Eulogy on the Life and Character of Andrew Jackson," July 1, 1845, in Crist, *Papers of Jefferson Davis,* 2:279–81.

28. Andrew Jackson in Richardson, *Messages and Papers of the Presidents,* 2:1160–62; Andrew Jackson in ibid., 3:1186; Freehling, *Prelude to Civil War,* 294.

29. Mayer, *Constitutional Thought of Thomas Jefferson,* xi.

30. William Porcher Miles, *Congressional Globe,* March 31, 1858, 35th Cong., 1st sess., 287; Henry Wise, *Richmond Enquirer,* October 12, 1860; Louis T. Wigfall, *Congressional Globe,* April 4, 1860, 36th Cong., 1st sess., 1488; Tocqueville, *Democracy in America,* 63.

31. Alexander Stephens in Cleveland, *Alexander Stephens,* 721; Davis quoted in Paludan, *Covenant with Death,* 28.

32. Vandiver, *Their Tattered Flags,* 24; Rhodes, *History of the Civil War,* 49.

33. Owsley, *King Cotton Diplomacy*; Jefferson Davis, in Rowland, *Jefferson Davis, Constitutionalist,* 2:73–75.

34. *Richmond Examiner,* February 26, 1862, in Daniel, *Richmond Examiner during the War,* 63; Senator James Phelan of Mississippi to Jefferson Davis, July 29, 1863, quoted in Royster, *Destructive War,* 185; Rable, *Civil Wars,* 108–10; Jones, *Rebel War Clerk's Diary,* 508.

35. Potter, *Impending Crisis,* 18–27.

36. William C. Davis, *Jefferson Davis,* 168–87.

37. Jefferson Davis, "Speech at Jackson, May 29, 1857," in Crist, *Papers of Jefferson Davis,* 6:124; John Calhoun, "Address of the Southern Delegates in Congress to Their Constituents," February 2, 1849, in Cralle, *Works of Calhoun,* 6:293; Jefferson Davis in U.S. Senate, December 10, 1860, quoted in *Rise and Fall,* 62; William C. Davis, *Jefferson Davis,* 117.

38. Jefferson Davis, "Remarks on the Special Message on Affairs in South Carolina, January 10, 1861," in Wakelyn, *Southern Pamphlets on Secession*, 124; "Speech of President Davis in Charleston, South Carolina, November 3, 1863," in Rowland, *Jefferson Davis, Constitutionalist*, 6:76; DeRosa, *Confederate Constitution of 1861*, 18–37.

39. William Ballard Preston of South Carolina before Virginia Convention, February 19, 1861, in *Richmond Enquirer*, February 21, 1861.

40. Capers, "Reconsideration of John C. Calhoun's Transition," 34–48; *Life of John C. Calhoun*, 69. Robert Barnwell Rhett ascribed the authorship of the volume to Calhoun. See Robert Barnwell Rhett to Richard K. Cralle, October 25, 1854, *American Historical Review* 13 (1907–8): 311; "American Oratory," *Southern Quarterly Review* 5 (1844): 375.

41. McCoy, *Last of the Fathers*, 135–43; John Calhoun, *A Discourse on the Constitution and Government of the United States*, in Cralle, *Works of Calhoun*, 1:157; Freehling, *Road to Disunion*, 213–52.

42. John Calhoun, *Disquisition on Government*, in Cralle, *Works of Calhoun*, 1:13, 32.

43. John Calhoun in United States Senate, February 19, 1847, in Cralle, *Works of Calhoun*, 4:133; Calhoun, *Disquisition on Government*, 1:33; Hofstadter, *American Political Tradition*, 67-91.

44. Genovese, *Slaveholders' Dilemma*, 47; Hartz, *Liberal Tradition in America*.

45. Kohl, *Politics of Individualism*, 108; John Calhoun in Burton, *In My Father's House*, ix; Calhoun in Cralle, *Works of Calhoun*, 1:29.

46. Freehling, *Prelude to Civil War*, 157–58; Thomas R. Dew, "Abolition of Negro Slavery," *American Quarterly Review* 12 (1832): 189–265; Faust, *Creation of Confederate Nationalism*, 8–9; Fredrickson, *Black Image in the White Mind*, 52–53; Eaton, *Freedom of Thought*, 30, 144–61; Genovese, *World The Slaveholders Made*, 134. Genovese argues that Calhoun was drawn by the logic of his argument to a defense of "slavery in the abstract" that resembled Dew's. See Genovese, *Slaveholders' Dilemma*, 47.

47. Freehling, *Road to Disunion*, 261.

48. Andrew Johnson, "Speech on the Seceding States," February 5, 1861, in Graf and Haskins, *Papers of Andrew Johnson*, 4:204; Andrew Johnson, in Graf and Haskins, *Papers of Andrew Johnson*, 4:217; Andrew Johnson, in Graf and Haskins, *Papers of Andrew Johnson*, 4:219.

49. "Remarks of Jefferson Davis on the Special Message on Affairs in South Carolina, January 10, 1861," in Rowland, *Jefferson Davis, Constitutionalist*, 5:22; "Andrew Jackson," *Huntsville Southern Advocate*, January 30, 1861.

50. Rainwater, *Mississippi*, 95.

51. Davis, "Reply to Stephen A. Douglas, May 17, 1860," in Crist, *Papers of*

Jefferson Davis, 6:322; "Inaugural Address, Feb 22, 1862," in Rowland, *Jefferson Davis, Constitutionalist*, 5:200; Davis, *Rise and Fall*, 2:478; Jefferson Davis to Robert Barnwell Rhett Jr., November 10, 1860, in Crist, *Papers of Jefferson Davis*, 6:369.

52. Foner, *Free Soil*, 11–39.

53. Jefferson Davis, "Inaugural Address, February 22, 1862," in Rowland, *Jefferson Davis, Constitutionalist*, 5:200, 205; De Bow, *Interest in Slavery*, 10; Jefferson Davis, March 2, 1859, in Rowland, *Jefferson Davis, Constitutionalist*, 5:49.

54. Jefferson Davis in *Charleston Mercury*, February 19, 1861.

55. Bolton, *Poor Whites*, 161.

56. Collins, *White Society in the Antebellum South*, 4–5; Lewis M. Stone in Smith, *History and Debates*, 332.

57. Escott, *After Secession*, 28; James W. Sheffrey in Virginia State Convention, February 27, 1861, *Richmond Enquirer*, February 28, 1861.

58. Oakes, *Slavery and Freedom*, 64. Bestor, "State Sovereignty and Slavery," 42, 60–61; Fehrenbacher, *Slavery, Law, and Politics*, 272; Finkelman, *Imperfect Union*, 322–23; Lee, *Confederate Constitutions*, 145.

59. *Augusta Daily Constitutionalist*, November 16, 1860, in Dumond, *Southern Editorials on Secession*, 170; Channing, *Crisis of Fear*, 258; Robinson, "Day of Jubilo," 80; Aptheker, *American Negro Slave Revolts*, 340–58; Jordan, *Tumult and Silence*, 1–7, 71.

60. Jefferson Davis in Rowland, *Jefferson Davis, Constitutionalist*, 5:30; Mary Chesnut in Woodward, *Private Mary Chesnut*, 181–90.

61. Fehrenbacher, *Constitutions and Constitutionalism*, 64. On conservative constitutional reforms at the state level, see Faust, *Creation of Confederate Nationalism*, 37.

62. Niemann, "Republicanism," 201–24; Fehrenbacher, *Constitutions and Constitutionalism*, 64–65; Rable, *Confederate Republic*, 49; Alexander Stephens in Frank Moore, *Rebellion Record*, 1:46; *Richmond Whig*, September 11, 1861, in Rable, *Confederate Republic*, 84; *Richmond Examiner*, February 26, 1862.

63. Niemann, "Republicanism," 217.

64. Jefferson Davis to Confederate Congress, November 18, 1861, Rowland, *Jefferson Davis, Constitutionalist*, 5:170; "Daughter of Dixie"; McPherson, *For Cause and Comrades*, 20–21.

65. Wiley, *Plain People of the Confederacy*, 69; Jefferson Davis to Confederate Congress, August 18, 1862, Rowland, *Jefferson Davis, Constitutionalist*, 5:322; Jefferson Davis to North Carolina governor Zebulon B. Vance, February 29, 1864, Rowland, *Jefferson Davis, Constitutionalist*, 5:322.

66. Jefferson Davis to Joseph E. Brown, May 29, 1862, CRG, 3:234–42; Jefferson Davis to Governor and Executive Council of South Carolina, September 3, 1862, Rowland, *Jefferson Davis, Constitutionalist*, 5:335; Davis, *Rise and Fall*, 507.

67. Jefferson Davis to General J. E. Johnston, February 28, 1862, Rowland, *Jefferson Davis, Constitutionalist*, 5:209.

68. Albert Gallatin Brown, December 28, 1863, 1st Confederate Cong., 4th sess., *Southern Historical Society Papers* 12 (1953): 133.

69. Thomas, *Confederacy as a Revolutionary Experience*, 58; Thomas Bragg Diary, February 27, 1862, SHC.

70. Jefferson Davis to Confederate Congress, February 3, 1864, Rowland, *Jefferson Davis, Constitutionalist*, 6:168; Joseph E. Brown to Jefferson Davis, May 8, 1862, CRG, 3:212; Benjamin H. Hill to Jefferson Davis, February 5, 1863, War Dept. Collection of Confederate Records, National Archives, Roll 67, at Jefferson Davis Association, Rice University.

71. Jefferson Davis to Joseph E. Brown, July 10, 1862, Rowland, *Jefferson Davis, Constitutionalist*, 5:250; Jefferson Davis to Braxton Bragg, March 26, 1863, Clements Library, University of Michigan, copy held at Jefferson Davis Association, Rice University.

72. Alexander Stephens to Linton Stephens, June 20, 1862, Alexander Stephens Papers, Manhattanville College Collection, copy at UGA.

73. Mr. Henry of Tennessee, February 2, 1863, in "Proceedings of the First Confederate Congress, 3rd Session," *Southern Historical Society Papers* 10 (1941): 26; *Speech of George A. Gordon of Chatham*, 13.

74. Jefferson Davis to Confederate Congress, November 18, 1861, Rowland, *Jefferson Davis, Constitutionalist*, 5:170; Jefferson Davis to Army of Tennessee, October 14, 1863, Rowland, *Jefferson Davis, Constitutionalist*, 6:61; Mitchell, *Vacant Chair*, 3–19; Mitchell, "Soldiering, Manhood, and Coming of Age," 43–45.

75. *North Carolina Standard*, January 2, 1861; *North Carolina Standard*, January 15, 1862.

76. James A. Seddon to Zebulon Vance, July 24, 1863, Zebulon Vance Papers, North Carolina Department of Archives and History; *North Carolina State Journal*, August 19, 1863; Frederick Fitzgerald to Edward J. Hale, July 24, 1863, Edward Hale Papers, North Carolina Department of Archives and History.

77. Woodward, *Mary Chesnut's Civil War*, 130; Davis, *Jefferson Davis, Ex-President of the Confederate States*, 2:160–64; Jefferson Davis to Robert E. Lee, August 11, 1863, Rowland, *Jefferson Davis, Constitutionalist*, 5:589.

78. Albert Gallatin Brown, December 28, 1863, in Frank Vandiver, ed., "Proceedings of the First Confederate Congress, 4th Session," *Southern Historical Society Papers* 12 (1953): 133; Jefferson Davis to Confederate Congress, December 7, 1863, Rowland, *Jefferson Davis, Constitutionalist*, 6:168; Jefferson Davis to Confederate Congress, February 4, 1864, Rowland, *Jefferson Davis, Constitutionalist*, 6:165.

79. Jefferson Davis in *Huntsville (Ala.) Confederate*, September 2, 1863; Jefferson Davis to the Army of Tennessee, Rowland, *Jefferson Davis, Constitutionalist*, 6:61;

Hodes, *White Women, Black Men*, 143, 140–41; Mitchell, *Vacant Chair*, 100–110; Jefferson Davis in *Charleston Mercury*, December 27, 1862.

80. Jefferson Davis, in *Charleston Mercury*, October 7, 1864.

81. Jefferson Davis in *Richmond Enquirer*, January 7, 1864; Faust, *Creation of Confederate Nationalism*, 46; Gov. John Gill Shorter to W. B. Hadewell, July 20, 1862, ADAH; Gov. John Gill Shorter to Mississippi Gov. John J. Pettus, March 5, 1862, ADAH; Jefferson Davis, "Speech to the Army of Tennessee, October 14, 1863," in Rowland, *Jefferson Davis, Constitutionalist*, 6:186.

82. Cawardine, *Evangelicals and Politics*, 56–58.

83. Powell and Wayne, "Self-Interest and the Decline"; *Richmond Examiner*, May 16, 1862, in Daniel, *Richmond Examiner during the War*, 54; *Charleston Mercury*, January 17, 1865.

84. Dodd, *Jefferson Davis*, 290–92; Neely, *Confederate Bastille*, 11, 16.

85. *North Carolina Standard*, May 6, 1863; Wesley, *Collapse of the Confederacy*, 151; Vandiver, *Their Tattered Flags*, 192.

86. Eaton, *Freedom of Thought*, 162–63; Pollard, *Life of Jefferson Davis*, 165.

87. Herschel V. Johnson to Jefferson Davis, February 27, 1864, Jefferson Davis Papers, Perkin Collection, DUL; Clay-Clopton, *Belle of the Fifties*, 239.

88. OR, ser. 1, vol. 16, pt. 2, 1118.

89. Powell and Wayne, "Self-Interest and the Decline," 29–46.

90. Davis, *Long Surrender*, 64; Nina Silber, "Intemperate Men, Spiteful Women, and Jefferson Davis," in Clinton and Silber, *Divided Houses*, 283–305, esp. 284.

91. William C. Davis, *Jefferson Davis*, 644–45.

92. Towns, "'To Preserve the Traditions of Our Fathers,'" 111–24; *New Orleans Picayune* quoted in Wilson, "Death of Southern Heroes," 6.

93. Jefferson Davis in *North American Review* 145: 256; DeRosa, *Confederate Constitution*, 31.

CONCLUSION

1. Stephens, *Constitutional View*, 2:448; Abraham Lincoln, "Address before the Young Men's Lyceum of Springfield, Illinois, January 27, 1838," in Basler, *Collected Works of Abraham Lincoln*, 1:112.

2. Abraham Lincoln, "First Joint Debate, Ottawa, August 21, 1858," in Johannsen, *Lincoln-Douglas Debates*, 53. Lincoln's evolving ideas on the Declaration and equality are ably described in Oates, *With Malice toward None*, 146–47.

3. Nevins, *Ordeal of the Union*, 3:454; Klement, *Limits of Dissent*, 173–77; Neely, *Fate of Liberty*, 64.

4. Marshall, *American Bastille*. Pioneering Civil War historian William E. Dodd remarked that the record on civil liberties was "all in favor" of the Confederate

president. See Dodd, *Jefferson Davis*, 224. For more recent, favorable assessments of Lincoln, see Belz, "Lincoln and the Constitution," 17–43; Neely, *Fate of Liberty*, 210–22.

5. Sharp, *American Politics in the Early Republic*; Blackburn, *Overthrow of Colonial Slavery*, 273–74, 218; Zilversmit, *First Emancipation*, 192–99; James, *Black Jacobins*, 162–63; Genovese, *From Rebellion to Revolution*, 49.

6. Frederick Douglass, "July Fourth and the Negro," in Philip S. Foner, ed., *The Life and Writings of Frederick Douglass* (New York, 1950), 2:181–203.

7. Katz, *Resistance at Christiana*, 92–103; "Impartial Citizen" in the *Liberator*, October 3, 1851, printed in Aptheker, *Documentary History*, 1:324.

8. Oates, *To Purge This Land with Blood*, 318; "William Lloyd Garrison at Tremont Temple, December 16, 1859," in Cain, *William Lloyd Garrison*, 158.

9. Abraham Lincoln, "First Inaugural Address," in Fehrenbacher, *Speeches and Writings*, 215, 220, 222.

10. Nevins, *Ordeal of the Union*, 3:190.

11. Abraham Lincoln, "Special Message to Congress," July 4, 1861, in Fehrenbacher, *Speeches and Writings*, 258–59.

12. Abraham Lincoln, "First Inaugural Address," in Fehrenbacher, *Speeches and Writings*, 220.

13. Abraham Lincoln to Alexander H. Stephens, December 22, 1860, in Fehrenbacher, *Speeches and Writings*, 194.

14. Foner, *Free Soil*, 13–18; Lincoln quoted in Foner, *Story of American Freedom*, 97.

15. *New York Tribune*, September 1, 1863.

16. Abraham Lincoln to Horace Greeley, August 22, 1862, in Fehrenbacher, *Speeches and Writings*, 358; Paludan, *Presidency of Abraham Lincoln*, 50–51; Donald, *Lincoln*, 362–66.

17. Grimsley, *Hard Hand of War*, 4, 144.

18. Hofstadter, *American Political Tradition*, 169.

19. Du Bois, *Black Reconstruction in America*, 87.

20. Wills, *Lincoln at Gettysburg*, 144–45.

21. Waugh, *Reelecting Lincoln*, 310–31.

22. Aptheker, *Documentary History*, 544.

23. Foner, *Reconstruction*, 70–71, 109; Fitzgerald, *Union League Movement in the Deep South*; Harding, *There Is a River*, 261–65.

24. Baltimore correspondent of *New York World*, quoted in Gillette, *Retreat from Reconstruction*, 218.

25. John R. Lynch, *The Facts of Reconstruction* (New York, 1970), 315.

26. Foner, *Reconstruction*, 583; Brecher, *Strike!*, 1–22; Bruce, 1877.

27. Reich, "Soldiers of Democracy," 1478–89; Litwak, *Trouble in Mind*, 405–79; Kelley, 119–51, McMillan, *Dark Journey*, 282–318.

28. Arnesen, *Waterfront Workers of New Orleans*; Herbert Gutman, "The Negro and the United Mine Workers of America: The Career and Letters of Richard L. Davis and Something of Their Meaning, 1890–1900," in Gutman, *Work, Culture, and Society*, 121–208; Rachleff, *Black Labor in Richmond*, 120–27. For a balanced account of the Populist movement and race, see Ayers, *Promise of the New South*, 249–82, and C. Vann Woodward's classic *Tom Watson, Agrarian Rebel*, 216–40, 431–50.

29. Karl Marx to Francois Lafargue, November 12, 1866, in Marx, *Karl Marx*, 274–75.

Works Cited

MANUSCRIPT COLLECTIONS

Alabama Department of Archives and History: Gov. H. W. Collier Papers. Benjamin Perry Papers. Gov. John Gill Shorter Papers. Thomas Watts Papers. Gov. John Winston Papers. William Lowndes Yancey file.

Jefferson Davis Association, Rice University: Jefferson Davis Papers.

Library of Congress: Crittenden Collection. James Henry Hammond Papers. Andrew Johnson Papers. Pickens-Bonham Collection.

Mississippi Department of Archives and History: Pettus Papers.

North Carolina Department of Archives and History: Edward Hale Papers. Zebulon Vance Papers.

Perkin Collection, Duke University Library: Herschel V. Johnson Papers. Lawrence Keitt Papers. Pickens Family Papers. Rutherfoord Family Papers. Alexander Stephens Papers.

South Carolina Department of Archives and History: Minutes of South Carolina Executive Council.

South Caroliniana Library, University of South Carolina: James Henry Hammond Papers. Francis Pickens Papers. Beaufort Watts Papers. Williams-Chesnut Manning Papers.

Southern Historical Collection, University of North Carolina: Thomas Bragg Diary. John Wilson Cunningham Papers. John Lipscomb Johnson Papers. William Porcher Miles Papers. Orr-Patterson Collection. Benjamin Perry Papers. Francis W. Pickens Papers.

University of Chicago: Stephen Douglas Papers.

University of Georgia: Brown Family Papers. Clay Family Papers. Howell Cobb Papers. Telamon Cuyler Collection. Hargrett Collection. Herschel Johnson Papers. Alexander Stephens Papers (copy, Library of Congress). Alexander Stephens Papers (copy, Manhattanville College).

Virginia Historical Society: Rutherfoord Papers. Henry Wise Papers.

NEWSPAPERS

Augusta Weekly Chronicle and Sentinel
Brunswick Advocate
Charleston Courier
Charleston Mercury
Clarke County (Ala.) Democrat
De Bow's Review
Edgeville Advertiser
Huntsville Confederate
Huntsville Democrat
Huntsville Southern Advocate
Jackson Weekly Mississippian
Milledgeville Southern Recorder
Milledgeville Federal Union
Mobile Daily Register
Montgomery Advertiser
National Intelligencer
Niles Weekly Register
New York Times
North Carolina Standard
North Carolina State Journal
Port Gibson Correspondent
Raleigh Weekly Standard
Raleigh Weekly State Journal
Richmond Enquirer
Richmond Examiner
Southern Banner
United States Telegraph
Washington Globe

PUBLISHED SOURCES

Abernethy, Thomas. *From Frontier to Plantation in Tennessee: A Study in Frontier Democracy*. 1932. Reprint, Tuscaloosa, 1967.

Adams, Henry. *John Randolph, a Biography*. 1882. Reprint, Armonk, N.Y., 1996.

Adams, John Q. *Memoirs of John Quincy Adams*. Edited by Charles Francis Adams. 1874–77. Reprint, Freeport, N.Y., 1969.

Address of the Southern Rights Association of the University of Virginia to the Young Men of the South. N.p., 1851.

"Address of Thomas J. Hudson at the Agricultural Fair." *Journal of the Mississippi Senate*. Jackson, 1858.

Address of William C. Harris before the Mississippi Senate, November 15, 1858. Jackson, 1858.

Address of William Lowndes Yancey to the Alabama State Democratic Convention. Montgomery, 1860. Curry Pamphlet Collection, ADAH.

Altschuler, Glenn, and Stuart M. Blumin. "The Limits of Political Engagement in Antebellum America: A New Look at the Golden Age of Participatory Democracy." *Journal of American History* 84 (December 1997): 855–85.

Ambrose, Douglas. *Henry Hughes and Proslavery Thought in the Old South.* Baton Rouge, 1996.

"American Oratory." *Southern Quarterly Review* 5 (1844): 361–91.

Anbinder, Tyler. *Nativism and Slavery.* New York, 1992.

Anderson, Benedict. *Imagined Communities: Reflections on the Origins and Spread of Nationalism.* New York, 1983.

Appleby, Joyce. *Capitalism as a New Social Order: The Republican Vision of the 1790's.* New York, 1984.

———. "Commercial Farming and the 'Agrarian Myth' in the Early Republic." *Journal of American History* 68 (March 1982): 833–49.

Aptheker, Herbert. *American Negro Slave Revolts.* New York, 1943.

———, ed. *A Documentary History of the Negro People in the United States.* New York, 1951.

Arnesen, Eric. *Waterfront Workers in New Orleans: Race, Class, and Politics, 1863–1923.* New York, 1991.

Ash, Stephen V. *When the Yankees Came: Conflict and Chaos in the Occupied South.* Chapel Hill, N.C., 1995.

Ashworth, John. *"Agrarians" and "Aristocrats": Party Political Ideology in the United States, 1837–1846.* Cambridge, 1983.

———. *Slavery, Capitalism, and Politics in the Antebellum Republic, 1820–1850.* Cambridge, 1995.

Atkins, Jonathan. *Parties, Politics and the Sectional Conflict in Tennessee, 1832–1861.* Knoxville, 1997.

Atkins, Lee Rawl, et al. *Alabama: The History of a Deep South State.* Tuscaloosa, 1994.

Avery, Isaac. *The History of the State of Georgia.* New York, 1881.

Ayers, Edward. *The Promise of the New South: Life after Reconstruction.* New York, 1992.

———. *Vengeance and Justice: Crime and Punishment in the Nineteenth-Century American South.* New York, 1984.

Bailey, Frederick W. *Class and Tennessee's Confederate Generation.* Chapel Hill, N.C., 1987.

———. "Class and Tennessee's Confederate Generation." *Journal of Southern History* 51 (February 1985): 31–60.

Bailey, Hugh. "Disaffection in the Alabama Hill Country, 1861." *Civil War History* 4 (June 1958): 182–94.
———. "Disloyalty in Early Confederate Alabama." *Journal of Southern History* 23 (November 1957): 522–28.
———. *Hinton Rowan Helper, Abolitionist-Racist*. University, Ala., 1965.
Baldwin, Joseph Glover. *The Flush Times of Alabama and Mississippi*. 1853. Reprint, New York, 1957.
———. *Party Leaders*. New York, 1855.
Banner, James M., Jr. "The Problem of South Carolina." In *The Hofstadter Aegis: A Memorial*, edited by Stanley Elkins and Eric McKitrick. New York, 1974.
Barney, William L. *The Secessionist Impulse: Alabama and Mississippi in 1860*. Princeton, 1974.
Basch, Norma. "Marriage, Morals, and Politics in the Election of 1828." *Journal of American History* 80 (December 1993): 890–918.
Basler, Roy, ed. *The Collected Works of Abraham Lincoln*. New Brunswick, N.J., 1953.
Bassett, John Spencer, ed. *Correspondence of Andrew Jackson*. Washington, 1927.
Bedsole, Virgil. "The Life of Jeremiah Clemens." Master's thesis, University of Alabama, 1934.
Belz, Herman. *Abraham Lincoln, Constitutionalism, and Equal Rights in the Civil War Era*. New York, 1998.
Benton, Thomas Hart. *Thirty Years' View*. New York, 1854.
Beringer, Richard, et al. *Why the South Lost the Civil War*. Athens, Ga., 1986.
Bestor, Arthur. "State Sovereignty and Slavery: A Reinterpretation of Proslavery Constitutional Doctrine, 1846–1860." In *Proslavery Thought, Ideology, and Politics*, edited by Paul Finkelman, 42–61. New York, 1989.
Betts, Edward, ed. *Jefferson's Farm Book with Commentary and Relevant Extracts from Other Writings*. Princeton, 1953.
Blackburn, Robin. *The Overthrow of Colonial Slavery, 1776–1848*. New York, 1988.
Bolton, Charles C. *Poor Whites of the Antebellum South*. Durham, N.C., 1994.
Bond, Bradley. *Political Culture in the Nineteenth-Century South, Mississippi, 1830–1900*. Baton Rouge, 1995.
Boney, F. N. *John Letcher of Virginia: The Story of Virginia's Civil War Governor*. Tuscaloosa, 1966.
Boucher, Chauncey. *Sectionalism, Representation, and the Electoral Question in Antebellum South Carolina*. Saint Louis, 1917.
Boyd, Julian P., ed. *The Papers of Thomas Jefferson*. Princeton, 1950–.
Bradford, M. E. *Remembering Who We Are: Observations of a Southern Conservative*. Athens, Ga., 1985.
Brecher, Jeremy. *Strike!* Boston, 1982.
Breen, Timothy. *Tobacco Culture: The Mentality of the Great Tidewater Planters on the Eve of Revolution*. Princeton, 1985.

Brown, Joseph. *Governor Brown on the Present Crisis.* N.p., c. 1860.
Brown, Richard H. "The Missouri Crisis, Slavery, and the Politics of Jacksonianism." *South Atlantic Quarterly* 65 (1965): 323–50.
Brown, Wendy. *Manhood and Politics: A Feminist Reading in Political Theory.* Littlefield, N.J., 1988.
Bruce, Robert V. *1877: Year of Violence.* New York, 1959.
Bryan, T. Conn. "The Secession of Georgia." *Georgia Historical Quarterly* 31 (1947): 89–111.
Buckle, Henry Thomas. *History of Civilization in England.* 1857. Reprint, London, 1922.
Burstein, Andrew. *The Inner Jefferson: Portrait of a Grieving Optimist.* Charlottesville, Va., 1995.
———. *Sentimental Democracy.* New York, 1999.
Burton, Orville Vernon. *In My Father's House Are Many Mansions: Family and Community in Edgefield, South Carolina.* Chapel Hill, N.C., 1985.
Burton, Orville Vernon, and Robert C. Mcmath, eds. *Class, Conflict, and Consensus: Antebellum Southern Community Studies.* Westport, Conn., 1982.
Butts, Donald. "'The Irrepressible Conflict': Slave Taxation and North Carolina's Gubernatorial Election of 1860." *North Carolina Historical Review* 58 (Winter 1981): 44–61.
Cabbell, Francis. *Early History of the University as Contained in the Letters of Thomas Jefferson and Joseph C. Cabell.* Richmond, 1856.
Caine, William E., ed. *William Lloyd Garrison and the Fight against Slavery: Selections From the Liberator.* New York, 1995.
Candler, Allen D., ed. *Confederate Records of the State of Georgia.* New York, 1972.
Capers, Gerald. "A Reconsideration of John C. Calhoun's Transition from Nationalism to Nullification." *Journal of Southern History* 14 (February 1948): 34–48.
Cappon, Lester J., ed. *The Adams-Jefferson Letters: The Complete Correspondence between Thomas Jefferson and Abigail and John Adams.* Chapel Hill, N.C., 1952.
Carey, Anthony Gene. *Parties, Slavery, and the Union in Antebellum Georgia.* Athens, Ga., 1997.
Cash, Wilbur. *The Mind of the South.* New York, 1941.
Cauthen, Charles. *South Carolina Goes to War.* Chapel Hill, N.C., 1950.
Cawardine, Richard J. *Evangelicals and Politics in Antebellum America.* New Haven, 1993.
Cecil-Fronsman, Bill. *Common Whites: Class and Culture in Antebellum North Carolina.* Lexington, Ky., 1992.
Chambers, Simone. *Reasonable Democracy: Jurgen Habermas and the Politics of Discourse.* Ithaca, N.Y., 1996.
Channing, Stephen. *Crisis of Fear: Secession in South Carolina.* New York, 1970.

Clausewitz, Carl Von. *On War*. Edited by Michael Howard and Peter Paret. Princeton, 1976.
Clay, Cassius. *The Life of Cassius Marcellus Clay: Memoirs, Writing, and Speeches*. 1886. Reprint, New York, 1969.
Clay, Henry. *Speech of the Hon. Henry Clay in the House of Representatives of the United States on the Seminole War*. Washington, 1819.
Clay-Copton, Virginia. *A Belle of the Fifties*. New York, 1904.
Clemens, Jeremiah. *Bernard Lile*. Philadelphia, 1856.
———. *Mustang Gray*. Philadelphia, 1858.
———. *The Rivals*. Philadelphia, 1860.
———. *Tobias Wilson*. Philadelphia, 1965.
Cleveland, Henry, ed. *Alexander Stephens in Public and Private, with Letters and Speeches*. Philadelphia, 1856.
Clinton, Catherine, and Nina Silber, eds. *Divided Houses: Gender and the Civil War*. Oxford, 1992.
Cole, Arthur. *The Irrepressible Conflict, 1850–65*. New York, 1934.
Collins, Bruce W. "Governor Joseph Brown, Economic Issues, and Georgia's Road to Secession, 1857–1859." *Georgia Historical Quarterly* 71 (Summer 1987): 189–225.
———. *White Society in the Antebellum South*. Chapel Hill, N.C., 1960.
Congressional Globe. Washington, 1834–61.
Connelly Thomas. *The Marble Man: Robert E. Lee and His Image in American Society*. Baton Rouge, 1977.
Cooper, William. *Liberty and Slavery: Southern Politics to 1860*. New York, 1983.
———. *The South and the Politics of Slavery*. New York, 1978.
Correspondence and Other Papers Relating to Fort Sumter. Charleston, S.C., 1861.
Correspondence between Henry A. Wise and Hon. Fernando Wood. Richmond, 1860.
Cott, Nancy F. *The Bonds of Womanhood: "Women's Sphere" in New England, 1780–1835*. New Haven, 1977.
Coulter, Merton E. *Georgia: A Short History*. Chapel Hill, N.C., 1960.
Crabtree, Beth Gilbert, and Patton, James W., eds. *"Journal of a Sesech Lady": The Diary of Catherine Anne Devereux Edmonston, 1860–1866*. Raleigh, N.C., 1979.
Cralle, Richard, ed. *The Works of Calhoun*. New York, 1888.
Crenshaw, Ollinger. "The Speakership Contest of 1859–60." *Mississippi Valley Historical Review* 29 (December 1942): 323–38.
Crist, Lynda Lasswell, ed. *The Papers of Jefferson Davis*. Baton Rouge, 1971– .
Crofts, Daniel. *Reluctant Confederates: Upper South Unionists in the Secession Crisis*. Chapel Hill, N.C., 1989.
Current, Richard. "God and the Strongest Battalions." In *Why the North Won the Civil War*, edited by David Donald. New York, 1960.
———. *Lincoln's Loyalists: Union Soldiers from the Confederacy*. New York, 1992.
Curry, J. L. M. *The Perils and Duties of the South, Substance of a Speech Delivered by*

J. L. M. Curry in Talladega, Alabama, November 26, 1860. N.p., n.d. Curry Pamphlet Collection, ADAH.

Daniel, John. *The Richmond Examiner during the War.* Richmond, 1867.

"A Daughter of Dixie." *An Appeal to the South.* N.p., c. 1861.

Davis, Burke. *The Long Surrender.* New York, 1985.

Davis, Jefferson. "Life and Character of the Hon. John Caldwell Calhoun." *North American Review* 145 (September 1887): 246–60.

———. *The Rise and Fall of the Confederate States of America.* New York, 1881.

Davis, Varina Howell. *Jefferson Davis, Ex-President of the Confederate States of America: A Memoir.* New York, 1890.

Davis, William C. *"A Government of Our Own": The Making of the Confederacy.* New York, 1994.

———. *Jefferson Davis: The Man and His Hour.* New York, 1991.

De Bow, J. D. B. *The Industrial Resources, etc. of the Southern and Western States.* New Orleans, 1853.

———. *The Interest in Slavery of the Southern Nonslaveholder.* Charleston, 1860.

Denman, Clarence Philip. *The Secession Movement in Alabama.* Montgomery, 1933.

DeRosa, Marshall. *The Confederate Constitution of 1861: An Inquiry into American Constitutionalism.* Columbia, Mo., 1991.

Dew, Thomas R. "Abolition of Negro Slavery," *American Quarterly Review* 12 (1832): 189–265.

———. *Review of the Debate of the Virginia Legislature of 1831 and 1832.* Richmond, 1832.

Dodd, William. *Jefferson Davis.* Philadelphia, 1907.

———. *Statesmen of the Old South.* Chicago, 1904.

Donald, David. "Died of Democracy." In *Why the North Won the Civil War*, edited by David Donald. New York, 1962.

———. *Lincoln.* New York, 1995.

———. "The Southerner as Fighting Man." In *The Southerner as American*, edited by Charles Sellers. New York, 1966.

Dorman, Lewy. *Party Politics in Alabama from 1850 through 1860.* Wetumpka, Ala., 1935.

Douglass, Frederick. *Life and Times of Frederick Douglass.* 1892. Reprint, New York, 1960.

———. *The Life and Writings of Frederick Douglass.* Edited by Philip Foner. 5 vols. New York, 1950.

———. *Narrative of the Life of Frederick Douglass: An American Slave Written by Himself.* 1845. Reprint, Cambridge, Mass., 1960.

Doyon, Roy R., and Thomas W. Hodler. "Secessionist Sentiment and Slavery: A Geographic Analysis." *Georgia Historical Quarterly* 73 (Summer 1989): 323–48.

Draper, Hal. *Karl Marx's Theory of Revolution: The Politics of Social Classes.* New York, 1978.

Drummond, Clyde. "Biography of Jeremiah Clemens: A Personal, Political, Military, and Literary Sketch of His Life." Master's thesis, Auburn University, 1934.

Du Bois, W. E. B. *Black Reconstruction in America, 1860–1880.* New York, 1935.

DuBose, John Witherspoon. *The Life and Times of William Lowndes Yancey.* Birmingham, 1892.

Dumond, Dwight L., ed. *Southern Editorials on Secession.* New York, 1931.

Dunaway, Wilma. *The First American Frontier: The Transition to Capitalism in Southern Appalachia, 1700–1860.* Chapel Hill, N.C., 1996.

Durill, Wayne K. *War of Another Kind: A Southern Community in the Great Rebellion.* New York, 1990.

Dusenbery, Benjamin M., ed. *Monument to the Memory of Andrew Jackson: Containing Twenty-five Eulogies and Sermons Delivered on the Occasion of His Death.* Philadelphia, 1846.

Dyer, Gustavus, and John Trotwood Moore, eds. *The Tennessee Civil War Veterans Questionnaires.* Easley, S.C., 1985.

Dykstal, Timothy. "The Story of O: Politics and Pleasure in the Vicar of Wakefield." *English Literary History* 62 (1995): 329–46.

Eaton, Clement. *Freedom of Thought Struggle in the Old South.* 1940. Reprint, New York, 1951.

———. *Jefferson Davis.* Baton Rouge, 1977.

———. "Mob Violence in the Old South." *Mississippi Valley Historical Review* 19 (December 1942): 351–70.

Eaton, John Henry. *The Letters of Wyoming to the People of the United States on the Presidential Election and in Favor of Andrew Jackson.* Philadelphia, 1824.

Eaton, Peggy. *The Autobiography of Peggy Eaton.* New York, 1932.

Edmunds, John B., Jr. *Francis W. Pickens and the Politics of Destruction.* Chapel Hill, N.C., 1986.

Eley, Geoff. "Nations, Publics, and Political Cultures." In *Habermas and the Public Sphere,* edited by Craig Calhoun. Cambridge, Mass., 1992.

Ellis, Joseph. *American Sphinx: The Character of Thomas Jefferson.* New York, 1997.

Escott, Paul D. *After Secession: Jefferson Davis and the Failure of Confederate Nationalism.* Baton Rouge, 1978.

———. *Many Excellent People: Power and Privilege in North Carolina, 1850–1900.* Chapel Hill, N.C., 1985.

———. "Yeoman Independence and the Market: Social Status and Economic Development in Antebellum North Carolina." *North Carolina Historical Review* 66 (July 1989): 275–300.

Faust, Drew Gilpin. *James Henry Hammond and the Old South: A Design for Mastery.* Baton Rouge, 1982.

———. *Mothers of Invention: Women of the Slaveholding South during the Civil War.* Chapel Hill, N.C., 1996.

———, ed. *The Creation of Confederate Nationalism: Ideology and Identity in the Civil War South.* Baton Rouge, 1988.

———. *The Ideology of Slavery: Proslavery Thought in the Antebellum South.* Baton Rouge, 1981.

Fehrenbacher, Donald E. *Constitutions and Constitutionalism in the Slaveholding South.* Athens, Ga., 1969.

———. *Slavery, Law, and Politics: The Dred Scot Case in Historical Perspective.* New York, 1981.

———, ed. *Speeches and Writings of Abraham Lincoln, 1859–1865.* New York, 1989.

Fellman, Michael. *Inside War: The Guerrilla Conflict in Missouri during the American Civil War.* New York, 1989.

Fields, Barbara Jeanne. *Slavery and Freedom on the Middle Ground.* New Haven, 1985.

Finkelman, Paul. *An Imperfect Union: Slavery, Federalism, and Comity.* Chapel Hill, N.C., 1981.

Fisher, Noel. *War at Every Door: Partisan Politics and Guerrilla Violence in East Tennessee, 1860–69.* Chapel Hill, N.C., 1997.

Fitzgerald, Michael. *The Union League Movement in the Deep South: Politics and Agricultural Change during Reconstruction.* Baton Rouge, 1989.

Fleming, Walter Lynwood. *The Civil War and Reconstruction in Alabama.* New York, 1905.

Fliegelman, Jay. *Prodigals and Pilgrims: The American Revolution against Patriarchal Authority, 1750–1800.* New York, 1982.

Flippin, Percy. *Herschel Johnson, State Rights Unionist.* Richmond, 1931.

———, ed. "From the Autobiography of Herschel Johnson." *American Historical Review* 30 (October 1924): 311–36.

Fogel, Robert William. *Without Consent or Contract: The Rise and Fall of American Slavery.* New York, 1989.

Foner, Eric. *Free Soil, Free Labor, Free Men: The Ideology of the Republican Party before the Civil War.* New York, 1970.

———. *Reconstruction: America's Unfinished Revolution, 1863–1877.* New York, 1988.

———. *The Story of American Freedom.* New York, 1998.

———. *Tom Paine and Revolutionary America.* New York, 1976.

Ford, Lacy K. "Inventing the Concurrent Majority: Madison, Calhoun, and the Problem of Majoritarianism in American Political Thought." *Journal of Southern History* 60 (February 1994): 19–58.

———. *Origins of Southern Radicalism: The South Carolina Upcountry, 1800–1860.* New York, 1988.

———. "The Origins of the Edgefield Tradition: The Late Antebellum Experience and the Roots of Political Insurgency." *South Carolina Historical Magazine* 98 (October 1997): 337–45.

———. "Popular Ideology of the Old South's Plain Folk: The Limits of Egalitarianism in a Slaveholding Society." In *Plain Folk of the South Revisited*, edited by Samuel C. Hyde. Baton Rouge, 1997.

Ford, Paul Leicester, ed. *The Writings of Thomas Jefferson*. New York, 1892–99.

Fox-Genovese, Elizabeth. *Within the Plantation Household: Black and White Women in the Old South*. Chapel Hill, N.C., 1988.

Fraser, Nancy. "Rethinking the Public Sphere: A Contribution to the Critique of Actually Existing Democracy." In *Habermas and the Public Sphere*, edited by Craig Calhoun. Cambridge, Mass., 1992.

Fredrickson, George. *The Arrogance of Race*. Middletown, Conn., 1987.

———. *The Black Image in the White Mind*. New York, 1971.

———. *"Blue over Gray": Sources of Success and Failure in the Civil War and Reconstruction*. Minneapolis, 1975.

Freehling, William. "The Divided South, Democracy's Limitations, and the Causes of the Peculiarly North American Civil War." In *Why the Civil War Came*, edited by Gabor S. Borritt. New York, 1986.

———. *Prelude to Civil War: the Nullification Controversy in South Carolina, 1816–1836*. New York, 1965.

———. *Road to Disunion, Volume One: Secessionists at Bay*. New York, 1990.

———. "Spoilsmen and Interests in the Thought and Career of John C. Calhoun." *Journal of American History* 52 (June 1965): 25–42.

Freehling, William, and Craig Simpson, eds. *Secession Debated: Georgia's Political Showdown in 1860*. New York, 1992.

Frost, John. *Pictorial Life of Andrew Jackson*. Philadelphia, 1847.

Gallagher, Gary. *The Confederate War*. Cambridge, Mass., 1997.

Geertz, Clifford. "Ideology as Cultural System." In *Ideology and Discontent*, edited by David Apter. London, 1964.

Genovese, Eugene. *From Rebellion to Revolution: Afro-American Slave Revolts in the Making of the New World*. Baton Rouge, 1979.

———. *The Political Economy of Slavery*. New York, 1965.

———. *Roll, Jordan, Roll: The World the Slaves Made*. New York, 1974.

———. "The Slaveholders' Contribution to the American Constitution." In *The Southern Front: History and Politics in the Cultural War*. Columbia, Mo., 1995.

———. *The Slaveholders' Dilemma: Freedom and Progress in Southern Conservative Thought, 1820–1860*. Columbia, S.C., 1992.

———. *The World the Slaveholders Made*. New York, 1969.

———. "Yeoman Farmers in a Slaveholder's Democracy." In *Fruits of Merchant Capital*, by Eugene Genovese and Elizabeth Fox-Genovese. New York, 1983.

Gienapp, William. "The Political System and the Coming of the Civil War." In *Why the Civil War Came*, edited by Gabor S. Borrit. New York, 1996.

———. "'Politics Seems to Enter into Everything': Political Culture in the North, 1840–1860." in *Essays in American Antebellum Politics, 1840–1860*, edited by Stephen Maizlish and John J. Kushma. College Station, Tex., 1982.

Gillette, William. *Retreat from Reconstruction, 1869–1879*. Baton Rouge, 1979.

Goldsmith, Andrew. *The Vicar of Wakefield*. 1766. Reprint, London, 1954.

Goodwin, Philo A. *Biography of Andrew Jackson, President of the United States, Formerly Major General in the Army of the United States*. New York, 1834.

Goodwyn, Lawrence. *The Populist Moment*. New York, 1978.

Gordon, T. F. *The War on the Bank of the United States*. Philadelphia, 1854.

Graf, LeRoy P., and Ralph W. Haskins, eds. *The Papers of Andrew Johnson*. Knoxville, 1967–.

Grammer, John M. *Pastoral and Politics in the Old South*. Baton Rouge, 1996.

Gray, Richard. *Writing the South: Ideas of an American Region*. New York, 1986.

Greenberg, Kenneth S. *Honor and Slavery*. Princeton, 1996.

———. *Masters and Statesmen: The Political Culture of American Slavery*. Baltimore, 1985.

———. "Representation and the Isolation of South Carolina, 1776–1860." *Journal of American History* 64 (December 1977): 723–43.

Greene, Fletcher M. *Constitutional Development in the South Atlantic States, 1776–1860*. Chapel Hill, N.C., 1930.

———. "Democracy in the Old South." *Journal of Southern History* 12 (1946): 2–23.

Greenwald, Bruce S., ed. "Unionists in Rockbridge County: The Correspondence of James Dorman Davidson Concerning the Virginia Secession Convention of 1861," *Virginia Magazine of History and Biography* 73 (January 1965): 78–101.

Grimsley, Mark. *The Hard Hand of War: Union Military Policy toward Southern Civilians, 1861–1865*. New York, 1995.

Gutman, Herbert. *Work, Culture, and Society in Industrializing America*. New York, 1977.

Habermas, Jürgen. *The Structural Transformation of the Public Sphere*. Cambridge, Mass., 1989.

Hahn, Stephen. *The Roots of Southern Populism: Yeoman Farmers and the Transformation of the Georgia Upcountry, 1850–1900*. New York, 1983.

Harding, Vincent. *There Is a River: The Black Struggle for Freedom in America*. New York, 1981.

Harris, J. William. *Plain Folk and Gentry in a Slave Society: White Liberty and Black Slavery in Augusta's Hinterland*. Middletown, Conn., 1985.

Harris, William C. *William Woods Holden: Firebrand of North Carolina Politics*. Baton Rouge, 1987.

Harrold, Stanley. *The Abolitionists and the South, 1831–1861*. Lexington, Ky., 1995.
Hartz, Louis. *The Liberal Tradition in America*. New York, 1955.
Heyrman, Christine Leigh. *The Southern Cross: The Beginnings of the Bible Belt*. New York, 1997.
Hill, Louise. *Joseph Brown and the Confederacy*. Westport, Conn., 1972.
A History of the Life and Public Services of Major General Andrew Jackson: Impartially Compiled from Authentic Sources. N.p., 1828.
Hobsbawm, Eric. *Nations and Nationalism since 1780: Programme, Myth, Reality*. New York, 1990.
Hodes, Martha. *White Women, Black Men: Illicit Sex in the Nineteenth-Century South*. New Haven, 1997.
Hodgson, Joseph. *Science the Handmaid of Republicanism*. Richmond, 1858.
Hofstadter, Richard. *American Political Tradition and the Men Who Made It*. New York, 1948.
———. *The Idea of a Party System: The Rise of Legitimate Opposition in the United States, 1780–1840*. Berkeley, 1969.
Holt, Michael. *The Rise and Fall of the American Whig Party*. New York, 1999.
Hoole, W. Stanley. *Alabama Tories: The First Alabama Cavalry, U.S.A., 1862–65*. Tuscaloosa, 1960.
———. "Jeremiah Clemens, Novelist." *Alabama Review* 18 (January 1965): 1–37.
Hooper, Johnson J. *Adventures of Captain Simon Suggs, Late of the Tallapoosa Volunteers*. 1845. Reprint, Chapel Hill, N.C., 1969.
Horton, Paul. "Submitting to the 'Shadow of Slavery': The Secession Crisis and Civil War in Alabama's Lawrence County." *Civil War History* 44 (June 1998): 111–36.
Howe, Daniel Walker. *The Political Culture of the American Whigs*. Chicago, 1979.
Hughes, John Starett. "The Madness of Separate Spheres: Insanity and Masculinity in Victorian Alabama." In *Meanings for Manhood: Constructions of Masculinity in Victorian America*, edited by Mark C. Carnes and Clyde Griffin. Chicago, 1990.
Hundley, Daniel. *Social Relations in Our Southern States*. Edited by William J. Cooper. Baton Rouge, 1979.
Hunt, Gaillard, ed. *The Writings of James Madison*. New York, 1900–1910.
Hyman, Harold. *A More Perfect Union: The Impact of the Civil War and Reconstruction on the Constitution*. New York, 1973.
Inscoe, John. *Mountain Masters: Slavery and the Sectional Crisis in Western North Carolina*. Knoxville, 1989.
Isaac, Rhys. *The Transformation of Virginia, 1740–1790*. Chapel Hill, 1982.
James, C. L. R. *The Black Jacobins: Toussaint Louverture and the San Domingo Revolution*. New York, 1938.
Jeffrey, Thomas E. *State Parties and National Politics: North Carolina, 1815–1861*. Athens, Ga., 1989.

Jenkins, A. M., ed. *Life and Public Services of General Andrew Jackson, Seventh President of the United States*. Buffalo, 1851.
Jenkins, William Sumner. *Proslavery Thought in the Old South*. Chapel Hill, N.C., 1935.
Johanssen, Robert, ed. *The Lincoln-Douglas Debates*. New York, 1965.
Johnson, Michael P. "A New Look at the Popular Vote for Delegates to the Georgia Secession Convention." *Georgia Historical Quarterly* 56 (Summer 1972): 259–75.
———. *Toward a Patriarchal Republic: The Secession of Georgia*. Baton Rouge, 1977.
Johnston, Milius. *The Sword of "Bushwacker" Johnson*. 1903. Reprint, Huntsville, 1992.
Jones, John B. *A Rebel War Clerk's Diary*. Edited by Earl Schenck Miers. New York, 1958.
Jordan, Winthrop. *Tumult and Silence at Second Creek: An Inquiry into A Civil War Slave Conspiracy*. Baton Rouge, 1993.
———. *White over Black: American Attitudes toward the Negro, 1550–1812*. New York, 1969.
Journal of the Convention of the People of South Carolina, Held in 1860, 1861, and 1862. Columbia, S.C., 1862.
Kammen, Michael. *A Machine That Would Go of Itself*. New York, 1982.
Kann, Mark E. *A Republic of Men: The American Founders, Gendered Language, and Patriarchal Politics*. New York, 1998.
Katz, Jonathan. *Resistance at Christiana: The Fugitive Slave Rebellion, Christiana, Pennsylvania*. New York, 1951.
Kelley, Robin D. G. *Hammer and Hoe*. Chapel Hill, N.C., 1990.
Kibler, Lillian. *Benjamin Perry: South Carolina Unionist*. Durham, N.C., 1946.
———. "Unionist Sentiment in South Carolina in 1860." *Journal of Southern History* 4 (August 1938): 346–66.
Killen, Michael. *Manhood in America: A Cultural History*. New York, 1996.
Klein, Maury. *Days of Defiance: Sumter, Secession and the Coming of the Civil War*. New York, 1997.
Klein, Rachel. *The Unification of a Slave State: The Rise of the Planter Class in the South Carolina Backcountry, 1720–1808*. Chapel Hill, N.C., 1990.
Klement, Frank L. *The Limits of Dissent: Clement L. Vallandigham and the Civil War*. Lexington, Ky., 1991.
Kohl, Lawrence Frederick. *The Politics of Individualism: Parties and the American Character*. New York, 1989.
Kojeve, Alexander. "Introduction to the Reading of Hegel." In *Deconstruction in Context: Literature and Philosophy*, edited by Mark Taylor. Chicago, 1986.
Kousser, J. Morgan. *The Shaping of Southern Politics*. New Haven, 1974.
Kruman, Marc. *Parties and Politics in North Carolina, 1836–65*. Baton Rouge, 1983.

Landrum, Grace Warren. "Sir Walter Scott and His Literary Rivals in the Old South." *American Literature* 2 (November 1930): 256–76.

Lee, Charles Robert, Jr. *The Confederate Constitutions.* Chapel Hill, N.C., 1963.

Leemhuis, Roger P. *James L. Orr and the Sectional Conflict.* Washington, 1979.

Lenner, Andrew C. "John Taylor and the Origins of American Federalism." *Journal of the Early Republic* 17 (Fall 1997): 399–425.

Lewis, Jan. *The Pursuit of Happiness: Family and Values in Jefferson's Virginia.* New York, 1983.

Life of John C. Calhoun, Presenting a Condensed History of Political Events from 1811 to 1843. New York, 1843.

Link, William A. "The Jordan Hatcher Case: Politics and 'A Spirit of Insubordination' in Antebellum Virginia." *Journal of Southern History* 64 (November 1998): 636–56.

Litwak, Leon. *Trouble in Mind: Black Southerners during Jim Crow.* New York, 1998.

Lynch, John R. *The Facts of Reconstruction.* New York, 1970.

MacPherson, James, ed. "Preface to Fingal." In *Poems of Ossian and Related Works.* Edinburgh, 1996.

Marshall, John A. *American Bastille: A History of the Illegal Arrests and Imprisonment of American Citizens during the Late Civil War.* 1869. Reprint, New York, 1970.

Marszalek, John F. *The Petticoat Affair: Manners, Mutiny, and Sex in Andrew Jackson's White House.* New York, 1997.

Martin, Bessie. *Desertion of Alabama Troops from the Confederate Army: A Study in Sectionalism.* New York, 1932.

Martin, John M. "The Senatorial Career of Jeremiah Clemens, 1849–1853." *Alabama Historical Quarterly* 43 (Fall 1981): 186–235.

Martineau, Harriet. *Society in America.* London, 1838.

Marx, Karl. *Karl Marx on America and the Civil War.* Edited by Saul Padover. New York, 1972.

Marx, Karl, and Frederick Engels. *Selected Works in Three Volumes.* Moscow, 1969–70.

Marx, Leo. *The Machine in the Garden: Technology and the Pastoral Ideal in America.* New York, 1964.

Mathews, Richard K. *The Radical Politics of Thomas Jefferson: A Revisionist View.* Lawrence, Kans., 1984.

Mayer, David N. *The Constitutional Thought of Thomas Jefferson.* Charlottesville, Va., 1994.

McCardell, John. *The Idea of a Southern Nation.* New York, 1979.

McCoy, Drew. *The Elusive Republic: Political Economy in Jeffersonian America.* Chapel Hill, N.C., 1980.

———. *The Last of the Fathers: James Madison and the Republican Legacy.* New York, 1989.

McCurry, Stephanie. *Masters of Small Worlds: Yeoman Households, Gender Relations, and the Political Culture of the Antebellum South Carolina Low Country.* New York, 1995.

———. "The Politics of Yeoman Households in South Carolina." In *Divided Houses: Gender and the Civil War,* edited by Catherine Clinton and Nina Silber. New York, 1992.

———. "The Two Faces of Republicanism: Gender and Proslavery Politics in Antebellum South Carolina." *Journal of American History* 78 (March 1992): 1245–64.

McGrane, Reginald C., ed. *The Correspondence of Nicholas Biddle.* Boston, 1919.

McHenry, Dr. James. *The Jackson Wreath or National Souvenir: A National Tribute of the Great Civil Victory Achieved through the Hero of New Orleans.* Philadelphia, 1829.

McKitrick, Eric L. *Andrew Johnson and Reconstruction.* Chicago, 1969.

McLaughlin, Jack. *Jefferson and Monticello: Biography of a Builder.* New York, 1988.

McMichael, Philip. "Slavery and Capitalism." *Theory and Society* 20 (Summer 1991): 321–49.

McMillan, Malcolm, ed. *The Alabama Confederate Reader.* Tuscaloosa, 1963.

McMillen, Neil R. *Dark Journey: Black Mississippians in the Age of Jim Crow.* Urbana, Ill., 1989.

McPherson, James. *Abraham Lincoln and the Second American Revolution.* New York, 1990.

———. *Battle Cry of Freedom: The Civil War Years.* New York, 1988.

———. *For Cause and Comrades: Why Men Fought in the Civil War.* New York, 1997.

———. "Why Did The Confederacy Lose?" In *Drawn with the Sword: Reflections on the American Civil War.* New York, 1996.

Meets, Stephen, ed. *The Writings of Benjamin F. Perry.* Spartansburg, S.C., 1980.

Memoirs of General Andrew Jackson, Seventh President of the United States. Cincinnati, 1845.

Message No. 1 of His Excellency Francis W. Pickens to the Legislature at the Regular Session of November 1862. Columbia, 1862.

Meyers, Marvin. *The Jacksonian Persuasion: Politics and Belief.* Stanford, 1957.

Miles, Edwin. *Jacksonian Democracy in Mississippi.* Chapel Hill, N.C., 1960.

Miller, Charles. *Jefferson and Nature.* Baltimore, 1988.

Miller, John Chester. *The Wolf by the Ears: Thomas Jefferson and Slavery.* New York, 1977.

Miller, Perry. *The Life of the Mind in America from the Revolution to the Civil War*. New York, 1965.
Mitchell, Reid. "The Perseverance of the Soldiers." In *Why the Confederacy Lost*, edited by Gabor S. Borritt. New York, 1992.
———. "Soldiering, Manhood, and Coming of Age: A Northern Volunteer." In *Divided Houses: Gender and the Civil War*, edited by Catherine Clinton and Nina Silber. Oxford, 1992.
———. *The Vacant Chair: The Northern Soldier Leaves Home*. New York, 1993.
Mohr, Clarence. *On the Threshold of Freedom: Masters and Slaves in Civil War Georgia*. Athens, Ga., 1986.
Moore, Frank, ed. *Rebellion Record*. New York, 1863.
Morgan, Edmund. *American Slavery, American Freedom: The Ordeal of Colonial Virginia*. New York, 1975.
———. *Inventing the People: The Rise of Popular Sovereignty in England and America*. New York, 1988.
Morris, Christopher. *Becoming Southern: The Evolution of a Way of Life, Warren County and Vicksburg, 1770–1860*. New York, 1995.
Morrison, Michael A. *Slavery and the American West: The Eclipse of Manifest Destiny*. Chapel Hill, N.C., 1997.
Moster, Harold, David Hoth, and George Hoesmann, eds. *The Papers of Andrew Jackson*. Knoxville, 1980– .
Neely, Mark E. *The Confederate Bastille: Jefferson Davis and Civil Liberties*. Milwaukee, 1993.
———. *The Fate of Liberty: Abraham Lincoln and Civil Liberties*. New York, 1991.
Neimann, Donald. "Republicanism, the Confederate Constitution, and the American Constitutional Tradition." In *An Uncertain Tradition: Constitutionalism and the History of the South*, edited by Kermit Hall and James W. Ely Jr. Athens, Ga., 1989.
Nelson, Dana D. *National Manhood: Capitalist Citizenship and the Imagined Fraternity of White Men*. Durham, N.C., 1998.
Nevins, Allan. *The Ordeal of the Union*. 4 vols. New York, 1950.
Norton, Mary Beth. *Founding Mothers and Fathers: Gendered Power and the Forming of American Society*. New York, 1996.
Oakes, James. "From Republicanism to Liberalism: Ideological Change and the Crisis of the Old South." *American Quarterly* 37 (Fall 1985): 551–71.
———. *The Ruling Race: A History of American Slaveholders*. New York, 1982.
———. *Slavery and Freedom: An Interpretation of the Old South*. New York, 1990.
Oates, Stephen. *To Purge This Land with Blood: A Biography of John Brown*. New York, 1970.
———. *With Malice toward None: The Life of Abraham Lincoln*. New York, 1977.
Olmsted, Frederick Law. *The Cotton Kingdom: A Traveler's Observations on Cotton*

and *Slavery in the American Slave States*. 1861. Edited by Arthur M. Schlesinger Jr. New York, 1984.

———. *Journey to the Seaboard Slave States*. New York, 1968.

Orians, G. Harrison. "Walter Scott, Mark Twain, and the Civil War." *South Atlantic Quarterly* 40 (July 1941): 342–59.

Osterweis, Rollin G. *Romanticism and Nationalism in the Old South*. Baton Rouge, 1949.

Owsley, Frank. *King Cotton Diplomacy: Foreign Relations of the Confederate States of America*. New York, 1917.

———. *States' Rights in the Confederacy*. Chicago, 1925.

Page, Thomas Nelson. *Social Life in Old Virginia before the War*. New York, 1897.

Paludan, Philip S. *A Covenant with Death: The Constitution, Law and Equality in the Civil War Era*. Urbana, Ill., 1975.

———. *The Presidency of Abraham Lincoln*. Lawrence, Kans., 1994.

Parks, Joseph. *Joseph E. Brown of Georgia*. Baton Rouge, 1977.

Parsons, Charles Grandison. *Inside View of Slavery*. 1855. Reprint, New York, 1969.

Parton, James. *Andrew Jackson*. New York, 1860.

Patterson, Orlando. *Slavery and Social Death*. Cambridge, Mass., 1982.

Petersen, Merrill. *The Great Triumvirate: Webster, Clay, and Calhoun*. New York, 1987.

———. *The Jeffersonian Image in the American Mind*. New York, 1960.

———, ed. *The Portable Thomas Jefferson*. New York, 1975.

Petit, Arthur J. *Mark Twain and the South*. Lexington, Ky., 1974.

Phillips, Ulrich Bonnell. *Georgia and States' Rights*. Washington, 1902.

———, ed. *The Correspondence of Robert Toombs, Alexander H. Stephens, and Howell Cobb*. Washington, 1913.

The Political Mirror or Review of Jacksonism. New York, 1835.

Potter, David. *The Impending Crisis, 1848–1861*. New York, 1976.

———. "Jefferson Davis and the Political Factors in Confederate Defeat." In *The South and the Sectional Conflict*, by David Potter. Baton Rouge, 1968.

Powell, Lawrence, and Michael Wayne. "Self-Interest and the Decline of Confederate Nationalism." In *The Old South in the Crucible of War*, edited by Harry Owens and James B. Cooke. Jackson, Miss., 1983.

Prentice, George D. *Biography of Henry Clay*. Hartford, 1831.

The Proslavery Argument. Charleston, 1851.

Public Meeting of Mechanics and Workingmen in Winchester, Virginia, January 9, 1861. Broadside, n.p.

Rable, George. *Civil Wars: Women and the Crisis of Southern Nationalism*. Urbana, Ill., 1989.

———. *The Confederate Republic: A Revolution against Politics*. Chapel Hill, N.C., 1994.

Rachleff, Peter. *Black Labor in Richmond, 1865–1900*. Urbana, Ill., 1989.
Rainwater, Percy Lee. *Mississippi: Storm Center of Secession*. Baton Rouge, 1938.
Ramsdell, Charles. *Behind the Lines in the Southern Confederacy*. Baton Rouge, 1944.
Randolph, Sarah. *The Domestic Life of Thomas Jefferson*. New York, 1871.
Reese, George, ed. *Proceedings of the Virginia State Convention in 1861, February 13–May 1*. Richmond, 1965.
Reich, Steven A. "Soldiers of Democracy: Black Texans and the Fight for Citizenship, 1917–1921." *Journal of American History* 82 (March 1996): 1478–89.
Reid, Henry, and John Eaton. *The Life of Andrew Jackson*. 1817. Edited by Frank L. Owsley Jr. Reprint, University, Ala., 1974.
Remini, Robert. *Andrew Jackson and the Bank War: A Study in the Growth of Presidential Power*. New York, 1967.
———. *Andrew Jackson and the Course of American Democracy, 1833–1845*. New York, 1984.
———. *Andrew Jackson and the Course of American Empire, 1776–1821*. New York, 1977.
———. *Andrew Jackson and the Course of American Freedom, 1822–32*. New York, 1981.
Rhodes, James Ford. *History of the Civil War, 1861–65*. New York, 1917.
Richardson, Nolan, ed. *Messages and Papers of the Presidents*. Washington, 1898.
Roark, James. *Masters without Slaves: Southern Planters in the Civil War and Reconstruction*. New York, 1977.
Robinson, Armstead L. "Day of Jubilo: Civil War and the Demise of Slavery in the Mississippi Valley, 1861–1865." Ph.D. diss., University of Rochester, 1976.
Rodgers, Daniel. "Republicanism: The Career of a Concept." *Journal of American History* 79 (June 1992): 11–38.
Rodriquez, Junius P. "Wired to the World: Antebellum Technology and the Origins of Southern Anti-technology Mentality." *Southern Studies* 5 (Spring and Summer 1994): 137–54.
Rogin, Michael Paul. *Fathers and Children: Andrew Jackson and the Subjugation of the American Indian*. New York, 1975.
Rose, Willie Lee. *Rehearsal for Reconstruction: The Port Royal Experiment*. New York, 1964.
Rotundo, E. Anthony. *American Manhood*. New York, 1993.
Rowland, Dunbar, ed. *Jefferson Davis, Constitutionalist: His Letters, Papers, and Speeches*. Jackson, Miss., 1923.
Royster, Charles. *The Destructive War: William Tecumseh Sherman, Stonewall Jackson, and the Americans*. New York, 1991.
Russell, William Howard. *My Diary North and South*. London, 1863.
Rutherfoord, John C. *John C. Rutherfoord of Goochland in the House of Delegates, February 21, 1860*. Richmond, 1860.

———. *An Oration Delivered before the Jefferson Society of the University of Virginia, April 12, 1843.* Charlottesville, 1843.

———. *Speech of John C. Rutherfoord of Goochland Co., Delivered in the House of Delegates of Virginia, March 1, 1858, On the Bill Authorizing a Loan to the Orange and Alexandria Railroad Co.* Richmond, 1858.

———. *Speech on the Banking Policy, February 9, 1856.* N.p., n.d.

Rutherfoord, Thomas. *Autobiography of Thomas Rutherfoord, Esq. of Richmond, Virginia, 1766–1851.* Richmond, n.d.

Ryan, Mary P. *Cradle of the Middle Class: The Family in Oneida County, New York, 1790–1865.* New York, 1981.

———. "Gender and Public Access." In *Habermas and the Public Sphere*, edited by Craig Calhoun. Cambridge, Mass., 1992.

Saville, Julie. *The Work of Reconstruction: From Slave to Wage Laborer in South Carolina, 1860–1870.* New York, 1994.

Scarborough, William, ed. *Diary of Edmund Ruffin.* Baton Rouge, 1972.

Schaper, Harold. "Sectionalism and Representation in South Carolina." In the *Annual Report of the American Historical Association.* Washington, 1901.

Schlesinger, Arthur, Jr. *The Age of Jackson.* Boston, 1945.

Schultz, Harold S. *Nationalism and Sectionalism in South Carolina, 1852–1860.* Durham, N.C., 1950.

Scott, Sir Walter. "Essay on Chivalry." In *The Miscellaneous Works of Sir Walter Scott.* Edinburgh, 1881.

Selections from the Speeches and Writings of the Honorable Thomas L. Clingman of North Carolina. Raleigh, N.C., 1878.

Sellers, Charles. *The Market Revolution: Jacksonian America, 1815–1846.* New York, 1990.

———. "The Travail of Slavery." In *The Southerner as American*, edited by Charles Sellers. Chapel Hill, N.C., 1960.

———. "Who Were the Southern Whigs?" *American Historical Review* 59 (January 1954): 335–44.

Shade, William. *Democratizing the Old Dominion: Virginia and the Second Party System, 1824–1861.* Charlottesville, Va., 1996.

Shallhope, Robert E. *John Taylor of Caroline: Pastoral Republican.* Columbia, S.C., 1980.

———. "Republicanism and Early American Historiography." *William and Mary Quarterly* 39 (April 1982): 334–56.

———. "Toward a Republican Synthesis: The Emergence of an Understanding of Republicanism in American Historiography." *William and Mary Quarterly* 29 (January 1972): 49–80.

Shanks, Henry T. "Conservative Constitutional Tendencies of the Virginia Secession Convention." In *Essays in Southern History Presented to Joseph Gregoire del Roulhac Hamilton*, edited by Fletcher M. Green. Chapel Hill, N.C., 1949.

———. *The Secessionist Movement in Virginia, 1847–1861*. Richmond, 1934.
Sharp, James Roger. *American Politics in the Early Republic: The New Nation in Crisis*. New Haven, 1993.
———. *The Jacksonians versus the Banks: Politics in the States after the Panic of 1837*. New York, 1970.
Sherman, William T. *Memoirs of General William T. Sherman*. 1875. Reprint, New York, 1984.
Shore, Lawrence. *Southern Capitalists: The Ideological Leadership of an Elite, 1832–1885*. Chapel Hill, N.C., 1986.
Shugg, Roger. *Origins of Class Struggle in Louisiana*. Baton Rouge, 1939.
Siegal, Frederick F. *The Roots of Southern Distinctiveness: Tobacco and Society in Danville, Virginia, 1780–1865*. Chapel Hill, N.C., 1987.
Simpson, Craig. *A Good Southerner*. Chapel Hill, N.C., 1985.
Simpson, Lewis P. *The Dispossessed Garden: Pastoral and History in Southern Literature*. Athens, Ga., 1975.
Smith, Adam. *An Inquiry into the Nature and Causes of the Wealth of Nations*. 1776. Edited by Edwin Canaan. Reprint, New York, 1994.
Smith, Daniel Blake. *Inside the Great House: Planter Family Life in Eighteenth-Century Chesapeake Society*. Ithaca, N.Y., 1980.
Smith, Mark M. *Mastered by the Clock: Time, Slavery, and Freedom in the American South*. Chapel Hill, N.C., 1997.
Smith, W. R., ed. *History and Debates of the Convention of the People of Alabama, Begun and Held in the City of Montgomery on the seventh day of January 1861; in which is Preserved the Speeches of the Secret Session, and Many Valuable State Papers*. Montgomery, 1861.
Sobel, Mechal. *The World They Made Together: Black and White Values in Eighteenth-Century Virginia*. Baltimore, 1987.
Southern Historical Society Papers. Richmond, 1941–54.
Southern Literary Messenger. Richmond, 1834–1845.
Speech of George A. Gordon of Chatham on the Constitutionality of the Conscription Laws, Delivered in the Senate of Georgia, 9th of December, 1862. Atlanta, 1862.
Speech of the Hon. L. Q. C. Lamar of Mississippi on the State of the Country Delivered in the Athenaeum. Atlanta, 1964.
Spratt, Leonidas W. *The Philosophy of Secession: A Southern View*. N.p., n.d.
———. *Resolutions on the Slave Trade*. N.p., 1858.
Stampp, Kenneth. *America in 1857*. New York, 1990.
Stephens, Alexander. *A Constitutional View of the Late War between the States*. Philadelphia, 1868–70.
Stevenson, Brenda. *Life in Black and White: Family and Community in the Slave South*. New York, 1996.

Substance of the Remarks of General Howell Cobb in a Speech Delivered in the Hall of the House of Representatives, March 11, 1864. N.p., n.d.

Sutton, Robert P. "Nostalgia, Pessimism, and Malaise: The Doomed Aristocrat in Late Jeffersonian Virginia." *Virginia Magazine of History and Biography* 76 (1968): 41–55.

Takaki, Ronald. *A Pro-Slavery Crusade: The Campaign to Reopen the Slave Trade*. New York, 1981.

Tatum, Georgia Lee. *Disloyalty in the Confederacy*. New York, 1934.

Taylor, John. *Arator: Being a Series of Agricultural Essays, Practical and Political: In Sixty Four Numbers*. 1813. Reprint, Indianapolis, 1967.

——. *An Inquiry into the Principles and Policy of the Government of the United States*. 1814. Edited by Loren Baritz. Reprint, Indianapolis, 1969.

Taylor, William R. *Cavalier and Yankee: The Old South and American National Character*. New York, 1961.

Thomas, Emory W. *The Confederacy as a Revolutionary Experience*. Englewood Cliffs, N.J., 1971.

——. *The Confederate Nation: 1861–1865*. New York, 1979.

Thompson, Wesley Sylvester. *The Free State of Winston: A History of Winston County, Alabama*. Winfield, Ala., 1968.

Thornton, J. Mills. *Politics and Power in a Slave Society, Alabama, 1800–1860*. Baton Rouge, 1978.

Tocqueville, Alexis de. *Democracy in America*. 1835–40. Edited by J. P. Meyer. Reprint, New York, 1969.

Towns, W. Stuart. "'To Preserve the Traditions of Our Fathers': The Post War Speaking Career of Jefferson Davis." *Journal of Mississippi History* 52 (May 1990): 111–24.

Tucker, George. *The Valley of the Shenandoah or The Memoir of the Graysons*. 1824. Reprint, Chapel Hill, N.C., 1970.

Twain, Mark. *Life on the Mississippi*. 1883. Reprint, Norwalk, Conn., 1972.

——. *Mark Twain's Autobiography*. New York, 1924.

——. "The Private History of a Campaign That Failed." *Tales, Speeches, Essays, and Sketches*. New York, 1994.

Twelve Southerners. *I'll Take My Stand: The South and the Agrarian Tradition*. New York, 1930.

Upshur, Abel P. "Mr. Jefferson." *Southern Literary Messenger* 6 (September 1838): 642–50.

Vandiver, Frank. *Their Tattered Flags: The Epic of the Confederacy*. New York, 1970.

Varron, Elizabeth R. "Tippecanoe and the Ladies Too: White Women and Party Politics in Antebellum Virginia." *Journal of American History* 82 (September 1995): 492–521.

Wakelyn, Jon, ed. *Southern Pamphlets on Secession, November 1860–April 1861.* Chapel Hill, N.C., 1996.
Wallenstein, Peter. "Incendiaries All: Southern Politics and the Harpers Ferry Raid." In *His Soul Goes Marching On: Responses to John Brown and the Harpers Ferry Raid*, edited by Paul Finkelman. Charlottesville, Va., 1995.
Ward, John William. *Andrew Jackson: Symbol for an Age.* New York, 1955.
Ware, Lowry Price. "The South Carolina Executive Councils of 1861 and 1862." Master's thesis, University of South Carolina, 1952.
The War of the Rebellion: A Compilation of the Official Records of the Union and Confederate Armies (OR), Washington, 1894.
Washington, James Melvin, ed. *A Testament of Hope: The Essential Writings of Martin Luther King, Jr.* New York, 1986.
Watson, Harry. "Conflict and Collaboration: Yeomen, Slaveholders, and Politics in the Antebellum South." *Social History* 10 (October 1985): 273–98.
———. *Jacksonian Politics and Community Conflict: The Emergence of the Second Party System in Cumberland County, North Carolina.* Baton Rouge, 1981.
———. *Liberty and Power: The Politics of Jacksonian America.* New York, 1990.
Waugh, John C. *Reelecting Lincoln: The Battle for the 1864 Presidency.* New York, 1997.
Weaver, Herbert, ed. *The Correspondence of James K. Polk.* Nashville, 1972.
Weiner, Marli. *Mistresses and Slaves: Plantation Women in South Carolina, 1830–1880.* Urbana, Ill., 1998.
Weir, Robert. "The South Carolinian as Extremist." *South Atlantic Quarterly* 75 (December 1975): 86–103.
Welter, Barbara. "The Cult of True Womanhood: 1800–1860." *American Quarterly* 18 (Summer 1966): 151–74.
Wender, Herbert. *The Southern Commercial Conventions.* Baltimore, 1939.
Wesley, Charles. *The Collapse of the Confederacy.* New York, 1937.
Wharton, T. J. *Journal of the State Convention and Ordinance Adopted in 1861, With an Appendix.* Jackson, Miss., 1861.
White, Laura. "The Fate of Calhoun's Sovereign Convention in South Carolina." *American Historical Review* 34 (July 1929): 757–71.
———. "The National Democrats in South Carolina, 1852–1860." *South Atlantic Quarterly* 28 (October 1929): 570–87.
———. *Robert Barnwell Rhett: Father of Secession.* New York, 1931.
Whites, Leeann. *The Civil War as a Crisis in Gender.* Athens, Ga., 1995.
Wiebe, Robert. *The Opening of American Society: From the Adoption of the Constitution to the Eve of Disunion.* New York, 1985.
———. *Self-Rule: A Cultural History of American Democracy.* Chicago, 1995.
Wiggins, Sarah Woolfolk. *The Scalawag in Alabama Politics, 1865–1881.* University, Ala., 1977.

Wiley, Bell. *The Plain People of the Confederacy*. Baton Rouge, 1943.

———. *The Road to Appomattox*. Memphis, 1958.

William L. Yancey at the National Democratic Convention, April 26, 1860. Pamphlet, n.p., n.d.

Williams, Benjamin Buford. *A Literary History of Alabama*. Rutherford, N.J., 1979.

Williams, Raymond. *The Country and the City*. New York, 1973.

Wills, Garry. *Lincoln at Gettysburg: The Words That Remade America*. New York, 1992.

Wilson, Charles Reagan. "The Death of Southern Heroes: Historic Funerals of the South." *Southern Cultures* 1 (Fall 1994): 3–22.

Wilson, Clyde, ed. *The Papers of John C. Calhoun*. Columbia, S.C., 1968.

Wilson, Douglas. *Honor's Voice: The Transformation of Abraham Lincoln*. New York, 1998.

———, ed. *Jefferson's Literary Commonplace Book*. Princeton, 1989.

Wilson, Edmund. *Patriotic Gore: Studies in the Literature of the American Civil War*. 1962. Reprint, London, 1987.

Wiltse, Charles. ed. *The Papers of Daniel Webster*. Hanover, N.H., 1977.

Wish, Harvey, ed. *Antebellum: The Writings of George Fitzhugh and Hinton Rowan Helper on Slavery*. New York, 1960.

Wood, Kirsten E. "One Woman So Dangerous to Public Morals: Gender and Power in the Eaton Affair." *Journal of the Early Republic* 17 (Summer 1997): 237–74.

Woodward, C. Vann. *Origins of the New South, 1877–1913*. Baton Rouge, 1951.

———. *Tom Watson, Agrarian Rebel*. New York, 1938.

———, ed. *Mary Chesnut's Civil War*. New Haven, 1981.

———. *The Private Mary Chesnut: The Unpublished Civil War Diaries*. New York, 1984.

Wooster, Ralph. *The Secession Conventions of the South*. Princeton, 1962.

Wright, Gavin. *The Political Economy of the Cotton South: Households, Markets, and Wealth in the Nineteenth Century*. New York, 1978.

Wyatt-Brown, Bertram. "Andrew Jackson's Honor." *Journal of the Early Republic* 17 (Spring 1997): 1–36.

———. "God and Honor in the Old South." *Southern Review* 25 (Spring 1989): 283–96.

———. *Southern Honor*. New York, 1982.

Zilversmit, Arthur. *The First Emancipation: The Abolition of Slavery in the North*. Chicago, 1967.

Index

Adams, John Quincy, 10
Alabama, 2, 4, 6, 42, 44, 45, 122; Democratic Party political culture in, 123–24, 128–30, 141; guerrilla warfare in, 135–41; Huntsville, 122, 136; Madison County, 135; Mobile, 135; North Alabama (Upcountry), 124, 126, 133–41; Peace Societies in, 135; southern-rights leaders in, 126–27
Alabama Legislature, 122, 125, 128
American Revolution, 22–23, 144, 146, 166–67
Anderson, Robert, 113, 118
Appomatox, 141
Army of Northern Virginia, 143
Army of Tennessee, 161
Ashmore, J. D., 43

Baab, William, 51
Baldwin, Joseph Glover, 6, 34, 41, 125, 131
Bank of the United States, Second, 5, 28, 33–37, 125, 159
Barbour, James, 49
Barbour, P. P., 35
Barclay, E. A., 86
Bell, John, 89, 136
Benton, Thomas Hart, 17, 34
Biddle, Nicholas, 5, 33, 34–36
Blair, Francis P., 33
"Bleeding Kansas," 42. *See also* Kansas

Bocock, Thomas, 163
Bonaparte, Louis Napoleon, 76, 79
Bonaparte, Napoleon, 24
Bonham, Milledge L., 120
Breckenridge, John, 111, 112
Brown, Albert Gallatin, 158
Brown, John, 76, 167
Brown, Joseph E., 6–8, 47, 56, 146, 159; conflict of, with banks, 87–88; conflict of, with Davis, 92–101; as Jackson-style politician, 84, 100; relationship of, with Georgia elite, 84–87, 91; and state aid to railroads, 88; and states' rights, 94–100; as Yale alumnus, 84, 87–88
Buchanan, James, 86, 109–10, 112, 113
Buckle, Henry Thomas, 73–75
Buford, Jefferson, 127, 128
Bull Run, First Battle of, 147
Burr, Aaron, 131

Calhoun, Floride, 30
Calhoun, John, 8, 9, 19, 29, 30, 32, 33, 35, 67, 110, 150; constitutional theory of, 151–64; *Discourse on the Constitution*, 151; *Disquisition on Government*, 152; on "Force Bill," 164; and popular sovereignty, 102, 116–17; on "spoils" system, 107
Chesnut, James, 39, 103, 116, 119
Chesnut, Mary, 39–40, 156
Christiana Riot (1851), 166

Christianity, evangelical, 124, 125, 137–41
Clay, Cassius, 52
Clay, Clement Claiborne, 45, 163
Clay, Clement Comer, 129
Clay, Henry, 24, 26, 36, 162
Clemens, Jeremiah, 6, 7, 122; accused of bargain with Whigs, 127–29; as Alabama legislator, 123; *Bernard Lile*, 131; on Compromise of 1850, 125–26, 128, 133; as Know-Nothing candidate, 129; *Mustang Gray*, 131–32; *The Rivals*, 132, 137; *Tobias Wilson*, 123, 137–41; as volunteer in Texas and Mexico, 125
Clingman, Thomas, 44, 67
Cobb, Howell, 53, 86, 97, 109
Cobb, T. R. R., 54, 146
Coffee, John, 21
Compromise of 1850, 7, 46
Congress (U.S.). *See* House of Representatives (U.S.); Senate (U.S.)
Constitution (Confederate), 151, 156, 160
Constitution (U.S.), 18, 102, 144, 145–64, 165–68
Crittenden, John, 133, 167
Crutchfield, O. M., 77
Curry, J. L. M., 44, 133

Dabney, Robert L., 70
Daniel, John M., 78, 150, 156
Davis, Jefferson, 6, 9, 52, 79, 84, 97, 99, 114, 120, 137, 165, 169; capture and imprisonment of, 163; conflict of, with Joseph Brown, 92–101; and conscription, 157; and constitutional doctrine, 8, 9, 145, 149–64; and days of prayer and fasting, 161–62; and democracy, 79, 147–49, 154; and morale, 143–44, 161–62; as president of Confederacy, 142; on Richmond Bread Riot, 150; *Rise and Fall of the Confederate States of America*, 147; suspends habeas corpus, 157; unpopularity of, 142–43, 169–70
De Bow, J. D. B., 2, 49–52
Declaration of Independence, 15, 165, 166, 168, 170
Democracy: Confederacy and, 144; in Greece, 2, 61; inequality and, 4–5, 49–50, 75–83, 121; in Jacksonian/Jeffersonian political culture, 4, 16–38, 54, 59, 60, 63, 66, 72–73, 83, 94, 108, 111, 120, 147–48, 152–54, 162; and scholarship, 2–4; slavery and, 1–4, 8–9, 65, 91, 125, 171; and virtual representation, 106; white men's, 2–4, 7, 41–42, 58, 66, 106; yeomanry and, 1–2, 5, 11–20, 89, 108, 154, 164
Democratic Party, 1, 38, 57, 63, 83, 103, 105, 112, 113, 125; Charleston Convention (1860), 53, 113; Cincinnati Convention (1856), 108–9; in 1850s, 40–56; in Mississippi, 148–49; as modern political organization, 2; and modernization crisis, 41–47; newspaper editors and, 46; northern War Democrats, 168; planter elites in, 4, 53–56, 82–83, 85–87, 128–30, 141; and popular will, 1, 123; and postbellum attacks on Lincoln, 166; role of, in Confederacy, 8; and rural life, 2, 5, 8, 37, 40–41, 43, 47, 52–53, 64, 73, 88–89, 101; scholarship on, 3; and slavery controversy, 46, 51–52, 90, 101, 111; Whig influence in, 45–46, 55–56, 85–88; and Whigs, opposition to, 6
Dew, Thomas, 35, 153
Donelson, Andrew Jackson, 31

Douglas, Stephen, 46, 89, 111–13, 165, 168
Douglass, Frederick, ix, 1–2, 166
Dred Scott case, 111, 155

Eaton, John, 21, 28
Eaton, Peggy, 28–32
Emancipation Proclamation, 169

Fillmore, Millard, 86
First Alabama Cavalry, 135
Fitzhugh, George, 53
Fort Monroe, 163
Fort Moultrie, 113
Fort Pulaski, 90
Fort Sumter, 4, 7, 113–16, 167
Franklin, Benjamin, 62

Garrison, William Lloyd, 153, 167
Georgia: Bibb County, 85; Black Belt in, 90; and coastal region, 93–94; secession of, 89–91; up-country (North Georgia), 84–93; Walker County, 93
Georgia Legislature (Milledgeville), 87–88, 90, 100
Gist, William, 55, 103, 105, 116, 118
Goldsmith, Andrew, 13, 26–28, 37
Greeley, Horace, 52, 169
Greene, Duff, 29
Grey, J. H., 57
Guerrilla warfare, 7, 97, 135–41, 165

Hamilton, Alexander, 131
Hammond, James Henry, 82, 106, 117, 119
Hanks, Dennis, 9
Harper's Ferry, Virginia, 76, 167
Harris, William, 49
Harrison, William Henry, 37
Hart, William, 80

Hayne, Isaac W., 103, 111, 114, 116
Helper, Hinton R., 52, 76, 90
Herndon, William, 9
Hill, Benjamin Henry, 87, 99
Hodgson, Joseph, 61
Holden, William Woods, 44, 47, 56, 91, 160
Honor: and Clemens, 7, 122–23, 125, 128–41; and Jackson, Andrew, 19, 21, 23, 29–33, 125
Hooper, Johnson J., 131
House of Representatives (U.S.), 43, 44, 52, 109
Household, 30, 69–70, 80, 124, 138–39
Hundley, Daniel, 67
Hunter, Robert M. T., 111, 114

Improvements, internal, 45–48, 59, 72–73, 88, 106

Jackson, Andrew, 2, 5, 8, 18, 26, 41, 47, 48, 54, 60, 72, 79, 83, 95, 103–4, 108, 120, 124, 147–49, 154, 164; and American Revolution, 22–23, 148; and Battle of New Orleans (War of 1812), 11, 19–21, 23, 25; Farewell Address, 36; Hermitage, 22, 35; and Indian Removal, 28; Indian Wars, 19, 24, 29; "King Veto," 34; and *Vicar of Wakefield*, 26–28, 37
Jackson, Andrew, Jr., 37
Jackson, Rachel, 28
Jackson, Sarah, 37
Jefferson, Thomas, 8, 26, 33, 36, 41, 43, 54, 55, 59, 72, 75, 76, 104, 144, 148, 154, 164; "eclectic" philosophy of, 13; and Embargo Act, 14; on England, 14; long-term influence of, 9, 11, 166–70; and Monticello, 12, 16; on "natural aristocracy," 19; *Notes on the State of Virginia*, 12,

Jefferson, Thomas (cont.)
    43, 65; and pastoral ideal, 12–18; and "revolution of 1800," 16; and slavery, 9, 12, 13, 16
Jim Crow, 171
Johnson, Andrew, 47, 54, 91, 134, 139, 153
Johnson, Herschel V., 86, 89, 98–99, 144, 162
Johnson, Nannie Rutherfoord, 69
Jones, Richard B., 142

Kansas, 42, 46, 87, 109
Kendall, Amos, 34
Kentucky, 9
Know-Nothings, 46, 74–75, 85–90, 129

Lamar, L. Q. C., 4
Lane, George, 135–36
Lecompton Constitution, 46
Lee, Robert E., 98, 116, 143, 145, 161
Letcher, John, 77
Lincoln, Abraham, ix, 90, 104, 111, 113, 118, 142, 157, 162; and democracy, 9–10, 165–69
Locke, John, 13
Lumpkin, John Henry, 86–87
Lynch, John R., 170

Macchiavelli, Niccolo, 75
MacPherson, James, 14
Madison, James, 16, 17, 55, 142, 144
Manhood: Brown, Joseph, and, 96; Clemens and, 123–26; Davis and, 80, 161; democracy and, 18, 22, 25, 28–32, 37–38, 42, 75, 133; Jackson, Andrew, and, 5, 8, 11, 12, 14, 17, 20, 22, 24–25, 30, 31, 36–37, 125; Jefferson and, 14, 17, 68; Rutherfoord, John C., and, 8, 57–83
"Marion Rangers," 122

Martineau, Harriet, 25
Marx, Karl, 91, 146, 171
McCall, Paul, 127–28
McClellan, George, 80, 98, 168
McDonald, Jasper, 39
McRae, John J., 43
Memminger, C. G., 30
Mexican War, 122, 132, 150
Miles, William Porcher, 45, 108, 145, 149
Militia: Brown, Joseph, and, 97; Clemens and, 134–35; Jackson, Andrew, and, 11, 15, 20–21, 23, 32
Monroe, James, 8, 55
Moore, A. B., 48, 133

Napoleon I. See Bonaparte, Napoleon
Napoleon III. See Bonaparte, Louis Napoleon
North Georgia (up-country), 84–93
Notes on the State of Virginia, 12, 43, 65
Nullification crisis, 32–33, 54, 103, 106, 109, 113, 148, 153

Olmsted, Frederick Law, 39–40
Orr, James, 104, 110, 119
Ossian, 13, 14

Page, Thomas Nelson, 64
Paine, Thomas, 12
Peninsula Campaign (1862), 80, 98, 169
Perry, Benjamin, 104, 106, 107, 120–21
Phelan, James, 150
Pickens, Francis, 6, 7, 102–3, 106, 120, 145; as ambassador to Russia, 111; and Calhoun, 110; and Executive Council, 117; and Fort Sumter crisis, 113–15, 118; and low country (1861), 115–16; as National Democrat, 103, 112; and South Carolina reapportionment, 107; and up-country, 118

Plantation household, 30, 69–70, 80, 124, 138–39
Planters. *See* Democratic Party: planter elites in
Polk, James K., 33
Pollard, Edward, 159
Pugh, J. L., 114

Railroads, 45, 47–48, 73, 88, 106
Randolph, Thomas Jefferson, 14
Reconstruction, 170
Republican Party, 39, 47, 50, 92, 139, 155
Revolution, American, 132
Rhett, Robert Barnwell, Jr., 105, 109, 111, 113, 114, 127–28, 154
Richmond Bread Riot (1863), 150
Ruffin, Edmund, 53, 60, 78, 81, 142, 163
Rutherfoord, Anne Bruce, 71, 73, 81
Rutherfoord, John, 63, 78
Rutherfoord, John C. (of Goochland), 6, 8; on democracy, 8, 58, 76; Enlightenment rationalism of, 66, 72–75; as father, 80–81; and Goochland County, 57, 58, 61, 68, 77; and Jefferson Society Address, 65–66; in Virginia House of Delegates, 8, 57, 70, 76, 78
Rutherfoord, Thomas, 61–63, 69

Scott, Dred, 111, 155
Scott, Sir Walter, 122–23, 131–32, 140
Scott, Winfield, 54
Secession, 112–13, 156; of Alabama, 122, 132–33; of border states, 113, 114; and democracy, 6, 53–56, 90–91, 102, 133; fear of slave rebellion and, 156; of Georgia, 89–92; Pickens and, 112–13; Rutherfoord, John C., as leader of, 77–79; of South

Carolina, 7, 54, 78, 102–3, 109, 112, 116, 121; of Virginia, 50, 54–56, 155
Second Bank of the United States, 5, 28, 33–37, 125, 159
Second party system, 41, 155
Seddon, James A., 160
Senate (U.S.), 7, 125, 127, 130
Seward, William, 85
Sheffrey, James W., 155
Sheridan, Philip, 57
Sherman, John, 52
Sherman, William T., 99–100
Shorter, John Gill, 162
Simms, William Gilmore, 119, 128
Singleton, Thomas, 65
"Slave Power Conspiracy," 155
Slavery, 8, 124, 170; Brown, Joseph, and, 89–92, 95, 98–99, 101; Calhoun, John, and, 151–53, 155; class conflict and, 47–54; Clemens and, 126–27, 136; Davis and, 144, 149–52, 154, 156, 158, 164, 169; democracy and, 1–6, 61; Democratic Party and, 4–5; Douglass on, 1, 166; evangelicals and, 140; Jackson, Andrew, and, 20, 23–24, 30, 32–33, 35–37; Jefferson and, 9, 11–13, 16; Lincoln and, 9–10, 167–69; Marx on, 171; Rutherfoord, John C., and, 69–71, 76–77, 82–83; sectional crisis and, 42–47, 50, 52; and South Carolina politics, 102, 110–11
Smith, Adam, 18
Smith, J. Henley, 84
South Carolina, 6, 51; Anderson County, 104; apportionment of (Constitution of 1808), 104–5, 107; Charleston, 113–15, 117; and democracy, 102–8, 121, 153; Edgefield County, 106–7, 119; Executive Council of (First), 7, 102; Executive Council of (Second),

South Carolina (cont.)
102–4, 116–17, 119–21; Greenville, 104; low country of, 104–5, 107, 113, 115–17, 119–21; Marion, 119; and National Democrats, 104, 106, 108–13, 115, 117; Piedmont, 107; Port Royal, 115; Richland, 119; and States' Rights Democrats, 104, 106, 108–13, 115; up-country of, 7, 104, 107, 115–21
Spratt, Leonidas, 51, 54
Stanton, Edwin M., 136
Stephens, Alexander, 109, 142, 156; and Brown, Joseph, 87–88, 93; and Davis, 98, 146, 159; and Lincoln, 165, 168; and slavery, 149, 168
Stephens, Linton, 87
Stone, Lewis M., 133

Taney, Roger, 34
Taylor, Frederick W., 17
Taylor, John (of Caroline), 17–18, 60, 66, 72
Taylor, Zachary, 127
Thomas, Thomas W., 87
Tillman, George, 106
Timberlake, John, 28
Tocqueville, Alexis de, 20, 41, 144, 149
Toombs, Robert, 85, 89, 109
Trescot, William Henry, 111, 113
Troup, George, 20
Tucker, George, 15, 16
Turner, Nat, 153, 166
Twain, Mark, 122, 131, 141

Union Leagues, 170
Unionism: Clemens and, 120, 123, 134–41, 144; Democrats and, 54–56; in Georgia, 90–91, 96; Pickens and, 111–12
University of Virginia, 59, 67

Vallandigham, Clement, 165
Van Buren, Martin, 31, 34, 46
Vance, Zebulon, 160
Vesey, Denmark, 153
Virginia and Kentucky Resolutions, 94, 144

Wage labor, 43
Walker, Leroy Pope, 98, 137
War Department (Confederate), 95, 142
War of 1812, 14, 20–21, 23
Washington, George, 16, 36, 95, 132
Webster, Daniel, 36
Whig ideology (England), 13
Whig Party (U.S.), 24, 63, 83; in Alabama, 127–28; influence in Democratic Party, 2, 84; Jackson-era politics, 26, 37–38, 42, 155; in Mississippi, 155; in North Carolina, 49
Wigfall, Louis T., 149
Winston, John, 47–48
Wise, Henry, 77, 79, 83, 149

Yancey, William Lowndes, 19; on Brown, Joseph, 94; and Clemens, 129, 134, 138; as secession leader, 53; on wage labor, 43
Yeomanry, 82; Brown, Joseph, and, 8, 84, 87, 89–92, 101; Chesnut, Mary, and, 39; Clemens and, 136; Davis and, 150, 159–60; democracy and, 2, 49–50, 108; Democratic Party and, 2, 40–42; Douglass on, 1; Jackson, Andrew, and, 11, 20, 22, 26–27, 33, 35–36; Jefferson and, 5, 11–17, 26–27, 53, 64, 154, 166–70; market economy and, 37, 43–45, 48, 51, 88; Olmsted and, 40–41; Rutherfoord, John C., and, 76–77; secession and, 6, 50, 52–53, 76–79

www.ingramcontent.com/pod-product-compliance
Lightning Source LLC
Chambersburg PA
CBHW011748220426
43669CB00020B/2948